SUGAR AND SLATE

About the Author

Charlotte Williams OBE is a Welsh-Guyanese award-winning author, academic and cultural critic. Her writings span academic publications, memoir, short fiction, reviews, essays and commentaries. She has written over fourteen academic books, notably including the edited collection *A Tolerant Nation? Exploring Ethnic Diversity in a Devolved Wales* (2003) and an edited text in the Rodopi postcolonial series on her father's work, *Denis Williams: A Life in Works* (2010). She is a Professor Emeritus at Bangor University and holds Honorary Fellowships at Wrexham Glyndŵr University, University of South Wales and Cardiff Metropolitan University. She is a member of the Learned Society of Wales. Her writing has taken her on travels worldwide but her heart and her home are always in Wales.

SUGAR AND SLATE

Charlotte Williams

With a new introduction by
Bernardine Evaristo

PENGUIN BOOKS

PENGUIN BOOKS

UK | USA | Canada | Ireland | Australia
India | New Zealand | South Africa

Penguin Books is part of the Penguin Random House group of companies
whose addresses can be found at global.penguinrandomhouse.com.

First published by Planet Books 2002
Library of Wales edition co-published by Parthian Books in association with
Berw Limited and their publishing imprint Planet Books 2022
First published with a new introduction by Penguin Books 2023

001

Typeset by Jouve (UK), Milton Keynes
Printed and bound in Great Britain by Clays Ltd, Elcograf S.p.A.

The authorized representative in the EEA is Penguin Random House Ireland,
Morrison Chambers, 32 Nassau Street, Dublin D02 YH68

A CIP catalogue record for this book is available from the British Library

ISBN: 978-0-241-99953-0

In association with Parthian Books and Library of Wales

Sugar and Slate, first published by Planet in 2002, was selected for the Parthian
Library of Wales series in 2022

www.greenpenguin.co.uk

Will you fly or will you vanish?
Caption from *Asafo! African Flags of the Fante*.

Contents

Contents

Introduction

Memoirs are an invaluable addition to how history is recorded or, more accurately, how we choose to selectively highlight and represent the past. The official historicization of the United Kingdom has tended to exclude the timelines of people of colour to the extent that it would be easy to think that we are not important enough for the record. Yet in a world where we are all racialized, and where people of colour are minoritized in majority-white societies, how we record the past is part of our national identity formation, as well as our personal concepts of belonging. In a culture where very few memoirs or autobiographies by people of colour are published, especially outside the celebrity sphere, each book that manages to surface is making an essential correction to the whitewashing of history; each book changes the historical landscape.

Within this context, *Sugar and Slate* by Charlotte Williams, first published in 2002, offers us a new and wonderfully unique perspective on one of the four nations of the United Kingdom, the country of Wales, both from a personal and a wider historical perspective.

Williams was born in Wales to a white mother and Afro-Guyanese father, Denis Williams, who was a visual artist of some note, an archaeologist and a writer. Her parents spent their early marriage living in London, moving in artistic circles that included fellow artists Francis Bacon and Lucian Freud, as well as fellow Caribbean émigrés Michael Manley (who became Prime Minister of Jamaica) and the writers Jan Carew and Wilson Harris. Her father's story is not the familiar one of a working-class immigrant consigned to working on the buses or in a factory, but that of someone who was a teacher at the Central School of Art and whose art was well exhibited. He was described by a leading critic as a "brilliant newcomer". Williams, pater, eventually relocated to Sudan to teach, and later to Nigeria, with the family following him to both countries until Charlotte's Welsh-speaking mother decided to return home and took her five daughters to live in Llandudno.

Williams begins the memoir with the sentence and sentiment, "It would have been so much easier if I had been able to say, 'I come from Africa.'" But her relationship to place is not so easily identifiable or reductive. In east and west Africa, she does not fit in and is regarded as a foreigner; so too in Wales where, as a biracial child in a predominantly white country, she is subject to the cruelties of racism, from both children and adults. Of course, as is the case, there was no language available to her as a child of the fifties and sixties to articulate this. Of racism, she writes, "I accepted it as my personal battle, not as anything particularly collective."

Sugar and Slate is an interrogation of Williams's identity, but it's also an investigation into nationality, Welshness, Britishness, class, gender and ethnicity, while offering the reader fascinating insights into Wales's untold black history, which has been overlooked by historians who only select white historical time-lines, and historians who explore Britain's black history but have omitted Wales from their research. One such example is that we learn about the religious African Training Institute, founded in Colwyn Bay in 1889 to educate African boys, drawing them from all over the African continent. Many of the boys, employed in various trades, were familiar figures around town. Their presence, and that of others, evokes a more multicultural history of Wales than most people imagine. I am reminded of the African Academy, founded a century earlier by religious social reformers in Clapham, London, in 1799, which attracted the sons and daughters of wealthy Sierra Leonians who were educated there. The Academy was fictionalized in the young adult novel *Jupiter Williams* (2011) by S. I. Martin.

Sugar and Slate, so named after the raw cane industry that underpinned slavery in the Caribbean and the once dominant slate production industry of Wales, is also an impressive study of her parents, written with the wise maturity of an adult who has thought long and hard about them. She acknowledges that her analysis is hindsight. There is her Guyanese father, more remote than not, both physically and psychically, but who takes her on memorable archaeological digs in Nigeria as a child; and her Welsh mother, from a country and language subjugated by England, and deeply rooted in the Welshness she wants for her children, over whom she is fiercely protective. In Wales, a country oppressed by the English, her children are also oppressed. The memoir is rich with complicated layers of connections and contradictions that defy simple reductionist statements about power and abuse, identity and marginalization, good and bad. Once ensconced in Wales, their father visits sporadically, until he leaves them altogether.

In later life, Williams moves to Guyana with her husband, connecting to her father's home country but, again, from the standpoint of an outsider, a foreigner, as well as being seen as an outsider within the expat community she ostensibly belongs to, but where she doesn't fit in as a working-class woman of colour. All of this further complicates her sense of belonging by adding a fourth country that serves as a temporary home.

I've never read a memoir quite like this one before. Although memoirs are typically about its author's life, and Williams has certainly lived a well-travelled one, it is also enriched with cultural and social history alongside the psychogeographical impact of migration and immigration. It presents a new, more multicultural version of Wales, and is a great companion read to the other Welsh book published alongside it, *Dat's Love* by Leonora Brito, in this landmark series.

Bernardine Evaristo
May 2023

Preface

I grew up in a small Welsh town amongst people with pale faces, feeling that somehow to be half Welsh and half Afro-Caribbean was always to be half of something but never quite anything whole at all. I grew up in a world of mixed messages about belonging, about home and about identity.

It's a truism that those who go searching for their roots often learn more about the heritage they set aside than the one that they seek. In the 1980s, serendipity took me to the Caribbean, to the country of my estranged father, and I began a journey I had not anticipated. It was a journey that took me across a physical terrain spanning three continents and across a complex internal landscape. If I set out with the idea to document something of my searching as a second-generation black Briton, what began as an account of a journey became an account of a confrontation with myself and with the idea of Wales and Welshness.

This is a story of childhood and youth, of Welshness and otherness, of roots and rootlessness, of marriage, connection and disconnection, of going away and of going home.

AFRICA

Small Cargo

It would have been so much easier if I had been able to say, "I come from Africa," then maybe added under my breath, "the long way round." Instead, the Africa thing hung about me like a Welsh Not, a heavy encumbrance on my soul; a Not-identity; an awkward reminder of what I was or what I wasn't.

Once at a seminar, one of those occasions when the word *Diaspora* crops up too many times and where there aren't too many of us present, the only other diaspora-person sought me out. His eyes caught mine in recognition of something I can't say I could name, yet I must have responded because later as we chatted over fizzy water and conference packs, he offered quite uninvited and with all the authority of an African: "People like you? You gotta get digging and if you dig deep enough you're gonna find Africa."

I wondered if my name badge carried some information lost to me or whether it was just the way I looked. I felt as if I had entered the realm of some kind of half people, doomed to roam the endless road to elsewhere looking for somewhere called Roots. I was annoyed. Maybe Alex Haley had committed us all to the pilgrimage. I found myself thinking about all those African-Americans straight off the Pan-Am in their shades and khaki shorts treading the trail to the slave forts on the beaches of Ghana. And then I thought about all those who couldn't afford the trip.

I thought about Suzanne. We were sitting drinking tea by the coal fire at home. "I has this friend see," she was saying in her strong south Walian accent, "with red hair and eyes as green as anything. She passes herself as white but Mam told her straight— you're black you is, BLACK! I know your mam and she's black as well so don't go putting on any airs and graces round 'ere." She had a way of talking over her shoulder in conversation with her imaginary Mam. She paused a little and then turned to Mam and said in a lowered voice, "Well I'm not wearing African robes for nobody, uh-uh, not me." Mam didn't respond and we fell silent. That's the Africa thing. It just pops up again and again like a shadow.

When I think about Africa, I think about the beginning of my self. I open my memory eye and there is only one long journey in which I am various ages between three and twelve years old. One composite toing and froing. Dad wrote,

> *Kate sweetheart,*
> *I take over the house on Saturday; that is, by the time you get this. I applied at once for permission to bring my family and for the necessary arrangements to be made. I suppose they'll now write to the Sudan Embassy, and then things would begin to move. Tell everyone you like now about the house. I didn't want them to laugh at you if it didn't come off, and of course, I didn't want the children to be disappointed. I feel absolutely*

magnificent—physically, mentally and about everything in general. I'm afraid my last letter to you was a bit nervous (about publishing etc) and I never ought to have sent it. I feel much more confident now in my own power. I do not need acquired skills to face the future with. I feel now I'm worth much more to myself and to everyone as what I am—an artist, and must try to work right up to the brim of my own possibilities. Five years is not a long time for work or for love but we'll use every moment of the time doing both. Then we'll see. I know this will make more sense to you. I love you. D

I am six years old. "We're going on a boat to Africa," Ma has announced. I tell Ann Morgans and Diane and Mrs Jones *fach*[1] who lives on the corner and they nod like when I said, "I'm going to Auntie Maggie's on Saturday." That's the way it was. Nobody we knew from within our small community had travelled. Well, only to Pwllheli and Prestatyn and the like. We lived out our lives bounded by the sea but very few had crossed it.

We sailed there by cargo ship the first time. A paint-peeled ocean-goer called the *Prome*; soft white letters printed on a charcoal background. It must have been toing and froing this ancient marine route for years by the time it carried us outwards from Liverpool dock. Ma glanced over her shoulder but kept going. Wales was behind her now and she could only move forward as she had done many times before. In the sweep of her skirts we were voyaging to a different world. Dad had already been in

---

[1] Welsh: literally "little Mrs Jones", but used as a term of endearment.

Africa for one lonely year when he sent for us. Just Ma and four small girls made our family then; *teulu bach*.[2] Just a small cargo on a big ship.

There is a curious intimacy about these cargo passages that one doesn't experience on passenger liners. A few cabins on loan to a handful of purposeful passengers for three weeks or so. Over hundreds of years small cabin-loads of explorers, missionaries, those in the service of the Colonial Office and their families have been transported in this way, their stories and their histories becoming intertwined by these sea crossings. They are the people who opened up the connecting routes, the ones who crossed the maps drawn out by Church and Empire. From 1868 Elder Dempster had a fleet of steamers following the infamous route to and from the Dark Continent. In later years we would travel to and from the coast of West Africa aboard luxurious dazzling white passenger liners: the *Apapa*, the *Accra*, the *Aureol*. But at first we went cargo to the Sudan.

It is surprising how you first notice difference as a child. A missionary family travelled with us on the passage I am remembering now. They were heading out to work in old Omdurman. They were noisy, and unlike us they spoke proper English. The mother had a loud challenging voice like a teacher, her mouth opening long and wide with every word. The father wore long socks with sandals, the type worn by older men today. He had too many words in his mouth as I remember and overly explained everything to their three children, who all looked and dressed

[2] Welsh: "small family".

exactly the same, in the way English children did. Then there were some very pale nuns, white as their starched collars, and some stiff Foreign Office people with World Service accents going to Aden. One of their group was a younger man, a fresher on his first tour to what must by then have been the vestiges of the colonial adminis- tration; part of the mopping-up job I suspect as Nkrumah brushed out the pink paint on the map of Africa. "Creative abdication" the British called it. Only pieces of these memories come to me now, pieces that shaped me. The memories don't fall out in nice neat lines as they seemed to do when there weren't so many of them.

We move out across the Bay of Biscay, where the storms lash the sides of the ship and pitch and turn us till we all lie down sea- sick for three days. Then into warmer waters and warmer days when schools of dolphins appear and swim alongside the ship, a happy squeaking escort that brings our entire passenger group out onto the deck. The crew put up a makeshift canvas swimming pool on the rear deck. I can smell the wet tarpaulin now, filled daily with salty sea water which moves in rhythm with the waves in the huge wide sea, so that we are tossed and showered and bobbed and ducked until we will never again misjudge the power and the perils of the ocean. The missionary children are not allowed to participate in the fun but content themselves instead with stand- ing nearby and staring. I can smell the ship's ropes and the bleached wooden decks. We find some hessian quoits that we wear as heavy armlets or anklets in our small-girl play, and we sing a Welsh song about a saucepan and a cat that scratches *Johnny bach*.[3] The wooden

[3] Welsh: "little Johnny".

rails of the ship's sides taste of the sea. Everything tastes of the sea. "Why do you have to put everything to your mouth, Cha?" Ma is saying. "*Ych a fi.*"[4] I'm not listening, only tasting and feeling.

There are areas of the boat barred to us. Over the rope boundary we can see oily black pulleys, coils of rope, rusting pieces of machinery and the sailors—rough sailors, the engine wallahs, the deck hands and the cooks and cleaners taking a cigarette or just emerging from the underworld to squint a few minutes' daylight. They are on the other side of things from us. They are very different from the smartly dressed officers who change from their blues to tropical whites and from whites-long to whites-short as the voyage takes us towards the Mediterranean. We spend whole days out on the decks, hair fuzzy and free, skin colour changing from pale to mellow browns. And by night we sleep in the belly of the ship lulled to sleep by the hum of the engines and the creaking of the old boat's aching structure as she rolls with the waves. We are suspended, with the echoes of our forefathers rumbling below.

Ma is happy on the sea. She prefers to travel this way. She likes these voyages; both the drift and the drive of them are part of her make-up, carried along with a helplessness she courted. "Why did you bring me here?" she would demand of Dad in the months to come. Yet this passage was part of her own inner drive to move out from under the claustrophobic pile of slate that was her birthplace. I would come to know her as sacrificer, sufferer, survivor. She had a steel will that had pushed her away from all the chapel

[4] Welsh: "Ugh!"

8

goodness, the village small talk, from the purples and the slate greys that invaded her inner landscape. In its wake came a fatalism that she could not shake off. It haunted her. But she was suited to the slow acclimatisation in the space of the voyage. The place between somewhere and elsewhere was so right for her.

I think about Ma as I wait in transit at Piarco Airport in Trinidad, caught up in those same kind of moments between somewhere and elsewhere. Eight hours from Manchester and one hour from Georgetown. I've been delayed for four hours in this limbo, wondering and waiting for an explanation as the BWIA[5] planes touch down and take off in a constant stream of traffic across the Caribbean. I once saw a programme on the telly about the man who has been trapped in the in-transit no-man's land of Charles de Gaulle Airport for years as no country will accept him. He lives his life out of the only small piece of hand luggage he pushes around on a baggage trolley and appears curiously content with his synthetic desert. He engages with a small cohort of familiar passengers who pass through regularly. "*Who am I?* I am that man at Charles de Gaulle Airport," he says.

I have rehearsed his scenario several times already. I suppose there could be worse airport lounges than Piarco to be held up in. It's got a friendly small-place feel to it and those coming in, those leaving and those just passing through, all muddle together like guests at a party. I've been here many times before and I've come to expect these delays as part and parcel of my journey. I've looked in my purse and worked out how many Eastern

[5] British West Indies Airways.

Caribbean dollars will keep me in Carib beers and sandwiches. Opposite me a Rasta guy is sleeping across four chairs. He is wearing an oversized woolly hat in "the colours" and his crumpled tee shirt has a map of Africa printed on the front. Somalia has become part of Mozambique, whilst Zanzibar has disappeared under his left arm. That's the Africa I know—all merged into one big place. I am quite adept at sketching Africa. I remember at school how swiftly I could draw the Dark Continent freehand, like a body map with the great veins of the Congo and the Nile and the Niger and the vast open deserts like skin.

Ma was never good in small spaces. I imagine myself small again, flung back into those snatches of memory that make up my Africa. Just once we fly to Africa and there are goody bags with BOAC[6] written on them for all of us. The insides of Ma's hands are red and there are beads of sweat sitting quietly on her nose. We are boarding the plane, which has a cold grey outside that looks like it will taste of pencil lead. There are lots of waiting people and bags ahead of us and it seems as if there may not be room for us. A woman with a loud English voice says, "Excuse me," and pushes past Ma to the front of the boarding queue. Ma just ups and grabs her by the neck of her blouse and starts to shake her like a piece of washing. "*Blydi Sais*,"[7] Ma says. "Just who do you think you are, Queen of the Cannibals? How dare you. How bloody dare you." Thumb in mouth, I try to shrink myself into the folds of her skirts. Ma is in a complete rage, shouting and

[6] British Overseas Airways Corporation.
[7] Welsh: "Bloody English!"

flapping her arms. Beads of sweat have broken out on her top lip too by now. Eventually the Captain comes to see what the problem is. "See that one," she says to him, "she thinks she can treat me like a dog, putting on airs like she's somebody." Lots more "How bloody dare yous" and "Who do you think you ares" follow before she can be pacified. The Captain calls Ma "Ma'am" very slowly. He tells her that they are first timers to the colonies and they don't know anything about Africa or about coloured people and so she lets it go, for now at least.

This battle would be part of what we were and what we would be, although I can't say I knew at that stage of my life what the battle was about. I guessed, like Dad said, it was because Ma was Welsh and she wasn't taking orders from anybody. But she was beautiful at sea. The cool openness on the decks, her wild beauty matching the elements; the blue of the waves and the blue of her eyes. Africa had called for Dad and now he was calling for her; Kate sweetheart, his love and his mentor. He loved the rhythms and poetry of her thoughts. Her ideas fell together like jazz, the blue notes resonating across the staves with their own logic, defying the predictable sequences and the rudimentary facts. He would not be without the magic that was her. She was shaping him; her mind was his umbrella and beyond this umbrella he dared not step. "*Paid a phoeni, Denis bach*[8] . . . Everything will be fine," she would say. She provided such spiritual security for him. She was our backbone.

Behind them they left London. The London of John Nash, Wyndham Lewis and Elgar that very gently nudged them away

[8] Welsh: "Don't worry, Denis dear".

with all its imperialist assumptions and its contradictions. That London would never be the same after the Picasso exhibition in the V&A took the country by storm, the influences of Africa cutting through the canvases like a knife. A London of immigrants. Sam Selvon's London; a cold, grey and miserable motherland.

There had been much pillow talk about the move out to Africa. They had discussed it over and over again, trying to anticipate the future. It could have been different. They could have stayed on in London; things were going well. Dad had a teaching job at the Central School of Art and several major exhibitions behind him with excellent reviews. I have a scrapbook from this time that Ma must have put together. Wyndham Lewis wrote in *The Listener* about a "brilliant newcomer"—his huge canvases hanging on the walls of the Gimpel Fils gallery bursting with colour and symbolism. Dad had painted *Human World*. It was magnificent, painted in equatorial reds, yellows, ochres and greens with tree-like people standing and glaring with large threatening eyes as if the Empire might stand up and strike back. It was pure savagery confronting civilisation. When I read the old fragment of *The Listener*, I saw all those assumptions that pushed them away; all those assumptions that lay deep in the lines.

In spite of the fact that Denis Williams speaks with an unmistakable Welsh accent, he is a Negro. But because of the Empire-building propensities of the Briton of yesterday he is British for he comes from British Guiana. Georgetown, the capital city, is where he lives. It is anything but the jungle: there are splendid boulevards lined with blood-red trees, a fine hotel (for

Sahibs only), a busy port. The Negroes are tennis and cricket
playing Negroes; Milton and the other national poet Shakespeare,
is what they are brought up on, but especially Milton.

How could this country have held him with all its double-speak? Wyndham Lewis was a Welshman, Ma told us later. "He was the one who said that the coloured men of London were all boxers and sailors and that we should move on," she said.

But Ma and Dad rubbed along the edges of a very glamorous London, moving in circles that included Francis Bacon, Lucian Freud and other equally well-known artists. Dad was artist-in-residence at the Slade for a while. He became the interesting chap to have at parties; a curiosity, a poodle, the comfortable stranger. Ma was not so easy. She was Welsh and uncomfortably different. "You're the English one," she used to say to Dad, knowing in her heart that she was the real dark stranger.

Their real life was a small cramped flat in Oxford Road, where Dad hung up his smarty-boy suit on the back of the door at night and set to work painting whilst Ma's wages from a job in a book warehouse kept them going. At night the West Indian chaps dropped by: Michael Manley, Jan Carew, Wilson Harris, Forbes Burnham, were all regular visitors. Gathered in that small space they talked about imperialism, about colonialism and independence. They were the Caribbean writers and artists and future leaders with visions and big thoughts, not boxers and sailors. They were planning a different world. And the stuff of their talk was the destiny of their own countries and news of Africa and Nkrumah in his fight for independence. That was their struggle;

they were not concerned with their position in the motherland. For them the motherland was only ever to be a temporary host, so although they knew the colour bar, they didn't need to take it on. They knew it was difficult to get lodgings and in many a bar they would be told, "Sorry but we don't serve you chaps in here." But it was all very polite; so very polite and so accepted.

When Welsh and Irish girls came to London looking for work they found the same lodging houses willing to let them in as the coloured chaps. It was Mrs Dovaston who took in Katie Alice and found Denis on Kilburn High Street and invited him back for tea. Ma said Mrs Dovaston's own granddaughter Josephine was a black girl and that her father had played the piano for Paul Robeson in America. I suppose she liked having coloured people round the house for Josephine's sake.

So Ma and Dad became lovers, eventually married and moved on. That's how we began to learn about movement. It was movement that was home. Home was not a particular place for us in the very early years. Home was Ma. We arrived into an exile; into a state of relocation that was both hers and his. And the journeys were more than physical journeys. They were travels across worlds of thinking, across generations of movements. These boat stories and seascapes, I now know, are part of a collective memory lying buried below the immediate moment.

Slowly the boat days grew longer and the small passenger group became politely accustomed to each other and shared table and time. The colonial boy with the books found his own space, aloof and largely indifferent to the rest of us. Just occasionally he had a way of announcing things authoritatively that spoke reams about his mission. "Khartoum," he said and paused for the audience to attend. "Lord Kitchener laid down that it should be built on a grid in the form of a Union Jack." And so he went on like he alone owned the knowledge. The cackle of the group heading towards Aden mingled with that of the missionary family in a noisy chorus. We were apart from all this. Ma was not one for mixing. Perhaps she was mistrustful of them. She would sit on the deck in her sunglasses with her scarf tied Audrey Hepburn fashion and watch over us.

From time to time, however, the group of passengers came together with some of the more senior members of the crew at the Captain's table. I remember one particular occasion at the Captain's table when the missionary group were brought to heel by Ma's tongue and made to treat us with the respect she demanded. She had maintained a chapel silence for some five long days when their proselytising caught her attention. Clearly suspicious of her association with the Dark Continent they had made presumptions about her soul. "What right have you to assume that I'm not saved?" she suddenly levelled at them across the dinner table. The shot flew through the air bringing an embarrassed silence that is now so familiar to us. It quietened their talk and averted their eyes. She had mastery. Ma and her Bible talk; she wielded Bible metaphor like a weapon. "Am I my brother's keeper?" she might sometimes ask. But more usually by careful inference she could confer the restraining power of scripture. She was not a preacher like her sister Maggie, but her speech was framed with spiritual reference. I never remember her having any small talk; it wasn't her way. I think that is how we understood her as Welsh at first. Contrary, confrontational, biblical and a passionate stranger. Ma's intuition was rarely wrong. She stood on guard against assumptions. I longed for her to be ordinary but she wore her difference like a banner. She was flamboyant. I see her in this wonderful rich patterned dress, a kind of Mexican dancer style with puffy, small, off-the-shoulder sleeves and a huge skirt. It was magical and it captured the wildness of her spirit; the rebel in her. The waves moved us towards the scorched country. Sand, scorch and semi-scrub; *Sudanic mulatto* Dad called it. Africa was pulling him in; it claimed him bit by bit and he was excited by all that it offered him. The country drew us to its desert plains, to the calls of the muezzins echoing across the city of Khartoum from the mosque towers that pierced the city skyline, towards the smell of neem, mimosa and camel dung. I can see those clear starry night skies from my seat at the back of Dad's Land Rover. I can taste the dust thrown up from the desert trails.

I am caught up in tiny moments, pictures of Africa flicker across my memory-eye in brilliant colour. As the ship nears ancient Port Said, tiny boats come alongside. At first just one or two, then there are many. Tall thin Africans with wild unkempt hair stand steady in the little boats as our ship comes to a slow halt. Matt black, midnight blue black, then indigo as their skins pick up the colours of the water. I have never seen anyone like them before. These are not Arabs; they are darkest Africa. I watch the dark strangers from the vantage point of the huge ship. I stand amongst the pale nuns and the Colonial Office people and the missionary family looking at the strange beings without recognition of what they are. "These are the Fuzzy-Wuzzies," the colonial boy says as though he has just looked it up in one of his manuals. "The Baggaras. We call them the Fuzzy-Wuzzies. My father used to say, 'Big Black Bounding Beggars that Broke a British Square'," he tells us, mustering all his self-importance. The Fuzzy-Wuzzies watch us, steady-eyed. Deep behind my eyes is fear and curiosity that asks questions of the beings within those dark skins. Their half-naked bodies, their primitive wholeness leaves my mouth hanging open. I can't taste their difference but I can see it. Their hair is dull and huge on their thin angular black faces and when they dive for the coins we throw overboard into the deep blue, the creatures emerge with their hair intact as though no water has penetrated the fuzzy mass. What devils of the sea they are to me. What a spectacle. The space between the *Prome* and the dock is filled with small boats and confusion. The entire crew is out flanking the side of the ship. We stand with our small brown faces, our own fuzzy-wuzzy hair, our white Welsh mother and the officers of Her Majesty the Queen. There is Africa below and we are safe Britannia. That's how I first saw Africa.

It said British in Dad's passport and British in Ma's and that meant all that was good and right and ordinary. Africa was the real stranger. The body map was not yet mine. It was all outside of me. I glimpsed it but I would not recognise my connection to it for years to come. And yet in those small moments an imprint was made; an unconscious but indelible imprint that means I stare at the Rasta man's shirt now and know something very deep gives it meaning to him and to me.

Afternoon Dreaming

Five-thirty in the afternoon and my Piarco anxieties are rising. I doubt that I'll ever be able to shake off the sense that things aren't going to go smoothly. Piarco might be the Crewe Junction of the Caribbean, but at one time it wasn't unusual to arrive at the transfer desk after a gruelling flight from London to hear the desk officer say, "I'm sorry madam but the plane is full," or "I'm afraid there has been a double booking." I've even been offered the jump-seat before today and spent what was actually a very pleasant two-hour flight peering out of the cockpit from between the pilot and co-pilot. I wouldn't say "no" to the jump-seat right now in exchange for the absolute assurance that I will be leaving here today. I turn up the volume on my Walkman, sit back and close my eyes. I dread that at any moment I could get caught up in yet another of those endless conversations with someone about who's who and who's related to who, in which we have to go all round the houses, or the islands, I should say. "Well yuh know Byron James . . . he brudder's boss-man Henry, right? Well Henry's wife is you fadder's cousin, right? Well . . ." on and on and round and round until we get back to find that we are all bonded in some infinite familial web. It's the same in Wales. As gateway to the

Caribbean, Piarco has almost become the official national meeting point with all the connecting work to do like that of an eisteddfod. I met the Mighty Sparrow here once—all gold rings and silk shirt and a big booming voice. He wrote his sprawling signature on the back of my return ticket, "Mighty Sparrow, King of Calypso". When I got to Georgetown I went straight out and bought his tape; when I left I had to relinquish my ticket and proof of any association with him. Life can be so cruel.

It's not too difficult to spot those who are going to Guyana. For some reason it's almost impossible to pass through this airport without at least one piece of your luggage getting left behind, so travellers en route to Georgetown are trying to carry their immediate needs along with every anticipated shortage in the Guyanese economy in their oversized hand luggage. And when the plane finally does begin to board, arguments will break out between passengers and cabin crew about which bags won't be allowed in the cabin and there will be a delay of at least another hour while the Captain is called to sort it out. I find myself mentally weighing up people's hand luggage as they begin to congregate around the departure gate; yes, they'll let that one on, or no, that one's got no chance. Then there are those travelling outwards from Georgetown. Like the wide-bottomed auntie who, despite the heat, is already dressed in her London coat, hand luggage straining at the seams to accommodate two dozen rock hard mangoes, a jar or two of achar and four bottles of XM rum—that little taste of Guyana for the relatives outside. I guess by now I am getting to be an accomplished observer.

Rasta-man's hand luggage isn't giving too much away but I try to read other messages about him. I watch as he turns over slowly and frees up the scene of Africa. I realise how easily he carries me back into Africa days—to some of my earliest memories of the Sudan and to my childhood memories of Nigeria. Two very different places have melded over time to become one Africa for me. I can't help wondering about Rasta-man's Africa; I'm curious about how he carries it with him. Is his Africa in the food he eats, in his music, his poetry? Does he talk it up in his everyday chat? Is it in his dreams or is it simply printed on his tee shirt? Why do we carry Africa around with us like this? I doubt he's ever been there, but what the heck; Africa is his spiritual home and he sleeps easy with it despite the hustle-bustle and noise all about him. He reminds me of a soldier, sleeping with part of himself on guard. I begin to relax with his sleepy pose and his sleeping Africa. There's his history and there's mine and I let them mingle together. As he sleeps with his picture of Africa, I pull out mine.

Colonizer's Logic
These natives are unintelligent—
We can't understand their language.

Chinweizu

Africa days punctuated by afternoon sleep. The heat demands "slow" or "sleep" and for the majority the choice is sleep. The women in the market pull their babies to their breast and lay down beneath makeshift stalls in a cool womb of shade. The window shutters close off the blast of the heat and the servants retreat to their quarters, first to eat and then to sleep. There's a lull. It's a time of quiet unaccompanied by the chorus of the night beetle or the rattle of the swamp toads that will come later. The forest is hushed too. Afternoon sleep is deep sleep. The driver sprawls across the front seat of the yellow municipal bus seemingly oblivious to the passengers who may soon join him in slumber. Stopped dead.

The afternoons are over when the six o'clock flower opens its evening face. Ma will make sweet tea with condensed milk served in glass cups and then teach us how to sew. Then the sounds of the night begin, the mosquito coils are lit and the fireflies sparkle in the dark spaces like the stars in the African sky. And in a brief twilight space Dad will type a few more lines of his book:

> *Siesta. The whole country flat on its back. The streets lay down like dead zebras: ochre striped with black, so secret and private you felt you had no right. Goats noiselessly reduced the careful hedges to skeletons; the hour your front gate is furtively opened and the animals let in to finish off the lawns; let in by the police, too, who show lethargic indignation in face of protest.*

In the cool of the evening Ma will read over Dad's manuscript and then they will argue while Joseph the servant boy makes pep-peh stew and hums a tune over his work.

But for now, along with most, they sleep and in those few hours long spaces open up to us like a reprieve. Time slows. The geckos and the wall lizards stand still in the intense light and baking heat. Only the children and the columns of ants move on. These are times of adventure and growth; times when all the rules are suspended as we little people are left on trust to shape our own worlds. In these free and open spaces we cross boundaries and discover our own Sudan and later our own Nigeria, our Africa.

I am about ten in the memory that comes to me now. I can see Ma sleeping, lying next to my father, back to back. She has been victim to the African sun again today. Sapped of all her strength, she lies naked on her side of the bed. I am curious about Ma's body. It is always strange but not a stranger to me. Its colours and its contours make no sense in this place yet it is warm and familiar.

I crouch with my small sister and observe her through the slatted wooden partition that separates off the private space of my parents' bedroom. Her arms and the top of her creamy back are splashed with freckles. Her marshmallow breasts slumber and her tummy, now five children stretched, relaxes into the crumples of the cotton sheet. I look at her red hair, freed from the French plait, tamed with time but still curling and twisting on the pillow. Ma is dreaming old dreams. I haven't been told her stories yet but I have seen them sometimes on her face and heard them when she calls out in her sleep. Her dreams tell of a yesterday I wish I could have known back then, I might have understood her better. The memories of her life in the small Welsh village thousands of miles away unfold themselves, first one, then another in a picture of words and silences.

I am nervous. I'm always nervous about the *seiat*.[9] Before every Wednesday comes I turn in my bed like a dog with a fever. I know I have written down every word the Reverend William Williams spoke. The others could never do it like

[9] Welsh: a mid-week religious meeting in chapel.

22

me, Katie Alice, take down every word as he speaks it. I am
the one chosen because I am quick like a piano player matching a song. "*O Israel, paham y dinistriaist dy hun?*"[10] That's
what he said and when I looked down my pencil had it
before me! But now I must write it out fine and nice on the
blackboard in the vestry so that at the *seiat* those who missed
the Reverend's words on Sunday can come and hear what
he had to say. And I will have to learn my piece by heart
ready for Wednesday. I will have to look upon the whole
congregation and read my verse aloud. And I will have to
try and make the words sound strong and smooth like he
does; to speak it like a poem of Eifion Wyn and let it go into
the people's hearts.

And we will all go down the hill from Bontnewydd to the
chapel hall and sit; boys on one side, girls on the other.
Those of us who have written on the board will be at the
front. I will see little John, my brother, sitting small with all
the other boys. John *bach*[11] who wailed and cried the place
down when father left us here and I couldn't go to him.
Johnny *bach del*.[12] But we're not allowed to speak. Oh no,
Miss Morgan will keep her sharp blue eyes on our backs to
see we don't ever have anything to say to the boys, not even
a glance to the other side of the chapel hall. If she were to
see me talking, even with my own brother, well she'd have

[10] Welsh: "O Israel, why hast thou destroyed thyself?"
[11] Welsh: "little John".
[12] Welsh: "pretty little Johnny".

me, she would make sure I'd be without my supper just like that! Not me, because I would try not to give Miss Blodwen Morgan any fuss and bother. Not like Mair Lewis does. I would never answer them back at Bontnewydd like Mair Lewis does, not out loud anyway. Only with my mind and in my heart. Even when they make me wear a silk hat to Sunday school, looking odd from the others, well I would just wear it like it was made for me . . . a crown to my red hair. A big silk crown.

It's like when Miss Morgan saw me looking in the mirror. Just combing out my hair I was, and she said, "Come away from there! Don't be fooling yourself that you are something! You are only fit for a farm labourer, girl! Farm boys, they're the likes for you!" She was cruel like that. Well I just looked her in the eye, quiet and strong, and I see what she really wants in a flash. She's after me to come and wash and comb her hair again after tea but she doesn't say so. She wants me to make her beautiful. But she isn't beautiful. Her spirit is hard and rough and so is her hair.

Like the time she pushed Nancy, the deaf and dumb one. Pushed her to go and blacklead the stove in the kitchen when everyone else had gone out. Left all by herself she was, *bechod*.[13] I was the one who taught Nancy to lip-read. I wanted to tell Miss Blodwen Morgan, "If you turn your face to Nancy you can tell her to her face what she's fit to do." Nancy can help with writing down the Rev. William Williams's

[13] Welsh: "pity".

words now and when I'm gone she'll be able to help the others with their homework in my place. We never say anything though. You don't answer back to anyone like that in Bontnewydd. Like this morning when we were washing ourselves in the entrance. Naked we were and Mr Thomas passes through from the side door and comes over to us and he touches us, touches our breasts. The man who starts up the hymns on Sunday does it too. There for all to see and we don't say a word, just keep on with our washing and things like nothing happened. Miss Morgan is all smiles with him though, Mr Thomas that is.

People from the town come to the *seiat*; the people from the shops. Some of the farmers too, and sometimes they bring their wives and children. Maybe they know of my father John William Hughes from Quarry View Stores and they've heard people say that he was a fine man who dressed smart and was friendly with all the people. Maybe they heard that when his wife died he let the shop his father had worked so hard to build just fall down until he was forced to shut it all up. And about how he's let himself go now and doesn't speak to anyone any more like he used to. They say he's got melancholia since his wife passed away. I didn't let that get back to Johnny *bach*. It's just people talking. People have got nothing more to do than to talk about everyone else's business.

I will read from my own hand to them. I can write very nice. That's why I got the prize at the eisteddfod for the League of Nations Essay, because of being able to write poems and the like. Osborne Roberts came as adjudicator that year and he said my essay was marvellous. I could be a bard but that's just silly to say because it's not for girls to do. So I will lick the chalk and in my best hand put up what the Reverend Williams said on the question about the colour of Jesus:

"Sut un ydoedd Iesu Grist?" meddai bachgen bychan croenddu wrth genhadwr mwyn ryw ddydd. "Oedd e'n wyn fel pawb o'm ceraint ynteu oedd e'n ddu fel fi?"[14]

The Reverend William Williams has spoken about how our people have gone to Africa to save the black people, *y bobl ddu*.[15] I saw a small black boy in one of the pictures he shows us. That's not the only black one I've seen. One time we went from Bontnewydd with my father and we saw black men playing music in Caernarfon town and my dad told me I must keep clear of them. But we collect every week in the box to help *y plant duon*[16] in Africa. I looked at the black boy in the picture for a long time. He's like us in Bontnewydd who haven't got a mam and a dad. His Jesus is just the same as our Jesus and we feel black just like him. It's not us to blame for that.

[14] Welsh: "What did Christ look like?" asked a little boy to a kindly missionary one day. "Was he white like my companions or was he black like me?"
[15] Welsh: "the black people".
[16] Welsh: "the black children".

Ma had no grace in the harsh Africa climate; it immobilised her physically and yet mentally she held us all despite her inner struggles. She guided us with the same strength that had driven her on from the orphanage. When she was eighteen, she had made her way to Liverpool and taken a job as a nurse. She spoke only a little English. "They thought I was stupid and so they sent me packing—sacked me," she told me only recently. "I couldn't understand things so I was just guessing at them and I made mistakes so Matron said, 'Get your things, we'll never make a nurse of you.'" Maybe they didn't understand that Wales was another country with its own language and its own people. From Liverpool she went to find her older sister, Maggie, in London. Maggie was working in service and couldn't offer Ma a home and so they walked the streets looking for accommodation until they came across Mrs Dovaston.

Then she was in Africa. She had freed herself, broken away from the confines of her past. Although Africa wasn't really a sanctuary for her, she could feel a kinship with the spirit of the people. She felt it through her own difference and she let it invade her. But Dad was a very different story. Africa both tempted and tormented him. It pulled at him in a way he couldn't resist but at the same time he couldn't let go of his European mind. Without that he feared he would be nothing but a savage and it was a savage he couldn't reconcile himself to. In his book *Other Leopards*, he writes the story of Lionel and Lobo, two names for one man. Lionel is the civilised one, the educated man, and Lobo is the savage. Lionel is the one constrained by Western logic, caught up in a way of thinking and presentation of himself that is not naturally his, by history or by spirit. Lobo on the other hand is free, wild, authentic. Dad is both Lionel and Lobo. I see that now, although I could never have understood it back then. His life was a struggle against his desire to be Lobo, but he was colonised by European thinking and European ways—the Lionel in him robbed him of his spirit that was truly African.

It's easy to explain it as Dad's inner self but maybe all of us who are dislocated tussle with Lionel. Maybe we, the dispersed ones, are all bit-Africans looking for the Lobo in ourselves: the free spirit, the savage spirit, the one who is reconciled with the past. I can see Dad's struggle in his writing: "Me lingering with the nostalgia of those sweet rhythms, memories three hundred years old; me back home now in Africa, there called brother by savage women . . . I'm no savage." Lobo lurks deep in his soul and his resistance speaks loud in the pages of his book. He is tormented.

During long, empty afternoons, Ma's inner defiance seeped into our souls. It was part of her and so it was part of us. We had to go out of the gate. We had to break the boundary like Ma. At first, in Khartoum days, we would leave the security of the compound and roam free until the muezzin's call to prayer drove us home. I was a follower in the outside world. I suppose I was still too young or too frightened of what would happen if Dad ever discovered the afternoons' secrets. Older and more experienced, in another Africa the design of the afternoons would be mine. But it was Evelyn, my older sister, who first opened the gates and opened our world.

Before his sleep Dad would say, "Behave yourself, child. Don't go jumping about like a monkey," or "Keep your tail cool, girl,"

"Keep your mouth quiet," and Ma would add her usual warnings about speaking to strangers at the gate or going out of the compound. And we did everything they said not to as though it was a licence to experiment. It was Dad who introduced us to the idea of swimming on grass, the afternoon he said before retiring to his bedroom, "Play inside. Keep off the wet grass, don't even put your damn foot near it." Our attention was now suddenly drawn to it in a different way. The gardener always flooded the lawn in the dry season to keep the grass green. The deep inches made a tempting Nile and we splashed and slithered about under the hot of the sun while Ma and Dad slept. We were caught out by our footsteps, our handprints and our belly prints, slowly emerging like an aboriginal painting as the water evaporated in the five o'clock sun.

When we were called to Dad's study I wasn't afraid. I knew I had the halo of Ma's spirit over me. I was always the charmed one, selected from amongst my sisters for Dad's displays of affection. He said I was like Ma and he never raised his voice or his hand to me. It was one of the few guarantees despite his array of unpredictable moods and harsh Victorian discipline. We might have opened the door of the study and found him willing to laugh it off. He could easily be so charming and gentle. When I saw that he was angry I knew that Evelyn would bear the brunt of his fury and I made a small defence of her. She would be doubly punished for her defiance and beaten like a dog. My remonstrations were weak. I recognised my inability to protect her from his fiery temper but for years I thought it was unwillingness. I understood her punishment spared me, but I would never be spared the feeling of guilt—guilt that I had participated in this bizarre ritual. Why did she laugh and not cry? To cry might have saved her. Why did she court his savage spirit? Why did Katie Alice? He tried to banish it from them; to punish them for entertaining Lobo. "Damn savage. What do you think you are, a savage?" he would ask. "Jackass. Blasted jackass, blasted fool, prancing around like an ape." Evelyn did cry quietly later and in the lines of his book Dad cries out too. I guess he was frightened of Lobo; tormented.

We tormented the men who came to empty the soil bucket in the afternoons. We called them the Jonnies. They would arrive not long after Ma and Dad lay down to rest. Like the wild goats that tended the hedges, their work wasn't spared the afternoon heat. The job was only fit for the afternoons when ordinary people slept and the filth of it could be hidden. The shit lorry approached the gate like a carnival float passing slowly by, with its occupants jumping on and off, steel bins clanking and crashing. We smelled them coming; the stench carried on the heat. Ma had told us how men in lorries like this came to steal small white children away so we ran inside when we heard them coming and watched from the concealed position below the bedroom window, waiting in whispers. The Jonnies entered the compound and had to pass by our hiding place to reach the toilet at the side of the house; pass once to collect and then pass back with the empties.

Our Jonny came into the yard, ragged shorts, matted hair, crow-black but chalky now with desert dust clinging, his white eyes buried like cowries in his black mask. We followed him with our small staring eyes and as he passed the open window we threw a curse through the grillework like a stone at the wild animal. We were the caged ones but when the Jonny stopped and glared back through the grille he looked to us like the trapped animal. We met his eye and cursed some more. Confronted, terrified and exhilarated, we spat and spat again; spat at his skin, at his dirty task, at him, at his blackness. He moved on silently to collect the barrel of excrement and then passed back. He paused at the open window laughing at our fear, shaking his free hand at us and we could do nothing but spit again. Spit him away. He started shouting, shouting loud like a baboon. We were screeching over and over, "The Jonnies! The Jonnies!" when Dad woke angry from his brief sleep and came rushing out into the yard. More matty haireds were now at the gate watching on as the Lionel in Dad came face to face with the Jonny man. A kind of Lobo stood before him, savage, wild, untamed, uncivilised. Dad shouted him down with three hundred years of history standing between them. We watched on, petrified. There was Dad, caught off guard, straight from his dreams, stripped and naked bar his white undershorts, remonstrating with the Lobo man. The afternoon sun lit up his clean brown skin against Jonny man's black. Dad's words, audible and English above Jonny man's babble, reverberated across the open yard and echoed across savannahs of afternoon sleep. Their angry voices rose with the heat. Dad's eyes were wide and his back was as stiff as his British top lip. Evelyn was giggling in terror. Then a gasp, a long collective gasp, as shit man swung the metal tub from across his back and raised it in his powerful arms into the air. A barrel-load of shit, suspended high above Dad's head, held there for seconds, heavy and waiting. Our mess. Our shit. The yard was silenced—goats, dogs, matty haireds, us, my father—all silenced; cowed to the primitive. Cowed to the savage spirit of Lobo. Then, with a sneer, Jonny man lowered the barrel and walked away.

The threat of the savage stayed with us. Dad would not let it go. There was the savage within and the savage outside. Ma and Dad were arguing; over food, over a visitor, over his writings. His tantrums rose up and down like a *marabunta*[17] banging its body on the ceiling looking for a way out. He was fun then furious. She was needy and challenging.

I think I knew something about Lobo back then. Just for a while. I knew what it was to be wild, to be boundless and savage. When I climbed, I felt the power of the trees in me so that I didn't know what was tree and what was me. I felt in me the same force that burst under the wings of the bird taking off in flight, the same force that tumbled the river water over the stones and that cracked lightning through the air. When I lay on the dank floor of the forest, I was the forest; nothing stood between the natural wildness and me. I guess that wasn't Dad's idea of savage though. The savage Dad fought against was rude and stupid, untamed and uncivilised—a threat. I thought his savage meant to be African. We weren't Africans. Weren't we saved as Ma had said?

Sometimes Dad would sketch Ma while she slept. I can look at those pictures now, but they are tinged with sadness. He captures the freedom of her nakedness—those pink breasts that suckled our little brown faces; her physical so at odds with us but her mental so in tune with what we were becoming. It was Ma who shaped our cultural memory, passed to us in her stories and her

[17] A type of large hornet with a painful sting.

way·of telling them; in the songs of her childhood that reached out to us and formed us. We were *cariad*.[18]

So I watch them sleep, their dreams intermingling. Dad fights with his people and Ma fights with hers and in those intense afternoon moments we were drawn out onto the forbidden road over and over again.

ON BAR BEACH—LAGOS 1966

The sea nearly swallowed Ma,
ate her whole
into its big translucent jaw.

I stood by her on Bar Beach
and then she was gone,
picked off with a long licking tongue
into the mouth of the deep and thunderous . . . gone
while I froze under the hot September sun.

Turned her over in its rolling laugh
and told her not to play with
Ajantala or Arawn,
fooled with her spirit,

tossed her rubbery doll's legs
into a sea ballet

[18] Welsh: "sweetheart", "darling".

and she shone in suspension,
sea drift
hair trickling across her face
like a bloodstain
held in mirrored moments
then out she came
spat out, angry,
cross with Denis.
He laughed like the sea
at Ma
and me.

Ajantala—mischievous, rebellious spirit child, Africa. *Arawn*—
being from the spirit realm, Welsh.

Africa to Wales

A CONGO COLONY IN WALES

Daily Graphic *of Wednesday July 13th 1892*

One of the prettiest spots of the many pleasant places on the main line between Chester and Holyhead is Colwyn Bay, not inaptly termed the "Naples of Wales". There the Congo Training Institute has been established under the patronage of King Leopold of the Belgians, to train African converts as missionaries, schoolmasters, and useful handicraftsmen. This Institute, which is only in its infancy as yet, owes its origin to a Welshman—the Rev. W. Hughes—who was sent out to the Congo by a missionary society, and was there when Mr. Stanley went to found the Free State. Seeing how rapidly the Europeans became victims of the climate, and how little could be done to Christianise and civilise the vast continent by the exertions of a few scattered workers, he cast about him to devise a plan for carrying on the work more efficiently and with less cost of human life. Before, however, he had matured a scheme he was reluctantly compelled to embark for England, nearly in a dying state. He took with him two coloured youths, one of whom he

35

*had redeemed from slavery . . . This opened a path by which the
problem of civilising Africa could be carried out.*

I've got a hundred Africa stories. I'm not so sure I have always
understood why they are so important to me; why they are more
than just a collection of memories. Some years after the African
man waylaid me with his comment about finding Africa if I dig
deep enough, a journalist friend and neighbour, Ivor Wynne,
took me to the graves of the Congo boys. It's a long-forgotten
piece of history, which has come to hold a lot of significance for
me. As I stood one Sunday morning in the overgrown graveyard at Llanelian I remembered that long ago Ma had told me
that there used to be a college for black fellows in Colwyn Bay,
but at the time it hadn't registered. Now it has become one of
those ancient trails I retrace over and over again as if to print
myself onto it.

I regard it as my own mini version of the Pan-Am pilgrimage
only all I have to do is take a right at the roundabout at Old Colwyn and walk up the road. When I visit the graves of the Congo
boys I feel just like those pilgrims to the slave fortresses at Elmina
in Ghana who stand in the ancestral spaces and recreate the past
in the present. It is as though through each retraced step the slave
experience is owned by them. They have to go back to make sense
of themselves in the present. In one single moment they are the
past, the present and the future all rolled into one—the recollection, the recreation and the restatement of the whole thing gives
them a profile. I once read that diaspora peoples without a collective historical event to refer to invent one in order to define their

presence in their inherited country. It took me a long journey to understand why the Congo boys are part of my Elmina. A hundred years separate me from the Congo boys, a small cargo shipped from the Dark Continent to little Wales.

N'Kansa and Kin Kassa were just eight and eleven years old when they were brought to Wales by their new guardian, the Reverend William Hughes. The boys arrived at Llandudno pier in September 1885 on board the steamer *St Tudno*, after a journey that had taken months of travel down long rivers and across vast oceans. The final leg was by pony and trap along Llandudno promenade, over Craigside and along the coast road to Colwyn Bay.

Their journey had begun in the upper Congo. They travelled by boat hundreds of miles down the Congo River to the coastal village of Banana, past Balabo, past Stanley Pool and Leopoldville, past Nyambe and Matadi: places that only lived in the stories of their elders. Stories about wars and about hunting, about spirits of the forest, about the giant Watussi and the Warundi, the small peoples of Batwa and about white men with eyes like dead fish who came with firearms and took away small boys and burned villages and killed old men and women. The Reverend Hughes himself spoke to them about these kinds of white men who left behind fatherless half-caste children who had to be hidden because of shame and fear.

Who can say what tribe the two boys were from? Maybe the Bantu peoples like the Bahunde and the Bahavu that occupied large parts of the Congo, or descendants of the Bayaka or Twa tribes that had spread over extraordinary distances. Most likely N'Kansa was either Bayaka or Twa. He came from the village of

Vunda, where he and his mother were slaves. These peoples, stigmatised as pygmies, had been slaves for hundreds of years; bought and sold by Arab tribes and by the Watussi for little pieces of iron and ivory and salt. Now at the end of the troubled century the chief of the village of Vunda agreed to accept a ransom for N'Kansa. The Reverend bought N'Kansa's freedom for a bale of grey baft from Rylands of Manchester, in value about four pounds and ten shillings. The story goes that N'Kansa went willingly with the Reverend. How could a child have known that without your tribe you become nobody?

William Hughes had left Wales like so many others in his time to evangelise and civilise the natives of Africa. Yet nothing of his studies at Llangollen Baptist College had prepared him for the Africa he found—so wonderful and yet so treacherous. "Soon after my arrival in the Congo," the Reverend wrote in his diaries, "I found it would be impossible to get proper hold of the young people without separating them as much as possible from former friends, old superstitions and other injurious influences." The Reverend believed there would be little point in scattering what was a dim light in the midst of such dense darkness. God's work was so easily destroyed by the power of evil that dwelt in these lands, it being too great for the few converts to overcome. Perhaps the Reverend realised that his work would always be frustrated by the strength of the beliefs of the people. Or perhaps he realised that his days in the Congo would always be numbered because of other injurious influences. It was said of Africa that many went in but few came out. Sickness and death claimed them;

black water fever, malaria, sleeping sickness, yellow fever and the like. When *daua*[19] entered their bodies even the witchdoctor might not succeed in casting out the evil spirits. N'Kansa and Kin Kassa carried the memory of the power of their witchdoctor deep inside them long after they reached Wales. They knew he could restore a field full of rye destroyed by a flood, he could make a tree struck by lightning sprout new leaves and produce milk. So great was his power that he had brought dead men, men already putrefying, back to life. Why couldn't the white man use the power of the witchdoctor and learn from his African ways? Their God only knows. Inevitably the Reverend Hughes fell ill, and he knew that if he didn't return to Wales he would surely die. Africa, the white man's burden and the white man's grave, they said. Africa would not spare him despite his worthy ministry.

Some say it may have been serendipity that brought these first two boys to Wales. Maybe not. It seems the boys were needed to nurse the sick Reverend on his journey to the coast. Perhaps he started out with the idea that they would accompany him a little of the way, but he became so ill en route that they were obliged to accompany him all the way to the coast. Perhaps he took pity on them and felt that he could not abandon them when they arrived at the town of Banana. After all, now they were without their tribe and a long way from home. Perhaps he had already written them into a plan that would allow him to continue his work without the

[19] Magic or evil spirit.

threat of illness and death. He had written to his sister in Colwyn Bay of his return and revealed to her "a most natural and practical scheme of mutual benefit". Instead of the great missionary exodus, he thought of bringing African boys to Wales, where they could be trained in the missionary work and eventually return home equipped to educate their own people. In this way nobody would perish because, the Reverend surmised, Africans seemed to be safeguarded from the evil effects of climatic changes because of their physical structure. It was believed at the time that the skull of the Negro was considerably thicker than the skull of a white man and, indeed, the Reverend's own observation had led him to conclude that the skin of the African was also much thicker. He considered his scheme a happy exchange, a fair trade, free of the miserable and disgraceful trades in human cargoes that were by then thankfully abolished. All his hopes were pinned on the establishment of a training institute in Wales.

The Reverend and the boys were carried across the ocean to the port of Liverpool on a cargo boat of the Elder Dempster Shipping Line and from there transported to Llandudno pier by a vessel owned by the North Wales Steamship Company. The proprietor of this company would later strike a deal with Elder Dempster and offer free connecting passages between the dock at Liverpool and Llandudno pier to any of the boys on the Reverend's scheme. Over the next few years this route would see a steady trickle of one hundred and fifty boys and one young girl come from African villages in Congo, Sierra Leone, Cameroon, Liberia, South Africa and more to Colwyn Bay. But first there was just N'Kansa and Kin Kassa.

I often wonder how the boys looked upon the people with wishy-washy faces as they approached the Liverpool dock or Llandudno pier. The purpose-built resort of Llandudno, designed as a holiday retreat, had only just been completed in those days. "*Hardd Hafan Hedd*", Beautiful Haven of Peace was how it was known; a fashionable Victorian tourist spot for the most respectable of people. I can imagine that Llandudno of 1885; its fine promenade and bandstand, the elegant sweeping crescent front of hotels, the sculptured gardens of the Happy Valley, and the Pier Pavilion where the flamboyant French conductor Jules Prudence Rivière would lead the orchestra with a jewelled ivory baton from his gilded chair. The tourists came from far afield. It is said that Napoleon III and Bismarck came to visit Llandudno and that the Queen of Romania spent many happy weeks there during the summer of 1890.

A stretch of the north Wales coast that included Colwyn Bay was often referred to as "the Naples of the North". The Reverend saw this as a most appropriate spot and chose it for its climate, its location close to the port of Liverpool and for its people, who the Reverend thought most pious and obliging. He chose Wales, he said, "because it is a land of chapels and churches, a land where there is a Bible in every house, and everyone can read it. English visitors notice the frequency and fervor of our religious services, the hearty singing and the zeal, enthusiasm, and responsive 'Amens', the general and reverent observance of the Day of Rest, with its Sunday-schools, to which old and young are to be seen wending their way Bible in hand."

The Reverend took the boys to his sister's home on Llanelian

Road when they first arrived and there they quickly settled into their brick and slate surroundings. N'Kansa and Kin Kassa were bright boys, eager to learn and to serve the God of the white man. Kin Kassa was the more reserved of the two whilst N'Kansa was funny and lively and readily picked up the tricks and ways of his little white companions. Very soon both the boys had learned to recite psalms and large passages from the Book of Revelation from memory, presenting them in the grand front rooms of large Victorian Colwyn Bay houses, and later, on a fund-raising tour of parishes across Wales. They were smartly dressed in tailored black serge suits with shiny buttons and wore white handkerchiefs in their top pockets. Little gentlemen; neckties framing their fixed expression. I've studied the old photos to see if I could see anything of the spirit of the boys but their faces are bland and lifeless. The Reverend stands between them in the picture looking like my Uncle John.

The two boys were stars wherever they went. They preached the mission in parish after parish throughout north and south Wales, where posters announced that the Reverend William Hughes would speak of his missionary travels and that the *bechgyn duon*[20] would sing in Welsh, English and in their native tongue. In the chapels they took up the hymnal and sang:

Doed Paganiaid yn eu tywyllwch,
Doed y Negro dua'u lliw
Doed addolwyr yr eilunod

[20] Black boys.

I weld tegwch Iesu'n Dduw
Deued llu heb ddim rhi'
Fyth i ganu am Galfari.

May the Pagans in their darkness
May the blackest of Negroes,
May the worshippers of idols
Come to see the glory of Jesus as God;
May they come in countless numbers
To sing forever about Calvary.

(Hymn 419, Vs 3, *Llyfr Emynau—Y Methodistiaid Calfinaidd a Wesleaidd*)

The Reverend sold photographs of them for a few pennies and people flocked to buy them.

Such was the interest they created amongst the sympathetic Welsh people, it may be said with truth that for two years the boys lived upon their shadows. These photos have also proved excellent advertisements in hundreds of Welsh homes and have enlisted the sympathy and affection of thousands. In many families where the portraits were shown, the children were so much interested on behalf of the coloured boys, that they took charge of collecting cards on behalf of the Congo Training Institute.

Eventually the Reverend was appointed as pastor of the Welsh Baptist churches at Old Colwyn and Llanelian and later Colwyn

Bay. The boys worked on his sister's farm, ate well, played and studied hard and became like sons to the Reverend Hughes. He took them on holidays to the beaches at Aberystwyth and they played free as sea birds and ran barefoot on the sands. They became a family.

Time went by and the Reverend's dream of setting up a training school became more urgent. In April of 1889 the newly formed Committee of the Congo Training Institute met in Llandudno. Within a year the Committee had secured a property, a large yellow brick building, on Nant-y-Glyn Road, Colwyn Bay and the Congo Institute was opened. A steady stream of new recruits followed the same journey the two small boys had taken out of Africa. Samba, Kofele M'besa, Alfred and Samuel Dibundu, Kwesi Quainoo, Eyo Ekpenyon Eyo, Oko Boco; and those with their mission names, Frank, Daniel, George, Samuel, Moses, John and James and more. Small cabin-loads came from all parts of Africa and the Institute grew in stature. Eventually its name changed from the Congo Institute to the African Institute, a reflection of the breadth of its activities. It seems odd to say now but the Institute became an influential meeting point for people from all over Africa. African dignitaries who had not been able to meet in Africa because of ethnic and colonial boundaries met up in Colwyn Bay. Some, including the great African nationalist Mojola Agbebi who toured in glorious African dress, came to give lectures. Agbebi was a powerful speaker and activist. At the time of his visit to the school, there were two students from Zaire, three from the Cameroon, three more from Calabar and two from the Gold Coast. There were two Liberians and two half-caste

Africans with Dutch parents, Roul VanderMost from Angola and a young woman called Ernestina from the Congo. And there was Paul Daniels, a black American from South Carolina on holiday from an orphanage.

Agbebi spoke at religious gatherings on behalf of the Institute and promoted the idea that the African was capable of advancement. He was educated to a level well above the average parishioner in Wales and spoke impeccable English. He advocated the voice of the African, not merely English sentiment rendered in an African language. The Africans stirred the hearts of the Welsh people. The Reverend himself preferred to pray in Welsh and the Africans in Wales gave a spur to the congregations' efforts to sing and pray in their own language and to protect their culture in the local chapels. Speaking Welsh was strongly discouraged in schools in Wales at the time when education was largely undertaken through English while some children caught speaking it were punished, but these Africans attested to the fact that English was not the only valid language.

The boys learned many things. Not only were they versed in the scriptures and trained in the ministry but they were also apprenticed to a craft in the town. One worked at the chemist, another at the wheelwright, others with a carpenter, a printer and a blacksmith. They were familiar faces in the town. A printing press was set up at the Institute and a Bible printed in Welsh with African phrases in it. Money began to flow in; patronage buoyed by Welsh missionary zeal, philanthropy and good will. Letters to the *Weekly News*, and even to the world press, proclaimed the "farsightedness of this radical and most novel scheme", which had never before been tried. Anywhere! The Institute aspired to train thousands of converts and do away with the need to send missionaries to the Dark Continent. It was anticipated that more colleges of this kind would be set up in Britain and other parts of the world. "The scheme of developing the natives will ultimately do away with the costly and unnatural foreigner. God will be more glorified," the Reverend argued and looked to the day when "Africans will be taught by Africans". He was convinced of the efficacy of his plan and so he fought the enemies of doubt and prejudice who cast a long shadow over his work and those who mocked and ridiculed and called the Institute the "Institution of the Cuckoo". In the land of Bibles and Sabbaths, the Reverend remained confident.

Most of the boys returned to Africa, scattered like seeds, spreading the word of God, but several died and were buried at Llanelian. As N'Kansa grew, so the desire to return to his homeland grew in his heart. The edges of his dreams were fringed with sadness. As he slept his spirit roamed the forests listening to the roar of the lion in the distance, he heard the hum of the songs of his ancestors on the lips of the huntsmen, he heard the women's stories as they planted manioc and he yearned for home. He longed for the storytellers, the warriors and the huntsmen of his village, for their nonsense and their laughter, when, drunk on pombe, they would dance—the dance of life, the dance of revelations, the dance of the twelve masks, welcoming in prosperity and health. He had heard of the death of his mother but his yearning was no less. "There is no home where there is no mother," the Reverend told him but N'Kansa still pined for his people. He knew the colours of his soul were not in the landscapes of Wales.

I've seen the grave of N'Kansa at Llanelian, I've seen the graves of Kin Kassa, of Samba and Daniel Harvey, of George Steane, Samuel Dibundu, Ernestina and others. Each of the graves a buried story. I feel that I know something about their voyage across the Atlantic. I think I know what it is like to be stranded at an outpost like Colwyn Bay; dislodged, dislocated. I imagine their lives played out in the little town with its ideas and images of the black man created through Bible culture. I know what it's like to be a curiosity. To be loved for your quaintness and your difference in a way that means you will never be normal. When I recreate this past I touch home with a particular kind of dislocation.

But there is more to the Congo boys' story than this. It lets me see an Africa with the eyes of Wales. I see the Welsh memory that comes from missionaries' stories of their travels, that comes from the chapels, the chapel hymns and the Sunday schools, from the collection boxes; from Ma—a story of Africa that passes on and on and on down generations in which strangely I have two parts. A story in which somehow I am both looking at and looked upon. I guess it's that type of story of Africa and black people that seeped into the cultural portrait of Wales. The missionaries went in the hundreds to the Dark Continent and all over the world, and brought home their tales to the parishes. Their ambitions were laid down forever in the lines of hymns—the most famous of all—"*Draw, draw yn Tsieina*":

> *Draw, draw yn Tsieina a thiroedd Japan*
> *Plant bach melynion sy'n byw*
> *Dim ond eilunod o'u cylch ym mhob man*
> *Neb i ddweud am Dduw*
> *Iesu, cofia'r plant,*
> *Iesu, cofia'r plant*
> *Anfon genhadon ymhell dros y môr*
> *Iesu, cofia'r plant.*

> Far away in China and the lands of Japan
> Live little yellow children
> Nothing but idols around them everywhere;
> No one to tell them about God.
> Jesus, remember the children
> Jesus, remember the children
> Send missionaries far across the sea
> Jesus, remember the children.

There were lots of them, men and women—Evan Evans, Eluned Morgan, Betsy Cadwalader—writing home about their travels and their yearnings for home. Like the Reverend William Hughes they worked hard to take the word of God to people with gods of their own. At the same time they had to present what they did in a way that might be palatable to their own people. They had to tell about their work in a way that condemned exploitation and plunder and disassociated itself from the forces of colonialism. These travellers must have seen themselves as leaders of a superior style of Empire building, a moral crusade. They used the same maps as the colonisers, took the same routes and byways, but they were not the ones who turned the villages blood red, scattered the peoples, stole and took away and left only damage, setting tribe against tribe and carving out territories and regions for themselves. The Welsh missionaries distanced themselves from this type of work; that would come to be seen as English misdeeds. Their mission was of a higher order. They managed to be both saviours of the natives and at the same time bolster a sense of Welsh pride and self-identity that had been so cruelly robbed and pillaged by the same English colonisation. They could boast that their work was unsullied by ruthless imperialism and so claim the moral high ground. "Little Wales" would have a finer, spiritual glory untainted by the savagery and slaughter of the English, at whose hands Wales itself had suffered centuries before. So the African and the Welshman were linked in a spiritual haven, a haven secure from the encroachments of the English.

Like Ma's black man, the African was a kindred spirit. Ma was reaching out to her own kind, sensing her own humanity through the African man I guess. But where did that leave me? Was it these Africa stories that settled in my cultural memory like sediment?

Alice and Dennis

Home. Ma got her own way. She wanted us to grow up in Wales. "I want the girls to walk down the street and be known," she told him. "I want them to see Mr and Mrs So and So and know them and be known by them. I want them to be part of something, to be whole." He argued with her but she got her way. She was sitting in Cwmdonkin Park in Swansea one summer, waiting for Bea to be born, when she made up her mind that Wales would be our home. "Breathe that air," she said, as though it had an inherent quality not found anywhere else in the world. If my parents had considered that having some black people around might have been an advantage we might have stayed in Swansea or Cardiff but we didn't. I grew up white, in Beit-eel, the house of God, in a small seaside town on the northern fringe of Wales.

The houses in our street didn't have numbers; it seemed more fashionable back then to have house names. Names that were supposed to conjure up the sense of the place—the sea, the wind, the mountains, the rivers and the lakes. There was Arran, Gwynant, Fron Deg, Haulfryn, a house called Awel y Môr that sang out about the sea's waves and then there was Beit-eel—the "house of God" in Arabic, not that anyone round our way would have known what it meant. I think it was the Reverend Hamilton, an old Christian minister who befriended our family in the Sudan, who suggested Beit-eel. Years before Ma eventually had the brass name-plate etched with black lettering made, she painted the name in white letters on a piece of plywood and placed it proudly on the front doorstep. Then she dragged two large boulders down from the mountain, painted them and positioned them triumphantly on top of each of the gateposts to announce the entrance to our shamba. Not long afterwards the front doorstep was adorned with the white painted skull of a donkey. I thought nothing of it. It seemed quite an attractive addition and stayed there until we left home. We were destined to be different if only by virtue of the donkey's head.

Ma staked out this territory for us on the edge of town like a Maroon community,[21] and set about building a sanctuary from the peculiar world that surrounded us. No one had lived in the house before. We were the ones to breathe life into its empty body. We built Beit-eel and Beit-eel built us.

Home. Ma in a starry sky dress all powdery and doughy and smelling of Nivea, safe and back home; and me, wrenched from an African womb, sitting in some strange and tiny space in Craig y Don school. Ma had betrayed me. How could she leave me to reshape myself amongst the wishy-washy faces?

I remember the wet afternoon lock-ins at school, looking out through the raindrops that kissed the window and trickled down big tears like mine. Dad slowly fading along with Africa, moving

[21] Maroons were runaway slaves who established communities beyond the control of the enslaving powers.

on a different time scale while I watched the flames slowly flicker in the schoolroom fireplace. He was busy building himself on African soil. While he puzzled the question of why the African man sold his brother into slavery, I puzzled a different anthropology. I lived between two worlds for a while, Africa uncomfortably imposing itself on my day-to-day life and me trying to banish it in my craving for acceptance. I summoned him in quieter moments. I could hear him reading to me after those sleepy afternoons in the tropics. He read the story of Alice, a girl who had Ma's name and many of her ways, a little girl in a strange and illogical world. I loved Alice and her encounters with the topsy-turvy. I recognised her transformations. And now I had fallen Alice fashion into this small-school world.

With my finger I make a peephole in the condensated wet windowpane and through it I see Falolou Road, Lagos, where a small boy runs with his stick and metal wheel. The spokeless rim of the bicycle wheel finds its own path on the dusty road as he gives it life with his stick. Who is taking whom? I run along with him. Two women are chatting in soft afternoon tones on the step of the house next door. One is parting the hair of the other into neat sections and forming twisted coils with dark cotton. She is halfway through her task. One side of the head is neatly sectioned, oiled and coiled. The other half is as yet untamed, a comb standing upright in the bushy mass. Their shoulders are bare, deep brown, large and round against the greens and yellows of the patterned cloth of their wraps. The woman working the hair has a baby bound tightly in her wrap, its head nodding sleepily, front to back, side to side. I pass by but I don't speak.

Alice and Dennis

Dusty bare-foot children with pot bellies and protruding belly buttons call out "*o-yimbo*", white person, or they just stand and stare. There are a few stalls along Falolou Road—women selling matches, kerosene, red soap, washing blue, mosquito coils, but business is quiet during the afternoon siesta. Most of the stall women have found a shady sleep for an hour or two. We find peanut lady awake. She sells on the pavement at the corner where Falolou Road meets the busy road leading to town. A coiled wrap of adire cloth shades her head, its coils of indigo blue finished with a stiff fan of cloth at the back. She scratches the side of her head and the whole headdress slides forward and comes to rest on her eyebrows. Her fire is just ash now but the embers still make some heat. She has made a little mountain with the red-skinned roasted groundnuts. We want a small-tin amount. She scoops up the nuts into the tin measure and levels off with the straight side of her palm. Then she rubs the roasted nuts between her palms and purses her fleshy black lips to blow. She tosses the nuts quickly between her hands and blows away the loosened skins that rise to fill the air about her like confetti. Not one nut falls to the dusty floor, to her wide dusty feet, her toenails stained with henna. She makes a neat crisp cone of newspaper and trickles the golden nuts inside. We will re-enact the nut lady's ritual in our own game later with bits of newspaper and small stones and a half tin that Joseph will give us. There are no brown skins in this place. Peanut brown we are. Roasted peanuts from another land. In Africa we were white and in Wales we weren't.

In the yard we find Joseph cleaning a chicken on the back step. Droplets of blood fall from its limp head to the concrete floor. We bring the chickens from the market alive and play with them in the yard until it is time for Joseph to make chicken stew. I won't eat chicken, even in pep-peh stew. Joseph tells us a chicken story. He always makes a story around the food he is preparing. Sometimes he tells us about a train that carries the heavy load of rice to the big ships and how some small grains of rice escape and grow beautiful in their own country, while the remaining grains of rice have to go in big sacks all the way to England. He weaves our names into each story he tells. The woman who keeps the chickens in the market is called Bea and she has a bad husband who beats her. Then he sings, "Beat-you Bea, beat-you Bea," or the rice train chugs up the hills and it says, "Cha-cha cha-cha, cha-cha cha-cha . . . Chaaaa". We love Joseph. He is our nanny. He cooks our food, washes and irons our clothes and he sits in the kitchen at night when Ma and Dad go out. We get out of our beds and go and find him in the kitchen and sit with him picking over the rice for the next day or play a game with the ant trails. With a stripe of soap on the floor he shows us how to redirect the trails of ants, splitting the ranks of the marching army or channelling them round and round the floor. Joseph is trusted. He is not a savage.

Not all the servants were like Joseph. I had to tell Ma about Tuesday, the houseboy in Khartoum. I would occasionally go to Tuesday's quarters in the afternoons while my parents slept and take him things from the house that he asked for. During those off-duty hours, he would discard his jalabiya and wear only thin cotton pants. He would lift me to sit on his hard knee and I would twist and turn because I wasn't comfortable. One day I told Ma about what Tuesday did to me and then he was gone. Dad said he was going to beat that damn savage and throw every last damn thing he thieved from us in the trench.

Miss Thomas said we should all pray for the children in Africa who have no food. She couldn't be referring to me because I was far too big, much bigger than the classroom life that buzzed around me. A boy called Paul and me were mis-shapes, rolled out of all the leftover plasticine. Like me, he didn't fit the available small spaces of the classroom. I had no real affinity with him beyond our shared size. I watched his pain gradually evolve into aggression as mine turned to resignation and then complicity. There might have been others like him in other classrooms, struggling with themselves, but there was no other of me in the whole damn school. My two older sisters were there for a short while but I didn't dare acknowledge them openly for fear of us all becoming too visible. To see my sisters was only to see things about my shameful difference that I was trying so hard to conceal. I had to ignore them. We spent our days apart, denying each other, and our nights bound together like beads on a string.

On my first day at school I was put to sit next to an angel with straight, mousy-coloured hair and large, mouse-like ears. She had long thin nostrils like lots of others in the room. Diane occupied a double desk that was in her classroom imagination a seat on the upper deck of a double-decker bus. As I sat down beside her she very kindly offered me a cigarette in the form of a hair clip. She had already carefully placed one between her own small pink lips, struck two pinched fingers along the edge of the wooden desk and lit her clip before offering a light to me. It helped to calm me and quieted my crying. I learned quickly that I must accept the bizarre, like the walrus that recited poems and the Cheshire Cat and the Mad Hatter and the Queen of Hearts and Mrs Templeton, Miss Ward and Mr Roberts (ap Wyn) and Ein Tad and peas and gravy and potato from an ice cream scoop, *Ach a fi*, folded arms and fingers on lips and toilets with no lids and Bronco toilet roll and gradually I found a way to be a pale-face too.

"*Neis te?*" [22] Ma would say when I told her about my school day as we walked home along Queen's Road. *Neis*. I would read out loud all the Welsh house names as we walked past; Gwynant, Fron Deg, Isallt, turning over her big pink hand with my small brown one, somehow the same but different, until we reached Beit-eel. Ma and I felt like one most of the time. We spoke the same, ate the same food, our eyes saw big pictures and we pushed aside the details. I had Ma's red threads in my hair and her freckles on my brown nose and I felt proud of them. But I knew I couldn't grow to be the same as her. She was angry inside and I was trying hard to be good. Until I learned to be a pale-face, things continued to be topsy-turvy.

NEIS TE?

"*Iesu tirion, gwêl yn awr
blentyn bach, yn plygu i lawr*"
we sang,
then ran
speckling the playground

[22] "Nice, yes?"

rice brown, rose red, slate blue
yellow kiskadee
all joyous jamboree
like flecks on my knitted cardie
jumping
chanting
rolling like pebbles on Llandudno beach
one movement
to and fro
dipping and turning
swallow style
free spirits under Mr Ellis' watchful smile
we tamed to his whistle
then inside, cheeks fire warm
eyes aglow to stories told
of faraway places, lands of gold
we, like coloured pencils neat in our tin
sit with chilblain toes
and mould the multi-coloured plasticine
to lifeless grey
and then I hear Miss Thomas say,
"God's children,
plentyn bach, plentyn du,
they're really all the same to me
they just blend in like milk and tea."

I graduated to Miss Thomas's class with the same cohort of
neat ponytails and bobs, short back and sides and sticky-out ears.

I longed for one of those ponytails that swung with the wind on sports day or a Kirby-gripped parting on the side. I longed for a pair of red shoes like Rosemary's and a vanity box and a handkerchief with embroidered edges. The girls were the natural angels and fairies, the fairy-tale princesses. They were beautiful. Diane was gossamer; her skin so delicate it was see-through. I could see the blue of her blood running through her tiny pencilled veins. She was gorgeousness all over. And Caradoc, freckles like Ma but more carefully painted on, with his hand up straight as a die to the teacher's questions. He knew everything. I was certain he would be a bank manager one day.

CARADOC JONES

Caradoc Jones
A carrot of a boy,
Sat next to me in school.
Called me chocolate biscuit
I called him ginger biscuit
Bloody fool.

Ma often came home from her topsy-turvy world shouting mad. Some *jack ass* had tried to cheat her, or talked down to her, or not served her properly. And she had told them she wasn't a dog, again, and that she wasn't going to be anybody's slave. Ma spoke out with all the conceit of territory. She would fight her own people for a place for us. I had to find different ways of coping. I had to be *neis* and I hoped that nice might just mean invisible.

One day I asked Miss Thomas if I could be excused to go to the toilet. She refused. I don't know if she thought I was looking for some diversion. I can't imagine for one minute how a hundred yards no-coat walk in the rain to some cold outside toilet could have been seen as such, but her answer was "no". The girls' toilets are no place for a pleasant diversion. The only school space out of bounds to the teachers is not a good spot to put yourself in if you are in any way vulnerable. I've heard Pakistani girls in Newport say they would rather wait to go home at lunchtime than chance their arm in these unobserved corners. I could never have waited so long. I was always dying to go to the toilet but I would stall because, most of the time, there were more important things to do. By the time I gave in and thought about asking it was bursting time. Miss Thomas said, "No, go and sit down," her face looking like she was sucking an acid drop. She was the kind of woman who couldn't do more than one thing at a time and this day she was clearly very busy counting out pencils. She usually said lots of daft things but I reckoned it best not to challenge her. It wasn't safe. Once I got into trouble for saying "Winston Churchill did nothing for us." I was repeating something I had heard Ma say at home but I didn't stop to think about who the "us" Ma was referring to, might be. Miss Thomas said lots about nation and about pride and winning the war and that "if it wasn't for him people like me might never . . .", on and on she went, full of gaps and pauses when she didn't know what words she wanted

Sugar and Slate

to use. She was looking a bit like she might start again when she refused my toilet request so I returned to my seat as Alice. "I don't want to be anyone's prisoner," Alice had told the White Knight, or was that Katie Alice talking?

I don't know where my idea came from but it was without a doubt related to the idea of being good. I know so because I was cultivating goodness and co-operation at the time. Perhaps all prisoners believe at some point during their incarceration that compliance will win over their captors and they will be set free. Back at my desk, I awaited permission but it didn't come. I was reading one of those books about children in foreign lands, Sue is Red Indian, and Ingmar lives in Sweden or something of the kind. Well Kimu was an Eskimo boy and his icy igloo didn't melt even though he had a fire in it. I deduced that surely Kimu's igloo was melting but with such tiny drops that nobody could see them.

And so the resolution to my situation came to me. Tiny drops must go unobserved, so if I could pee one drop at a time I could get away with it. It was so obvious and so wonderful a plan Alice might have thought it up herself.

I was shocked, and so were many others, when a loud, warm cascade faster than the Swallow Falls at Betws-y-Coed splashed over the sides of my chair and formed a huge shameful pool on the parquet floor.

"What did you do that for?" Miss Thomas asked like a Mad Hatter.

"Isn't it obvious?" thought "Alice".

Pandemonium broke out. Diane tightly folded her arms in disapproval, a Kirby grip still dangling from her open mouth. Paul was making a big show of jumping over the pool when he lost control of himself and accidentally pushed one of the dainties into it. She cried and so did I.

Miss Thomas could only find a large pair of boys' white football shorts and some ugly black pumps for me to change into while the "dainty" appeared to be completely restored to her beautiful self. The ugliness of it all went deep. I was struggling on the margins of femininity already and she pushed me right over the edge. Exit Alice. I knew that I was something other than a little girl like the rest of them but I didn't know quite what. When I returned to the classroom in the humiliating garb I had to stand with my bottom pressed against the radiator all morning. "But I'm dry, Miss Thomas," I protested. She was counting the pencils back into the box.

Eventually it became more comfortable to accept a boy-like persona. I couldn't make Alice fit. Physically the boy-girl idea fitted better. That's how Dennis came in. It was during one of those wet afternoons when some of us got sent to the huts to mix with the "backward" children, a jumble of kids of all ages herded together like ants by a circle of soap. My cousin Si spent his whole life imprisoned in the huts crayoning and planting bulbs; co-operating because everyone was so kind and *neis*. One hot summer day some of the kids had tried to burn the huts down. I don't know if it was an ultimate act of rebellion, an uprising from the ranks, or if it was an attempt by the "normal" kids to oust the occupants of the huts. They used Michael Morris's round spectacles to set fire to the bits that had been slowly splintering off from underneath the wooden structure. Scorched black it was. You could smell the smoke from Standard Four. I wasn't near the huts that day. I only went there once because it was a wet afternoon. The weather was as grey as the boys' pants. I was flicking through the pages of a comic when I saw Dennis. I could see he wasn't coloured like me but he was definitely some kind of white-black boy. It was his hair that grabbed my attention first, not his defiant manner or the fact that he had my dad's name. Dennis the Menace's black hair was fuzzy and wild and free. My heart sang to look at him. He was the only person I had ever seen that looked anything remotely like me. I both loved him and hated him like the bits that made me black. I loved his wildness; I loved the permanently angry look across his face, I loved his belligerence, his clumsiness, the way he got things all wrong, but above all I loved his hair. I loved him because he was all so like the real me but I knew this had to be a secret because Dennis wasn't good. I lived in fear of my relationship with Dennis being exposed. There was always the possibility of being suddenly outed. It wasn't only Dennis—any associated reference to blackness haunted me. The word *Africa* alone did it to me for years and later a whole series of words cut through—darkie, monkey, black, and any word that started with "nig" or that sounded even vaguely like "coon" or "wog". Banana could make my cheeks fill up hot. I was so ashamed. The words could be lurking anywhere. When all my defences were down, when I was just off duty, some damn fool teacher could quite innocently say something like, "How now brown cow," and I would have to live with it later.

I've been trying to remember when this all began but I can't. It sort of built up slowly. I used to chant, "Eeny meeny miney mo, catch a nigger by his toe," along with the rest of them. I never imagined that I was the Golly on the Robertson's jar or the Black Jack on the sweet wrapper. There was a playground song that I found a great comfort in:

> *If you're white you're alright*
> *If you're brown stick around*
> *If you're black git back, git back, git back.*

I wasn't black, I was brown, peanut brown. Africa was black, not me. The song announced the order of things and it made me safe. I was Dennis alright, a white-black boy even if the rest of them couldn't see it.

Mr Jones Standard Three and Mrs Jones Standard One were having an affair. They whispered and sparkled to each other through the connecting doors when we were supposed to be eyes closed whilst we recited, "*Ein Tad, yr Hwn wyt yn y nefoedd,*"[23] in one slow voice. While they mingled, the boys showed us their white willies under the desk. Well, not their real willies; just pretending they were, by sticking a finger out of their flies. Bobbie Evans didn't understand the game and he showed all us girls his real maggot. We laughed all day. It was Mrs Jones who said kindly one day that my hair was like coils of spaghetti. So, "Spaghetti Head" they called me for a while. It made a change. Tinned spaghetti she must have meant because people didn't eat the real stuff then.

School was a real muddle. I would just about manage to stave off the Africa business when Dad would reappear for the summer

---

[23] The first line of the Lord's Prayer, "Our Father, who art in heaven".

and remind the whole damn school of my supposed origins. If you were black you must be from Africa and that's all there was to it, although nobody stopped to ask me what it was like there. Dad was home on Sports Day and stayed until the heather flowered on the mountain and then it was time for him to go back. I was Queen of Sports Day. Queen for a day. For one day of the year I was untouchable; the best, and everyone agreed. Dad said we would be nothing if we didn't achieve and we'd end up as some stupidy black girls working in Woolies. Dad was always going on about winning and being the best at things. I'd see him standing in the crowd in Craig y Don park when I stood on the starting line knees slightly bent, arms and fists poised like a boxer, tense and waiting for the ready-steady, and he'd nod at me knowingly. The smile on his face told me I would win; that we'd both win. Then, the whistle blew, "GO," and like a leopard springing into the free open space, I was boundless again, long easy strides carrying me out of the compound across the savannah and away. Me alone right out in front, cool, comfortable, going to win. And the whole crowd, the whole school, cheering me on, squealing and screaming with delight at the one they had backed to cross the winning line. I knew all about this kind of race. Dad was cheering me on with "Go it alone! Go it alone!" There was no one like me, no one like what I might become, no message to tell me what to be other than Dad's "Go it alone" and Dennis and Alice.

There's a children's poem by Talhaiarn called "*Brenin y Canibalyddion*"[24]—"King of the Cannibals". It appeared in

---

[24] Reproduced in *Drws Dychymyg*, ed. Elinor Davies (Gwasg Gomer, 1980).

children's books up until recently. It's a lively, raucous poem that
thunders along at a pace like drumming:

Mi draethaf chwedl fach i chwi
Yn loyw, hoyw, ffraeth a ffri,
Am frenin mawr ei fraint a'i fri,
Sef Brenin y Canibalyddion.
Ei hyd oedd ddwylath a lled llaw,
A'i ben 'run llun â phen hen raw;
'Roedd ganddo swyddogion, wyth neu naw,
A'i balas a wnaed o bridd a baw;
A'i enw oedd Brwchan-wchan-iach,
Llumangi-hyllgi-wichgi-wach,
A'i wisg yn crogi fel hen sach
Am Frenin y Canibalyddion.

Yn howcio, cowcio, llowcio'n lli,
Chwipio a hicio a chicio'r ci,
Yn strim-stam strellach yn ei sbri
Bydd Brenin y Canibalyddion.

'Roedd trigain o wragedd yn ei dŷ,
Pob un yn ddu, pob un yn hy,
A deugain o hyll-dduach ddu
Gan Frenin y Canibalyddion.
Ac felly i gyd 'roedd ganddo gant
I foddio ei fyd ac i foethi ei fant;
A genid bob wythnos ddau o blant,

A'r Brenin a ganai gyda'i dant,
Gan ddawnsio i Wisgan-isgan-aw
A Sipog-lethog-lwythog-law,
Nes syrthio ar ei gefn i'r baw—
Ow! Frenin y Canibalyddion.

I'll tell you a little story
Clearly, brightly, wittily and freely,
About a king, great his privilege and fame,
Namely the King of the Cannibals.
His height was six foot and a hand's breadth,
And his head was like the top of an old spade;
He had officials, eight or nine,
And his palace was made of earth and dirt;
And his name was Brwchan-wchan-iach,
Llumangi-hyllgi-wichgi-wach,
And his clothes hung like an old sack
On the King of the Cannibals.

Gabbling, gobbling, guzzling away,
Whipping, gnashing, and kicking the dog
Higgledy-piggledy merrily,
That's the King of the Cannibals.

There were sixty wives in his house,
All of them black, all of them bold,
And forty more, uglier and blacker
Had the King of the Cannibals.

66

And so altogether he had a hundred
To make him comfortable and to suit his taste;
Every week two children were born,
And the King would sing with his harp
And dance hoppity-boppity-bumpily-dumpily
Merrily-cheerily-gladly-madly
Until he fell on his back in the dirt—
Oh! The King of the Cannibals.

In later verses the grotesque King ends up eating his entire harem and several of his princes. "And their throats were cut one and all, every hideous horrible man and woman." I resisted the few available images offered out to me. There was nowhere to go but wishy-washy. I never saw a proper black person in a book. I never saw a black person in the street. I never saw a black person on the telly except the Black and White Minstrels when we went round to Auntie Maggie's. I never heard anything about black people and I didn't want to. There was no one even remotely like me.

It's raining, heavy tropical rain on the Piarco tarmac, sheets of it. No planes are taking off for now. Looking out through the raindrops on the window, I imagine Brenin y Canibalyddion dancing his thunder dance. He's got me thinking about the whole role model business again. It's not that King of the Cannibals could ever have been my role model but I imagine the dainties thought he was.

Beit-eel

Beit-eel was a haven. Within its private space it was possible to be without mask or masquerade, beyond the gaze of an outside world greedy with curiosity. It was out of bounds to their questions, their demands for conformity. In Beit-eel we could be unaccountable and free and beyond inspection. I walked through my childhood carrying a heavy burden of expectations in my satchel. I was an ambassador and a pioneer and I knew it. It was a big responsibility. The need for recognition, for credibility and acceptance was always present—for myself, my family and something called "my people", whoever they were.

I knew I stood for something but I had no idea what. Without any sense of a shared culture you're destined to invent yourself in your own style—to make it up as you go along. It must have been so much easier to have a label like Jewish or Chinese; whatever tribulation it might bring at least it stood for something, a culture that was recognisable. But black stood for nothing, nothing at all, and coloured stood for even less. "Black" implies some type of group identity and there weren't any groups where I grew up.

Dislocation. Caught up in a vacuum with little reference to anything that you are or that you might be. Historyless, re-assigned and reshaped; a curio.

For the last three hundred years or so there has always been a smattering of us Maroons in isolated spots throughout Wales. In the parish of Conwy lies the record:

1762

Owen Jones, Vicar

Baptized Robbin Conway, a Black Man

who belongs to Esqre Holland.

Owen Jones was a slave, probably a child slave, the property of one of the most well-known families in Conw(a)y. There was Valentine Wood of Chepstow; an ex-slave who in the last century published a book about his life entitled *The Amazing Adventures of Valentine Wood*. There was George Williams of Blaenafon; an engine driver who was married to a Welsh woman and by the time of the census in 1891 had a son who was also an engine driver and four daughters in the local school. Lots of stories like this lie dormant in the pages of parish records across Wales.

There is one story from Caernarfonshire that goes back two hundred and fifty years. It's the story of John Ystumllyn, otherwise known as Black Jack/Jac Du who was kidnapped on the African coast around 1745. He was about eight years old when he was brought to north-west Wales as a child servant. He was the first black man ever seen in Criccieth. The story goes that he spoke no proper language but howled and screamed like a dog. Eventually he acquired two languages, presumably Welsh and English. He was baptised at either Criccieth or Ynyscynhaearn church; he learned to write and was taught gardening as his trade. He became an excellent gardener, with a great love of plants. Local people knew him as a meticulous and skilful worker, adept at mastering almost everything he saw others doing such as making model boats, wooden spoons and baskets. It is said that Jac Du was an active, healthy-looking youth and "even though his skin was black, the local maidens used to dote on him and would compete for his favours". The one who won his heart was a maidservant named Margaret, and they were married at Dolgellau church in 1768 with the son of the Vicar of Criccieth acting as best man. Jac was appointed steward at a local big house and took the name Jones. He died in July 1791 and was buried at Ynyscynhaearn. Like the rest of the community he had become a stern chapel-goer and some say that on his deathbed he spoke of his only regret as being that during his irreligious past he had dared to play the violin on Sundays. He and his wife had raised a large family of seven children. Ann, their elder daughter, married a Liverpool musician. One of their sons, Richard, became huntsman to Lord Newborough and was described as a quiet, unassuming man, who used to wear top hat, velvet jacket and high white collar. He died in 1862 at the age of ninety-two and was buried at Llandwrog near Caernarfon, where his descendants were said to be still living well into the 1880s.

There was no such thing as "black" where I grew up;

Llandudno wasn't that kind of place. We were "the coloured family" in polite English. The history of the Welsh language had not provided any obvious reason to avoid the term "*pobl ddu*"[25]—the descriptor hung comfortably like any other on the end of one's name. *Du*, black. *Jac Du*, Black Jack, but then not a lot of people spoke Welsh in Llandudno. I grew up coloured, half-caste, and it took me a long time to realise that to be half-caste wasn't to be half of anything. It took me even longer to realise that to be mixed was not to be mixed up, or was it? How would I have known? You have to have knowledge of a wider experience to make sense of your own and that just wasn't available. The space I carved out was mine alone and my sisters were carving out their own identities in the same way. It was all invention and charade. I grew up not knowing which bits of my life were universal and which bits were particular to just us. That's how it happened that we had an inside life and an outside life, a private and a public, and in the public we had to make it seem as though it all fitted in wonderfully. We lived in a respectable town, in a very respectable road and "race" was one of those dirty words nobody would dream of bringing to their lips.

"Are you from Africa? I bet it's hot in your country. Are you feeling the cold? Do you eat this sort of food where you come from? Are you that colour all over? Can you speak English? You people are so good at dancing. Is that your father? He's a proper gentleman, isn't he? What part of Africa is he from? Can't tell when you're dirty, can we? You don't need to wash so often I

[25] Black people.

71

suppose? That's some suntan you've got there. Have they all got small ears like you? Let me feel your hair. People like you don't blush, do they? I mean, there's no point."

You mean I spent all those years with my cheeks burning and nobody knew any different?

We had no name for that kind of stuff; the word "racism" hadn't been invented. Only in retrospect can I add up my experience in this way. I guess back then a lot of it seemed inadvertent and innocuous, sporadic and disconnected. I accepted it as my personal battle, not as anything particularly collective. We were all busy suppressing the reality of it, both them and us. Take the words "blackie, darkie, rubber lips, gollywog, wog, nigger, coon"; shocking and upsetting as these words were, they rarely came our way. And we learned fairly early on to cope with those kinds of names. Kids, drunks or some disgruntled old person might occasionally let the side down but in our town we all colluded in the wonderful deceit of what I suppose you could call "polite racism".

Small-town thinking has its own way of managing difference. It both embraces it and rejects it. In its ambivalence you become at one and the same time highly invisible and punishingly visible. "We never really noticed you were coloured," they would say in condescending tones, or "You're not really black, you're just brown," and we would all be relieved of the onerous impoliteness of being black. We would trade bits of ourselves for their white acceptance, denying ourselves to provide reassurance against the intrusion of difference. But it was the background assumptions embodied in the questions that caught me so unawares. The

72

everyday assumptions of inferiority that eventually ground me down until I didn't know who or what I was.

I remember one day travelling home from school with my sisters, hair sharp and shiny with huge bows at the end of our plaits and our uniforms beyond criticism. Ma sent us out looking good. We sat as ambassadors for "our people" on the four o'clock bus— just one misdemeanour would be generalised to all black children everywhere, just as their supposed disadvantage landed on us. Perhaps these signals were lost on the bus conductor who, weighed down with his own mental baggage about black kids, shouted across to us, "Barnardos'? Okay you can go free."

The Barnardo's passport didn't irk too much, it was one of few things that we could turn to our advantage—free entry to the Palladium and Savoy cinemas, free ice cream, free chips; it all seemed quite fair. After all, it was their game not ours. Yet the reality was that our semi-detached life was shared by some of the most respectable families in the community—solicitors, teachers, doctors. We lived in a very up-and-coming middle-class part of town. The middle-class bit didn't apply to us; black families are somehow classless. We were classless, clubless, and groupless. Just ourselves; sometimes special, sometimes not. But never ordinary.

Yet I longed for the ordinary. Ordinary like Ann and Diane and the twins from the corner shop and Jimmy whose father worked for the council. I envied their dinky-doo lives, when I could peephole it from their backdoor step. "Dinky-doo", that's what we called it—fitted carpets, net curtains, three-piece suite, gardens with borders and flowers, closed doors and closed-up lives. There was just nothing dinky-doo at all about Beit-eel. It was an outpost of some mythical African state. We had lino floors throughout that we polished every Saturday morning with dusters tied to our feet like skates. We had a rug in the lounge which Ma had haggled for in a Khartoum souk that sent clouds of dust into the air when we beat it with tennis rackets in the back garden. There were some large pieces of uncoordinated furniture bought from Ball and Boyd's auction rooms, a Chesterfield with a broken arm that flapped down (always at the wrong time) and a bed settee with a Welsh quilt thrown over it. Other families had a lawn-mower or even a gardener; when the grass in our garden got too long we cut it down with a kitchen knife. We didn't have a best room or a parlour like Ann Morris; there was a downstairs and an upstairs and we pushed back the furniture and flung back the curtains to play school, shop or to stage a show. It all went on in our front room.

Other people put up pictures of animals and photographs of the family or the ancestry on their walls. We had a tomb rubbing from the pyramids in Egypt and above the fireplace hung Dad's painting *The Moolit*. *The Moolit* was a painting of the celebration of the birth of the prophet Mohammed in watercolour greys, orange, sienna and rust and touches of lapis lazuli blue. There were women in white robes dancing amongst a thousand glistening lights and the buried skulls of the ancients in the foreground. The artefacts of Africa were all around us but Dad wasn't. I longed for a dad and a mam or a daddy and a mummy. Instead we had Ma. Her Africa was in Wales and she wanted it for us.

True to say, Ma's language odded (that's one of Ma's words I

74

think) her all the more. She listened to the radio in Welsh and she always thought in Welsh. You could tell because her English wasn't proper English at all. She had a kind of circular speech; she started a sentence at the end and worked backwards. She added her adjectives after her nouns and she let intonation fill in great holes in the sentences. She spoke with the assumption that we shared a time and a place with her, the assumption of a shared memory that was marked out with places and events and people we should know. In her coded memory there was a whole range of collective meanings, a pattern of ancestral motifs and a plethora of moments to which we only had limited access. She spoke with a history. She belonged. The language was hers and so was the place; past, present and future. Our inheritance was partial and distorted but freely given. In intense family moments of love, anger, grief she soothed us with the poetry of her language.

We in turn spoke the English of Welsh people. English as a second language when we had no other first language. A jumble of words of spurious origin littered our speech. *Felyfeclin?*[26] *Rigarig?*[27] *Hen gnafon drwg?*[28] until it was impossible to disentangle what language they were or if they had a literal meaning at all outside of home. Dad's language too suffered in the same way. "What dat damn *rig-a-rig* goin' on down dere? Yuh banging round like a damn *felyfeclin*. Quieten down man or yuh gun get a

---

[26] Most likely a corruption of "*melin fetlin*", Welsh for steamroller.
[27] Welsh: from "*ragar-ryg*", the corncrake, a bird with a carping call; used to describe someone who doesn't stop talking.
[28] Welsh: literally a "bad lot", but means "rascals" when used affectionately for naughty children.

chwip dîn."[29] There must be lots of people quietly carrying this language interference; the Creolised, syncretic language registers that relate to station stops across Wales. We spoke Llandudno Welsh or was it Llandudno English?

Looking back ours was always a woman's house. Ma found it, Ma bought it after the Cymdonkin Park conversation and Ma was in it most of the time. "We can go away for five years and come home with nothing Denis *bach*, or we can put some money into a place in Wales," she said to him. "Send money home and we'll have something to show for it at the end." She thought he would eventually come and live in Wales. He thought she would stay in Africa with him. So they compromised. They to'd and fro'd.

Seasons came and went and so did Dad. That's why ours became a woman house. There is no head of table in a woman house, no master chair, no closed-door room. In our woman house there were just chairs, open rooms, we went for a pee with the door open if we wanted to, dried our knickers over the bath and wore our nighties downstairs to watch *Sergeant Bilko*. Dad's home visits interrupted this happy rhythm with his Victorian discipline and etiquette. We were all "pleases and thank-yous" and "would you minds" when he was around. This was the legacy of his Caribbean past. The Victorian morality, his manners, the directness of his speech and even perhaps the fact that we all had Victorian names. His speech had all the elaborate decoration of the Caribbean though we heard nothing of the place at all. Sometimes, just sometimes, a Calypso song would be on his lips,

[29] Welsh: "smack bottom"; a "hot smack" Ma used to say.

76

"Yellow bird way up in banana tree". "Long time gyurl meh neva see yuh" . . . but that was all. He had left it all well and truly behind in his exodus to Africa. He spoke only of Africa and his mission there. Perhaps the answer to the question "Is your father from Africa?" should have been "Yes" all along.

We formed a strong woman phalanx against his mannish ways. His tantrums and his tempers were just as unpredictable and fierce as they had always been but not quite so effective. We had the edge on him because this was our own territory. He could slam doors and shout, but in Llandudno Ma was queen. He was the outsider, he needed us to mediate this alien environment so we had something to trade. He was a welcome guest, a visitor granted permission to join in. We hosted him and we enjoyed his stay but he never belonged. He never could.

But Ma was happy when Dad was about. His presence located us publicly and, if only temporarily, explained our brown faces to all those who thought we were adopted. And he loved Wales although it had something of a fairytale quality to him. One time he flew into London and bought a silver metallic Volkswagen Beetle straight out of the showrooms and drove it up to Wales. That year we explored the interior; Betws-y-Coed, Dolwyd-delan, Machynlleth, Dolgellau, Llangollen. We invaded the countryside, horn tooting, arms waving at those who stared as we breezed through. We were a travelling show and like the Congo boys, a curiosity that people came out of their houses to see. Black people and countryside don't go together in white people's thinking.

At the end of every afternoon we washed and dressed for the

early evening promenade along the seafront like the visitors, or up the paths into Gloddaeth Woods, or through the tropical gardens of the Happy Valley. When we went shopping, the shop assistants in Dunphy's the grocer's would nod respectfully at him as he stood a foot or two behind Ma in his detachment from the mundane, hands gently clasped behind his back. Alf Roberts, the tobacconist next to the Savoy cinema, said Dad was a proper gentleman. And in the sawdust butcher in Craig-y-Don where Ma always spoke Welsh to the man behind the till, they spoke English because Denis was home and they didn't seem to laugh nearly as much.

He was as charming as he was difficult. His laughter filled us with a pleasant relief and he was a beautiful storyteller. Most of his time was spent writing his book, pounding away on his portable Olivetti on the card table in the bedroom above our heads. Pages and pages of the African Lobo struggling to get the European Lionel out of his head, struggling against incorporation, against the loss of his true self. He would rehearse his arguments with Ma in the kitchen while she cooked the roast dinner in the evenings. "You can't be a man if your head has been cut off by colonialism. How can you speak, act, create anything if your every thought has been shaped for you by the European? If you can't think a thought that hasn't already been cast with meaning by the coloniser; if your language has been relegated to the status of babble." Ma understood. He went on. "Without the head, the snake is nothing but rope . . . that's what the Africans say. That's how they've done it, Katie Alice, they've got inside our heads. Hundreds of years of the European God shoved down the throats of its peoples until their spirit is disturbed so that the church has put them in a trance—believing that tomorrow the missionaries' promises will come true and they will be lifted out of their miserable state. Rubbish, man! Rubbish!! Guns and gods broke up Africa, European guns and the European God."

Guns, gods and Africans in our back kitchen and all I wanted to be was ordinary.

On one of his home visits Dad was finishing his novel *Other Leopards* and he wrote:

Between Europe and Africa there is this desert. Between the white and the black this mulatto divide. You cannot cross it, whoever you are, and remain the same. You change. You become, in a way yourself mulatto—looking both ways. Looking back to the vertical, sideways to the timeless mystery . . . Catherine, it will have to be, if ever I see those mountain eyes again. I'd tell you then what you asked and I never answered; I'd tell you who I am, since now I know. I am a man hunting and running; neither infra nor supra, not Equatorial black, not Mediterranean white. Mulatto, you could say, Sudanic mulatto, looking both ways. Ochre. Semi. Not desert, but not yet sown. Faecal, so far; shadowless. Never mind though Kate, there are whole heaps of things. Like you've always said.[30]

I guess that was his dilemma. Dad was never staying. One afternoon he was getting ready to meet me from school when he

[30] From *Other Leopards*, Hutchinson, 1963.

caught sight of his reflection in the wardrobe mirror, dressed as he would be in his carefully pressed trousers, a shirt, a moss green jumper from Marks and Spencer and his tan suede jacket. He was patting his hair into place when his reflection threw back at him a monstrous vision of Lionel. Lionel, a gentleman, a muse on the white man—top hat, velvet jacket, high white collar—a Jack Du. "All this fuss about being African only you're really white." The words in his book rushed at him. "You're white inside and you can't man me because the whiteskin woman's on y'mind. You come to me with the whiteskin woman on y'mind. You come to me half man and thinking I don't know. There's nothing wrong with you Lobo. I'll get the whiteskin woman outa your mind . . ."

He stared at this dandy reflection, hardly believing it to be himself, and he saw across miles of desert to the London schools where he'd learned European art and all the while he wanted to paint *Human World*. He thought about his work, *Painting in Six Related Rhythms*; a remarkable piece of which Wilson Harris had said, "It glows like a jewel among 200-odd paintings, a witness of a technical and spiritual revolution where tension is contained and balanced and the spirit of the man is independent and free." *Free?* Free to attend the gentlemen's parties in suits and neckties and drink fine wines? "Hell man, wha' hap'nin tuh meh?" He saw the death of himself and began wildly tearing off his clothes. "WHAT KIND OF A GHOST IS THIS?" he shouted. Ma came running from cleaning the bath. "WHAT IS A BLACK MAN DOING IN THIS MAUSOLEUM?" pulling and tugging at his jacket, throwing it across the room, shedding his incorporation, throwing out a picture of integration that he dreaded and despised, "I CAN'T LIVE WITH THIS FAIRYTALE!"

I'd like to say that same night, but I think my memory is askew—one night shortly after shall we say—one of those quiet Llandudno nights a small *haboob* was mustering, whipping up the sands on the West Shore, driving out the lovers nestling in the dunes. It can be that way in the Naples of the North. Our road was sleeping, Dad too—he had finished his writing for the day. He was fast asleep by the time the wind picked up, stole through the open bedroom window and gently lifted the sheets of his manuscript, one by one, out into the night. By the time we were awakened by Dad's shouts, almost half of the manuscript had taken flight. Pages and pages wafted past Mrs Parry's house and past Mrs Jones *fach*'s where the road bends to meet Conway Road. Pages filled the air, curling and billowing down into Jones the Butcher's garden like white ibis in flight. Pages of Dad's self just wafting away. We girls were out in our nighties and stocking caps like Wee Willie Winkie shouting and shrieking and making noisy efforts to gather what we could without damaging the pages. Dad was distraught. I see him standing by the gates of Beit-eel, flanked by the white stone pillars, trying to look dignified in his bare feet and pyjama pants, his wonderful brown chest bared to the world. Lights came on in neighbouring houses and Mr Morris appeared in his striped pyjamas with Missus just behind him in curlers and blue quilted dressing gown. More page collectors quickly emerged. Ivor Wynne had raised the alarm, his reactions finely tuned from years of rapid response to any sound or siren that might produce a story. Such was the life of a journalist. They were there, stripped of their respectable day, chasing and plucking the pages of Dad's life caught up in the privet hedges of little Wales. As we handed over what we could retrieve—black ink smudges across the white pages—I think we knew he could never stay. Dad was angry with Africa not Wales, but Wales reminded him of the source of his anger.

We made the local paper next day, of course, thanks to Ivor Wynne. The headline read: "HIGH FLYING FIRST NOVEL".

Weddings, Mixed Blessings

There is nothing like a marriage for turning private affairs into public issues. After all, that's what a wedding is: a public declaration of a union—for better or for worse. But there are marriages and there are mixed marriages and the latter inevitably signal a whole lot more to their public than the mere fact of two people promising to live out their days together.

Early in the last century, Cardiff, like Liverpool, had been identified as an area of Britain where there was a need to tackle the fast-growing "colour" problem. And so in 1929 the Chief Constable of Cardiff proposed a legal ban on miscegenation, the fancy word for racial intermixing. The ban was modelled on the South African apartheid system and put forward something like their Immorality Act of 1927. The fear and the threat of intermarriage follows even the smallest concentrations of black people; it has done throughout history. I suspect isolated cases like Jack Ystumllyn would never disturb anybody too much beyond the level of gossip, private jokes or ignorant comments, but the possibility of anything more widespread is going to bring to the surface any number of animosities. It was the same threat of miscegenation that finally put paid to the African Institute in Colwyn

Bay. That's not the recorded story of course; the Institute was formally closed down on the grounds of financial mismanagement. But the real reason was because the quaint little lads grew into not so quaint big men and they started to date local women. It was okay while the African boys were small, but when they came to be young men they posed a new kind of threat to the community. The boys had been coming steadily for ten years since 1885, coming and going back to their African countries, although a number of them died in Colwyn Bay. Kin Kassa and N'Kansa both died, so did Samba and Daniel, Kwesi Quainoo, Samuel Dibundu and George and Joseph Abraham and several others. Died of colds and flu and small accidents and things just as the missionaries were dying of diseases in Africa. The black man's burden you could call it. Others went back to their lands taking with them small gifts from the local people in recognition of how much they were loved. Washing soap from Mr H. Hughes, a grocer in Colwyn Bay, the same from Miss Kate Hughes. An iron chisel from Mr Greenfield, two medical books, twenty-two shillings and sixpence and a medicine case from Dr G. Herbert Rutter. Books, pencils, silk handkerchiefs, tools, ink bottles, ties and collars and the likes from other local people. And a poem from Mr Bostock.

FAREWELL LINES TO THE CONGO
STUDENTS LEAVING COLWYN BAY

Go back, dear friends, to Afric's land
Where the dark primeval forests stand
And deserts scatter their golden sand,

Where the ancient Nile and Congo sweep,
And over the cataracts proudly leap
To pour their vast waters into the deep;
But when from us you are far away
Remember old friends in Colwyn Bay.
Return to the land where lions roar
Where crocodiles swim or bask on the shore
Where men gather gems and golden ore,
Where cinnamon, nutmegs, and cloves abound.
Where ivory tusks are often found,
And ostriches flee across the ground;
But don't forget wher'er you stray,
The friends who remain at Colwyn Bay.
We wish you—thro' life—truest happiness:
May Providence smile, prosper and bless,—
And every good work be crowned with success!
May the Dark Continent soon be light!
May slavery cease! May men do right,
And only for truth and liberty fight!
May your Christian Endeavour never decay,—
Remember the lessons at Colwyn Bay

Was it those same local people who rapidly withdrew their loans and favours when the *John Bull* poster proclaimed "BLACK BAPTIST, BROWN BABY"? (This quickly became corrupted locally to "BLACK BAPTIST, BROWN BASTARD") It might have been a simple love story. A liaison between one of the African boys and a local girl and there was a brown baby. The

Institute was bankrupt within days, the house was closed up and the remaining boys sent home. After ten years, the Reverend had lost his battle against the forces of prejudice. The coupling of black with white had pushed them too far. Whilst the public records might tell of a financial scandal, it was miscegenation that struck to the heart of this tolerant community as it did right across Wales.

It was during the early sixties when my eldest sister Janice met the chap she would later marry, William "Billy boy" Housley, and for a good many years she became, strange as it sounds to me now, Mrs Housley. He was tall and handsome; dark curly hair, sparkling blue eyes and everything about him enchanted us. Beit-eel had been without the smell of a man for too long. He wore blazers and jumpers and open-necked shirts and sometimes a cravat. He was a man of the world, a maths scholar and an artist par excellence. He once told a crowd that mattered, "I'll never be Welsh because I can't paint in Welsh," but paint he could. We all loved Billy from the day we met him and we hovered around him like hummingbirds. We fed vicariously off Jan and Billy's love and their stories. We could only imagine their world from our captivity; the talking circles of college friends who would gather every Saturday afternoon in the Venetia coffee bar to chat loudly about art and love and life. And late in the evening the same crowd would move on to the Rendezvous Rooms to dance and party till morning. It all sounded so romantic and exciting. Jan was going jazzier by the day. She wore figure-hugging shifts or oversized jumpers and cut-off tight trousers with stilettos. She backcombed her straightened hair to a beehive with a swept-over side-fringe that ended in a kiss curl. She spent hours in the mirror, and then more hours in the bathroom getting ready to go out with Billy, all the while entertaining us with a medley of Helen Shapiro and Shirley Bassey songs. She had a wonderfully deep and resonant voice, and when she hummed her nostrils would flare out and small ornaments would vibrate and fall off the mantlepiece. Jan saw herself as an exotic beauty. She said, "They shouldn't call us half-caste, that's a terrible word. We're continental." Everything was continental that year, even the coffee cups in the Ven.

The Housleys were part of Llandudno's community of small business people. They owned one of two tiny shops that flanked the doors of the Savoy cinema where they sold wool for knitting and crochet. The shop brimmed over with the fleecy, the flecked, Arans, merino, mohair packed in six, twelve and twenty-four times four-ounce packs. For six days a week Mrs Housley sat at the centre of this blossom, knitting or crocheting incessantly. Not baby clothes or cardies or toilet roll covers—nothing so simple. Mrs Housley made dolls, kitted out in hand-knitted pastel shades of Victorian garb which were year-in year-out a big hit with holidaymakers. That's so Llandudno, a town dedicated to the manufacture of an imagined Victorian era. I never owned a Housley doll although she must have flogged hundreds of the woolly-faced little effigies every year. And I never saw Mrs Housley in anything knitted; she didn't wear wool. She only ever wore costumes, polyester jackets and skirts or at times a plain shift dress topped with a jacket or coat in colours that so fittingly matched every sea-front hotel in Llandudno. And she wore hats; a frizzle of net to frame the powder-puffed, one-and-nine-penny rouge-touched face. I never saw her jacketless, but she wore the type of blouse that was all front so to speak; a panel of pleated net or lace just large enough to cover her ample bosom with the yellowing bri-nylon back concealed from the eye. A wonderful deceit, like Llandudno itself.

I didn't know Mrs Housley was a spiritualist until long after Jan married Billy. Her other "occupation", which she didn't disclose too much about, was reuniting the living with relatives and friends on the other side. I must say, even as a young child I always found the experience of talking with her somewhat unnerving. She had this way of tilting her head to the side and staring at me with a strange grin on her face. Just staring and not saying anything—not to me anyhow. She was accompanied everywhere by her invisible Native American-Indian spirit guide with whom she would have occasional hushed conversations.

The wedding, which took place in the autumn of that year, was a bizarre affair. The ceremony was held at our local church at Llanrhos, on the edge of town. We had walked there to Sunday school for years to co-operate in the purification of our souls by some good but misguided women and then nicked Oxo cubes from the little shop nearby to re-adulterate our souls on the way home. Our church was host to this weird and wonderful pairing, a pairing that wasn't just about Janice and Billy but one that would seal our union to all that was Llandudno. Our family and the community were to collude in this open act of miscegenation which would of necessity open up a space for us in our home town. The wedding was after all a demonstration of our commitment to them; a public declaration of our settler status. The town embraced us for it. For years I would hear, "Oh yes, the older sister married the Housley boy, you know," with such positive connotations.

In Nigeria all the women of a family wear the same cloth to a wedding. All wearing the same cloth but personalised into their own particular style. It shows family. I suspect there was no such intention behind our rig-outs. Ma had got a good deal on a bolt of pink brocade from Clares Department Store in town. It did show family though, that and our brown faces. I was a fairy in pink, a princess at last. The excitement trembled within me and when I turned the page of the hymn book it ripped itself off. "It just happened," I whispered to Isabel. Things like that seemed to happen around me, Dennis the Menace never far away. Evelyn cried throughout the service though I never understood why. Pink tears on pink brocade.

Both Ma and Auntie Maggie wore fur. One looked like a beaver and one like a badger. "*Côt marr-vellus, te?*" Maggie exclaimed to herself in best Llandudno-Welsh as she stood in front of the hall mirror. The small Welsh badger had been over since early that morning squealing with excitement and tickling our bare legs. Everything was "*Da iawn*" and "*Bobol bach*" and "*Duwks, barr-gin te?*" Maggie liked things material as much as she liked things spiritual. She was a born proselytiser and took every opportunity to preach her own unique brand of hellfire and brimstone, but for all her work, in her home town of Bethesda they called her "*Maggie Bunt*"[31] in recognition of her true calling.

---

[31] Literally "Maggie Pound", an indication of her love of money.

As wedding gifts she carried with her a box of Bronnley soaps and verbal warnings about the perils of sex, admitting openly that Father, as she referred to her husband Matt, had had his wicked way with her only once and after that she had kept her legs and her eyes firmly closed. "*Horrible, te?* I've been a wooden woman ever since." By the Seventies she still had a lot to say on this matter but by then her focus had shifted to "contradictive pills" which she saw as the evil of the age. Auntie Maggie was so before her time. She only had one child herself—a small adult male (Dave was never a child)—and I don't think she thought it wise to have more than one.

The little church was full. The Housleys didn't have family, they were immigrants to Wales. But they had people and they turned out in some numbers. They sat on the groom's side in a glow of colour. That day I caught my first view of what constituted our family at that time. Pews of them. Welsh Moors flanking the left side of the church like a shadow. I looked behind me searching out a glimpse of the collective chromosome, a hint of the hereditary endowment so that we could take stock of John William Hughes and Mary Jones, our joint ancestry who made our story. This dynasty was the Bethesda genealogy in its purest form. And what a congregation of identical miniatures. Small people; round-faced, high-pitched, sharp-nosed, sharp-eyed strangers who claimed me with every glance and every movement. Ethel and Enid, Beryl and Ted, John and Eileen, Caradoc and Margaret, Dafydd and Avril, Menna and more. Some cousins by marriage, Wil Da-Da, Elwyn with his father's mother, Pritchard Pritchards, Richard Richards, Hugh Hughes. And Uncle Walter too. Uncle Walter had a war injury, or so one of his many stories went, which had left him with damaged vocal cords and a distinctive husky, gravel voice that sounded like a tractor engine starting up. When he whispered across the pews the whole church could hear him. When we sang, together we made one glorious unifying voice, except for Walter's strained wheeze. He was short and fat and wore small, round, bottle-end glasses that neatly fitted the sockets of his eyes. *Serious* bottle ends that magnified his eyes to frightening proportion. He was the man in the family for us before Billy, our only model of the white male species. This was our family. The Welsh interior had come to town.

Beit-eel embraced them all within her small rooms that day with a proximity that ensured a mingling of the tribes and a mingling of the languages. There was an October chill in the air, but the wedding party spilled in and out of her open doors. Some smartly dressed and well-spoken chaps from Billy's student life made speeches and fun. Billy, the new man in the family, sat comfortably in an oversized armchair smoking his pipe and Ma and the Aunts made food. Father (as in Uncle Matt) carved the joint. We were allowed champagne and Evelyn cried some more. Uncle Walter helped everyone to drinks and then again and then some more. He had a way with drink. It was his ambition to own a pub and eventually he did, the King's Arms on Bethesda High Street. But that would be another story.

Beneath her discarded fur Mrs Housley had on a dazzling costume. She was rouge red with the excitement of the day; buzzing and chirping and marvelling as she would about most things. "Isn't that nice, ducky," she cooed in the way that Lancashire folk do. She seemed to swell visibly with the heat of the room. She mesmerised me completely. I could almost feel her heartbeat. She was omnipresent. Her eyes twinkled blue like her diamanté necklace. My eyes watered with the smoke of Billy's pipe and she glistened all the more. She held me captivated in her stare. I watched as coils of pipe tobacco smoke rose above the heads and drink loosened the tongues until song and laughter and argument and conversation became one.

When the Ogboni *agbada*[32] glided in through the living-room door, intuitively I knew it must have had something to do with Mrs Housley. The *agbada* had always hung on the back of Ma's bedroom door for decoration. It entered slowly, swaying like one of those larger than life mammies on Agege Market. Any awkwardness of human movement was concealed below the magnificent gilded robe. It had been brought to life and now it moved with its own life. It filled the centre of the room with its majestic gyrations. Its arms danced slowly in gathering gestures, beckoning us all closer. The wedding party roared and clapped a greeting as if they had been expecting the arrival. The new guest bowed low and then high in long, slow movements. Suddenly, as one, the group of aunts let out a piercing, deafening screech, stamping their feet and ululating like the women of a North African Zaar. The mother of the Zaar, in the embodiment of the dazzling diamanté Mrs Housley, began to sway backwards and forwards, her eyes rolling to the back of her head. Some strange

[32] A ceremonial dress of the Ogboni cult in Nigeria.

frothy babble emanated from her mouth and in a voice clearly not her own, she, as Llandudno personified, called down Ogun, then in turn Shango, Olórun and Èsù. Down came the deities of the ancient kingdom of Oyo one by one seeking out empty vessels within the room.

It was as if one of the great ancestors had entered into the very soul of the talking drum, standing as it always did beside the fireplace. The drum, moved by its spirit host, threw itself into the arms of Uncle John and he began to tap out a beat: *Bap Bap, bap bap bap bap*, the hard edge of the drum being rapped with the carved wooden stick. *TrrrrRap, bap, bap, bap*, calling out repeatedly, hard and short. Johnny *bach*'s head moved its own dance, up, down, round, back and then stop: the room held in this pause. Then it started again: *RAPAPA TA RAP RAP RAP*. Small pearls of sweat appeared on his face and then a sweet look of release. From my small-world seat beneath the canopy of adults, I felt the bigness of this drumming, it reached down inside of me and filled me and pulled me up into the circle of dance. All present were drawn into the dance by the mother of the Zaar. She did not dance herself but Mamma Housley orchestrated the great Ogboni puppet as we danced round it, in and out between its great skirts. Ma was dancing a dance of joy and the moonstone beads on her neck smiled into the room. Great libations were offered to the invited ancestors. The spirit of Wales was dancing with them and within this great celebration I was being created more whole. Johnny *bach* squeezed the strings of the talking drum in his armpit and moved his body to reach the middle tones. *Gangalang,*

gangalang, grrrumbang, the sounds coming from somewhere deep and far away. They heard no answer. Again they called out, demanding a reply.

Gangalang? Gangalang? shouting out over the Carneddi. Then, and only then, did the sounds come, sudden and powerful like the thunder of Shango cracking open the skies. The bongo drum, as if charged with the energy of Èsù the trickster-god, jumped from the top of the bookcase into Auntie Beryl's waiting lap. In an unconscious rediscovery of ancient mantras they made sounds that reached down to the floor of the bush, vibrated through the bellies of snakes, reverberated from tree to tree. Sounds that defied Shango and Olórun, sounds that wakened Eryri. Beautiful conversations drum to drum, calling and answering. Then drumming man found a new expression; he was carried now by some terrible vocal forms and had to set them free. His whole body became drum; man and drum as one, a shaking, moving, rhythmic form. He was swaying, his eyes closed and teeth clenched until his own agonising wail from the yard of Bontnewydd came back onto his lips and his years of pain were released into the room.

The air was filled with madness. Someone had donned the donkey head from the front doorstep and circled in and out between us braying. The mother of the Zaar called upon each in turn, and each took up a masquerade adopting a persona; sometimes of their choosing, sometimes not. Sometimes their devils sought them out and they had to exorcise them. The room pulsated with the drumming. Maggie Bunt and my sister Bea entered as identical twins dressed as badger and beaver, dancing synchronistically. Ted had covered his face with the ebony mask from the wall at the top of the stairs. Black Ted. Ted Du, now he was, Talhaiarn's King of the Cannibals chanting in a monotonous and raucous voice,

Yn howcio, cowcio, llowcio'n lli,
Chwipio a hicio a chicio'r ci,
Yn strim-stam strellach yn ei sbri
Bydd Brenin y Canibalyddion.

Sometimes the spirit that arrived in the room was so mysterious that the gathering shouted out for explanation. "Who are you? Where are you from? Who is your mother? Are you Welsh? Are you proper Welsh?" Then, "Yes we know of you, but tell us who you really are!"

I saw Evelyn searching for herself among the crowds of women in *The Moolit* hanging above the fireplace. She was roaming through the ochre streets under the lapis lazuli sky, white robes covering all but her eyes. When the power of the talking drum reached into the soul of my sister Isabel she became Yamanja, the ultimate African mother. In that moment as she glimpsed her own beauty, all her childhood anguish fell from her shoulders, devoured by the tigers on the sitting-room rug. What kind of *anta banta* day was this? What kind of Bethesda *juju*? What scene of domestic barbarism had Llandudno summoned up?

Eventually the celebration threw up a new and most wondrous sight. Janice, wedding ivory discarded, entered trance-like dressed as Mrs Housley, a strange *Windrush* lookalike with an alien spirit within her. And that was how she left Beit-eel. We waved the new Mrs Housley and Billy away as Olórun, the god of the sky's face flushed with the changing light of evening. But the Zaar didn't finish then. It rolled on into the night hours. The flood of music spilled out onto the road and so did a procession of dancers heading towards the *cwm*[33] behind the house. The Congo boys turning in their graves on Llanelian Road knew their ancestors had been called down. The music bound us all. We were here. We were here to stay and we had brought our own little piece of Africa with us.

As the grand ceremonial procession drummed on past Mrs Morris's house, off into the Celtic jungle at the bottom of the cwm, I thought I espied a bespectacled Ogboni, prostrate and exhausted, on the floor of the dense bush, *agbada* part discarded like some great anaconda skin, a store of empty beer bottles at his side, laughing in that familiar hoarse whisper.

[33] Welsh: "valley".

Chalky White

Years had passed since Janice was lost to the tribe while the rest of us waited patiently to be discovered by the opposite sex. No general recognition had been granted for the idea of interracial dating and Jan and Billy were as much an oddity locally as Jack Ystumllyn and his bride must have been. Worse still, there was as yet no official sanction of the idea that black could indeed be beautiful. Images of black beauty were thin on the ground. When I was a teenager a date was the ultimate measure of beauty—the only real public recognition that you were in any way desirable. I yearned for a date. I longed to be discovered, waiting for Columbus to pitch his boat in Llandudno Bay.

Llandudno was a town that swelled to twenty times its size in the summer and shrank to a miserable, lonely graveyard in winter. A town where every summer our hopes were raised that life might just begin and every winter we faced our grim reality. Too young to appreciate the rugged beauty of the abandoned landscape, in winter we were simply bored and boarded up. The best most of us could hope for was a seat in the one-and-nines on a Saturday afternoon to watch some outdated John Wayne film, knowing that when the credits came up at five-thirty the weekend was over. It's not surprising that we longed for the summer when young Italians and Irish would come and work in the hotels and the bars and when there was just a vague chance that a gang of mods from Manchester would blaze into town on their scooters for the weekend.

One summer Chalky came to town.

WIN A FIVER! FIND CHALKY!

This is Chalky White [a photo of Chalky with cap pulled down over face, reading the *Daily Mirror* newspaper]. *Today he will be in Llandudno. He will be carrying a rolled up copy of the* Daily Mirror *under his arm. If you spot Chalky approach him and say,* "YOU ARE CHALKY WHITE. I CLAIM MY REWARD." *You could be today's lucky winner!*

Llandudno was pitched into Chalky frenzy. Unemployed people joined the army of holidaymakers in the search for the elusive Chalky. At lunchtime the schoolkids poured out of the school gates and roamed the crowded streets looking for him. Chalky White and I whiled away hours waiting to be discovered. A group of boys from my class took to calling me Chalky White on account of my initials and the fact that I definitely wasn't Chalky. They would whisper as they passed me, "I claim my reward."

I was not the kind of girl that boys would have thought to take out. I knew they didn't see me as beautiful. I knew they couldn't see the white in me although I tried my best to show it. It wasn't only them either; *I'd* bought into a whole way of thinking about black people that didn't amount to anything very positive—things about fuzzy hair, thick lips, big backsides, the usual. It all added up to the word "ugly". It wasn't just that I wanted to be blonde, straight haired, blue eyed and beautiful which, let's face it, every girl did—white or black—but it was a whole host of confusing things that I carried around in my head about my body that was even more damaging. I thought only black people had curly pubic hair and brown nipples which made keeping out of the showers at school a necessity. I thought my skin was thicker and my muscles stronger than any white girl my age which meant I must be more resilient to injury. That led to a whole lot of boasting and a whole lot of accidents. I thought black people couldn't get sunburned. And I was secretly scared of black men; not that I had come across too many in Llandudno.

In any case, dating was a measure of beauty so I was outside of all that. I accepted my part in an unspoken agreement between the races. There were other things I could be—funny, friendly, clever, happy, sporty, musical, loud and gregarious—but not beautiful. I had this confirmed recently when an old school friend described me as an ugly duckling at school and I wondered at what point she had decided I had been transformed. "I was always the same," I said to her. "I didn't change, you did."

The fact was, if a boy asked me out it might somehow have been an affront to the whole school population. That no one had was in itself a deterrent. But more likely, in the natural order of things there were a host of girls standing in the line in front of me; even the plainest of them assumed she would be ahead of me in the pairing-off ritual. It was the general assumption of my inferiority in the beauty stakes that guided all our thinking. Or was it something else? Something forbidden? I remember much later a boy I eventually dated telling me, "None of us knew we could ask girls like you out." The fact that he wasn't a schoolboy made this liaison possible. He might have turned into a real boyfriend but neither of us knew how to *be* publicly and there was nowhere to go, so we didn't.

There was just one occasion however, that a boy from school did take me out. A vee-necked, fresh-faced boy who lived in an area of town where you didn't have to be very bright to secure a place in the top streams at the grammar school and follow Daddy into some safe profession like accounting. I bet I could find any one of them now with some nice-wife, nice-house, nice-life story shopping in Marks & Spencer on a Saturday morning. He didn't ask me out himself; a guy called Johnny Pritchard, the leader of his group did, on his behalf. To my mind Johnny Pritchard had a popularity he didn't deserve due in no small measure to the fact that he drove a car to school. He rode on the privilege of class and money and with all the weight of this privilege he suddenly stepped out in front of me one day in the corridor at school, a posse of sycophantic creeps standing behind him. He announced loudly that Richard, the fresh-faced vee-neck who I didn't know at all at that point and who was nowhere to be seen, wanted to go out with me and that I was to meet him at seven-thirty on Friday night outside the Palladium. I felt my cheeks burn purple brown like the heather at the end of September. I couldn't have said "no" if I had wanted to.

I believed I should be grateful to have been chosen. Had Columbus arrived?

I hardly dared believe he would show up by the time I found myself outside the Palladium that Friday. There were a few of us standing on our spots waiting—either nervously or nonchalantly depending on experience—for our dates. I was fifteen. I felt near perfect on the make-up front, blue sky eye shadow with a heavy pearlised brow bone and pearlised pink lips. I modelled myself on the girl in the Silvikrin advert. I named her Tessa, cut her out, stuck her in my scrapbook and built a whole imaginary world around her. They didn't make panstick in my colour which meant I had a chalky complexion like Tessa, although she didn't have a clear line where her face ended and her neck began. My hair was swept back into the tightest headache-inducing ponytail, a clip pinning it securely to the back of my head for fear it would end up looking like a hearth brush. I searched out the hair shafts below the stiff fringe and found thankfully that they were still straight. It had taken me all day to do. I could still feel the faint sting from the hot comb burns high on my forehead. Hair pressing and straightening was a closely guarded family secret. I couldn't conceive of this being public knowledge even to this day. I told my closest love of this shameful act only after we had decided to be married. It was like owning up to having a prosthetic or false teeth.

We brought the hot comb back from Africa. We didn't use pressing oils because no one had told us we needed to; Ma had no role in any of this hair business. We just heated the comb on the kitchen stove and applied it directly onto our naked hair. We didn't have pomade to finish it off so we used olive oil which we bought in very small bottles from Boots the Chemist and that smelled to high heaven under the heat of the combs. It all had to be hidden; the combs, the oil, and the baboo that was simply a home-made nylon stocking cap we used as a hairnet. *Baboo?* Is that a real word or one of Ma's? The hot-combing ritual took up much of Sundays. Sometimes Sunday morning before Ma started the cooking, some-times after lunch when we had washed up the dishes. Sundays; hot comb, the black and white afternoon film on the telly, more hot comb, boiled eggs for tea and a nasty bout of Sundayitis.

At secondary school there was no end to things I couldn't do because of the hair. Swimming and showering for a start, but there's much more to the hair thing than that. Ask anyone who's been there. A couple of years ago I met up with an aunt on my father's side still living in London and I decided to broach the subject with her. "Do you hot comb, Auntie, or do you have your hair relaxed?" I asked. Clearly reluctant to take on the subject, she took a long pause before answering. "I still do the hair every Sun-day, my dear, with the hot comb. You know I live amongst Europeans so I must keep it private still." I felt like a member of an underground sect.

Vee-neck didn't turn his head towards me as he drew up in his car, as though I should know he had arrived without beckon or greeting. Neither did he take his eyes away from the road when I got in the car. We drove round for a while, concealed behind the visors of what turned out to be his father's car, cruising unfamiliar routes. We didn't do Mostyn Street or the Promenade. He didn't say too much; he talked a little about his chums at school but he could have been talking to anyone. I began to understand it was a clandestine affair. I wasn't particularly surprised or disappointed, just accepting. I had no expectations. I just hoped this was ordinary but something told me it wasn't.

Eventually he stopped the car on the West Shore. The sea breeze wafted gently in from his rolled-down window and cooled my hot cheeks. Small relief. I wanted to walk along the sands where I could see other couples strolling in the evening air. I wanted to be out on a regular date. I wanted to be Tessa and not to disappoint. My sister, Isabel, was in love with Elvis and sometimes I would have to enact a part in her *Blue Hawaii*. I wanted to play my part again now; the beach was a perfect setting.

Then the questions began, like bullets from a gun, and at that time I had no defences. I didn't like questions. I still don't.

"They say you people don't wash your hair for months. Is that true?"

I did my best but I had taken a hit in my most vulnerable spot from his first round of fire. "What do you eat in your house?" He was serious and I was answering seriously. There was nowhere to hide. He tortured me in this way for about an hour, seemingly oblivious to my discomfort. As darkness came and his chances of being spotted narrowed, he got more relaxed and confident in his long heritage of superiority, while I got more tense. His cheeks didn't seem so red in this light. I actually thought he was a nice-looking boy really and I blamed myself because it made me feel better.

"Do your sisters get any boyfriends?" "Do they do it—y'know, have it off?"

"Girls like you are supposed to be good at it, aren't they?" "Are you brown all over? Nipples as well?"

"Is the hair on your fanny tufty?"

The sexual nature of his questions added to the agony. Each bullet penetrated deeper than the one before. I was trapped and yet so misguidedly, so stupidly, grateful to be out on a date. I laughed a little to hide my pain. It wasn't a case of "never show the enemy you're wounded", nothing so sophisticated. I was operating my "be good and you might get free" strategy.

I don't know what eventually prompted him to come clean with me, but he did. Maybe he was overcome with guilt although I doubt it. I think he just wanted to quell any romantic expectations I might have.

"Look," he said to me finally, "I've got a girlfriend of my own you know. Carys. Johnny Pritchard set this whole thing up as a joke. I didn't know anything about it until today. I never asked to go out with you. I never would. I don't fancy you. It's just a bit of fun. He dared me to pick you up and drive you round for a while that's all. Nothing more than that."

"That's okay," I said feigning nonchalance, and then added in a show of misplaced gratitude, "I wasn't even sure you'd come at all."

I can't especially remember being dropped off. I didn't feel humiliated; that would have been arrogant. I was relieved to be let off the hook. I made my way home, walking slowly up Conway Road. The lights were still on in Mrs Jones *fach*'s house when I reached the corner of our road. I couldn't arrive home too early without having to provide explanations so I sat for a while beneath her privet hedge. I needed time to think about what I might say to the girls at school the next day. "Ma said I couldn't go" would be as good a cop-out as any and deny ever having been out with him. That was the easy bit compared to facing vee-neck, or worse still Johnny Pritchard. How stupid can you get? I felt ashamed that I could ever have presumed that I would have been asked on a real date. I felt a fool that I had answered his questions so honestly. I knew I had given the enemy precious information and I knew I had betrayed my sisters. I couldn't bear to think about what might be done with the information. I felt sick. I shoved the whole scene down deep inside with a whole load of other crap that I was pretending wasn't there. I couldn't stay away from school because I always had to be so bloody good.

Much later, revisiting this episode in my mind, I was able to find a way of thinking about Johnny Pritchard and his elaborate hoax. At first I couldn't understand why he would pick me for his sport. I was just a fourth former, a mere minion. I couldn't bring myself to think that this charade was for the entertainment of the entire sixth form. That would be unthinkable. I would never be able to keep that down with all the other garbage. I toyed with the idea that maybe he picked the vee-necked stool pigeon because he fancied Carys himself. Sweet sandy-haired Carys, a Welsh middle class, one of the original *crachach*.[34] But surely there must be easier ways of splitting up a couple. No. Slowly, very slowly, it occurred to me that Johnny Pritchard fancied me himself. Fancied me with a passion: wanted me for himself, wanted to know me

---

[34] Welsh: "elite" in a pejorative sense.

and what I was. I realised that Johnny Pritchard had been caught up in the deep creek brown of my eyes, my laughter and my spirit. But he didn't dare act on it. Hundreds of years of ugliness lay dormant in his fears. He was filled with a hatred and a longing, both pulled and repulsed by the possibility. I was angel and devil to him, light and dark, and he had to exorcise me and own me. A nasty case of negrophilia if ever I saw one. Johnny Pritchard had to separate the potential of our connection, his white from my black and then colonise it. But Johnny Prick-hard just did not dare. He could not confront his own desire so he sent his stooge.

We all got caught up in the damage. It's funny how the tide can turn; how the scapegoated so easily become scapegoaters. When you are pushed to the bottom it's easy to resent those down there with you or those you think are below you. They are the ones that become the biggest threat to your survival. There was a black girl who appeared in our life for a short moment of time. I remember her now as clear as I remember Johnny Prick-hard. She wasn't in my school and I didn't know her, nor could I. But we did meet just once.

She arrived at Beit-eel one day with her social worker. It must have been dawning on them at the Barnardo's home that coloured kids had different hair and different skin to Europeans. Either that or this farsighted social worker had thought of it for himself. So he brought her to us. I have no idea how he found Beit-eel; he just turned up one day and we all came to the door to look. It was obvious that Simone was a reluctant participant in this encounter. She stood at a sheepish distance with her head lowered, avoiding any eye contact. She had bleached white patches on her skin and her hair was tatty. She was teenage shy and who could blame her. She had been sent to this colourless outpost in Llandudno and was as isolated as we were.

The social worker wondered if we could help her with her "hair and things". I suppose her hair was the obvious link but none of us knew what the "things" might be. I suppose in theory it could have been a fruitful alliance. She could have joined our Maroon community although the gulf between us was immense. We thought the damage was all hers. It was easier to spot than ours. She was a Barnardo's kid—classless, homeless, parentless, placeless—who just happened to have a brown face.

The day Simone came to have her hair done she was by herself. We showed her the hot comb and the olive oil and she touched them like they were emblems of an ancestry she had never had. A small smile crept over her face in anticipation of the ceremony. We were like the women on Falolou Road. Isabel took charge of operations and managed to make the procedure look very professional, dividing and clipping Simone's nappy hair with the confidence of having attended to her own for the last ten years. Simone's hair was unaccustomed to being straightened and at first resisted the heat of the comb, springing back into its original crinkly form. The kitchen filled with the familiar smell of singed hair, burning flesh and burned oil but gradually her woolly mass responded and lay down quiet in a distinguishable English shape. The Afro was tamed to a bob, a fringe of soft curl at the front, no frizz and no crinkled hair shaft to give the game away. It was pressed-out, nylon, doll hair. We talked hair with Simone but that was the limit of our shared experience. We warned her of the transient normality hot combing provides. A hint of rain, a steamy kitchen or bathroom, early morning mist or even a nervous sweat could have you transformed like Cinderella. It was so easy to be publicly outed by a sudden frizz, hair quickly shrunk and mis-shapen by a change in the climate. "Never sleep without a baboo," I admonished her, "or your hair will be too bushy in the morning. Don't let anyone touch your hair and don't lean on things because you'll leave a greasy mark."

It was not too long after the Simone hair-day that I caught sight of her in the town. She saw me and looked away. But something passed between us. Her hair, restored to its fuzzy mop, was a betrayal I could not accommodate. She didn't of course have a hot comb and nowhere to buy one. We knew how precious this little commodity was. She had been unable to sustain the miracu-lous transformation and was too polite or too scared to come back to ask for more. Even if she had a comb, she might not have been able to manage by herself. Yet I despised her for it. She repre-sented something I feared. She was an unwelcome invasion, a reminder of just what might shame me in this dreadful clamour-ing for small-town respectability. Every bit of her dragged me down and took away from my favoured position. I couldn't take her on; I was on the front line myself. She reminded me of what it was I was trying to escape from. All the Barnardo's assump-tions. Rivers of them.

It's all so subtle, the corruption of one's self-image. I've got hundreds of stories about hair and they all revolve around the same thing. Some people say the pressing and the straightening is about making your hair more manageable but it wasn't about that at all; not then. We'd seen the women on the Falolou Road and their hair plaiting and tatting but that didn't give us a lead. We were after European tresses, we were after being the same as everyone else, we were chasing after the only images of beauty that were presented to us. We were trying to fit in. None of us could see the way in which Dad's Lionel was eating away at our thinking. Down on the beach we were all playing for the *Daily Mirror* money, "YOU ARE CHALKY WHITE, I CLAIM MY REWARD."

Beach-front days. Beach Crusaders. "Come-and-be-joyfuls", Isabel called them. Every summer they set up their mission down by the jetty between the second and third row of breakwaters from the pier, cruising the beach like red man o'war jellies. "Oh happy days, when Jesus was . . .", hand clapping and rocking like a gospel choir on the spot where the previous winter Maggie Roberts got laid while the rest of the gang looked on. Rows and rows of white-haireds in deckchairs lining the prom like a gathering of the Agatha Christie Society; all white spongy legs, pink faces and purple hair. Dot Taylor might be one of these and you'd never know. Her colour has faded to Llandudno peach now. She has been there all along, growing and changing and fading. Dot's father was the first black man to settle in Llandudno so Ivor Wynne's story goes, way back at the turn of the last century. He was a boxer with a travelling show, all the way from Baltimore in America. Eventually he married a Welsh girl and settled in Llandudno. They had five brown-girl daughters just like us, who grew up in the town but very soon left. All except Dot and her sister Elsie. I never saw them during all the time I was growing up and then one day they just became visible to me. I wish I had known them when I was young because they might have given a hint of what I could become. Ma couldn't help with that. Dot's old now. Her hair is permed and dyed purple-grey. An old Llandudno lady like the rest of them, all chalky white and blended in, sitting on the beach with the water gently lapping her feet.

S'CUSE ME . . .

I felt too big, just outa shape,
a blot on monochrome landscape.
On my desk I idly wrote:
"I love you Jimi
I really do
When I grow up
I'll be like you"
and then took note
that in this land of slate and coal a Hendrix II
might have no role.

I wasn't cool, I wasn't right
I wasn't black, I wasn't white.
In my dreams I thought
"Please Honey
can't you change my style
make me over
like Voodoo Chile?"
but still I sought

in the midst of chapel, chips and *chwarae teg*
to make myself a shape that's shared.
Tight mouth, tight hair. I tried to wear
high heels and Marks and Spencer gear.
Willing me she sighed
"American Tan?
Rosebud Lips?
Relaxed and waxed
and pear shaped hips?"
but still she tried . . .
Miss Morgan Thomas still wonders why
black bottoms curve and not the thighs.

I grew up loud, I grew up strong
In my small town, I felt all wrong
'till Hendrix cried
"Don' worry Chile
don' wonder why
just be like me
. . . kiss the sky"
suddenly I realised
on open hills within my view
a purple haze on purple heather grew.

(Scribbles from a 1969 diary)

Purple Haze

QUEEN'S COLLEGE YABA, LAGOS 1966

Under punishment for noise-making
with Bose Nicole, a storyteller
who calls me princess.
Kneeling outside the staffroom
gravel chips embedded in our knees scarred bougainvillea red,
hands raised above heads crowned with blue wool berets
mercifully protecting their aubergine skin.
Against what?
While the white teachers drink tea and eat stew.

Bose wears hers down to her eyebrows always,
like the military boys preparing for the war that itches on the streets.
Yele Lakeru wears hers on the back of her head
swollen with pickie-pickies; an ant's nest.
I wear mine English style over my straightened hair.
Do they still wear berets in England?

We had been studying pictures of Gainsborough and Holbein,

pondering kings and queens, great statesmen, the Prince of Wales.
"I will pass the London matriculation" Yele shouts,
"I will write about the vestments of Henry VIII, the ermine, the silk,
the lace from Verona."
Words tickle across her lips like ants slipping out of the swollen nest.
Slowly Bose rises, stands full square like Henry VIII on desktop.
Arms akimbo, she begins "One time in the Kingdom of Oyo"
We, vigilant like the soldiers on the road, attend to her story telling.
"One time in a forest city, five missionary men arrive with tales
    of a strange god,
an all powerful god, one god, a true god, a god above all others"
She makes her body big like an Oba.

" 'Abandon your false gods' " they say to the city's elders,
'worship the one and true god
and you will be saved. And you will be saved'."
Bose nods out the words, we copy, nodding like pigeons.
"Turn away from evil influences and from the spirits
Burn your idols and worship the great god, the one and true god.
You will be saved."
The elders listen carefully like hunters.

The elders are silent. Their mouths fall open in disbelief.
"Eh eh" we chorus, "Eh eh" like the ancients.
" 'You ask us to leave our ancestral gods and follow your god?
You ask us to burn our sacred image? You ask us to turn our back
    on our rituals?' "
She throws the questions at us like bread and we peck at each one.

" 'We must rest, we must eat. We must consider the power of your god. Come let us eat'."

Bose in repose, a long pause, we wait. She considers.

" 'Come eat!' " The elders beckoned the missionary men but they refused.

" 'We cannot partake of your food, we cannot eat with savages,

We cannot eat the food of those who worship false gods'."

The elders listen carefully like hunters.

Bose cups her ears like a hunter. She stares around, we stare after her.

" 'You refuse our food. We must be interested in your god and yet you cannot share in the very thing that sustains all life?

You reject our offerings but we must accept yours?

Are we swine? How can we take interest in your god if you will not eat?' "

A delicious stew is prepared. A stew that brings water to the mouths of everyone in the Kingdom

A gleaming, sweet sweet stew like Mama Tunde's yam stew but better.

We are swaying with Bose, we are hungry, our bellies ache.

So the missionaries agree. They take their fill. Their lips gleam with grease

their fingers shine with fat, they smack their lips, their bellies swollen and they ask for more

Eating like baboons until only a few bones remain in the bottom of the pot.

"Finally the old man of the city speaks," Bose whispers. We duck our
   heads in reverence.

" 'My friends, the meal is over, you are satisfied.

I see that you have eaten your predecessor who came and insulted
   our gods and our ways.

So my friends now you know of another great god'."

Bose voice growls belly deep, stool pigeons stare askance

"There is no god like one's stomach and that's why we must sacrifice
   to it every day!"

We are bowing with laughter. We grasp our bellies, we stomp like
   pigeons,

we shout, "We are hungry! We are hungry!"

And so we are under punishment for noise making.

No stew.

(inspired by Chinweizu's *African Parable of Resistance*)

A lot of things have been written and said about black families in
Britain. It's said a good many Afro-Caribbean families are single-
parent families, that they live in poverty, that the kids don't do
well at school and that they use drugs, become criminals and end
up in care. It's an image that goes along with high-rise flats, council estates scarred with graffiti, litter, drunks, prostitutes and
roaming dogs. And there's an image of our version of this family
too; the white mum bringing up the black kids alone. Women
abandoned by no-good black men left with kids with confused
identities; truants, school failures, kids who drop out, get pregnant

and get married young. I suppose the deck was always stacked against us. I'm sure we must have registered in all the statistics but that kind of collective label hadn't reached our ears in Llandudno. We were just one family blazing our own trail. Dad did finally leave and overnight we learned the meaning of free school meals, vouchers for school uniforms, jumble sales and the man from the social. We fell suddenly into the ranks of poor Britain but we carried it off with style. We couldn't afford to do otherwise. When poverty collides with blackness you have to get tough to survive. I doubt we did survive, but after Hendrix I knew there was something different.

The turbulent sixties were ending and everything seemed to be cracking open at the edges. It was post-Vietnam, post-hippy, post-Empire fall-out. Things had changed—the black world was striking back. There were cries for independence from all over the Caribbean. Civil wars, famine and apartheid racked Africa. There was Angela Davis, Malcolm X and the '68 Olympics when the American sprinters made the black power salute on the podium and gave a message to the world about the civil rights movement. Somewhere Enoch Powell was changing our fate with his "Rivers of Blood" speech. On the telly during coverage of the Vietnam War we watched as a man was executed by being shot in the head. "Human rights!" screamed Isabel, holding both sides of her head. Aberfan had sunk under a huge pile of slurry and Cliff Michelmore's voice broke up as he told us. We all cried—the tragedy was getting closer to home. It seemed as if whatever had been holding things together was being blown right open and the aftershock was reverberating across Britain like the chukka chukka sounds from Hendrix's guitar.

It didn't feel to us like a new global emancipation; not so much a new dawn as a dark day. Bits and pieces filtered into our front room and we grasped at things that fitted our teenage aspirations— Hendrix, *Hair*! and the new dark shades of Biba make-up.

Things had started to go awry the summer of sixty-six. Ma left us alone in Beit-eel while she visited Dad in Uganda. He had taken a visiting professorship for a semester at Makerere University. She didn't know, but he had summoned her there to tell her the marriage was over. There was someone else, something else, something better. It blew her apart. On our side of the Atlantic things were equally explosive for different reasons. Evelyn sat on the bed one morning and smoked her first cigarette while we all looked on enviously, then she burned the figure of eight in her black babydoll nightie; eight for the eight "O" levels she had passed. But nothing could hide her disappointment at failing the one she wanted most. She was a damn artist after all, we all knew that. It was a bad day, the whole *us and them* of it crashed home. More rubbish to push under the pillow. We were beginning to buy into conspiracy theory. "It's all shit," she shouted, "SHIT!" She was careering out of control, badly in need of a little direction and we, the crew, were going with her just like those Africa afternoons. It was time to hit back, time to strike out. *Human World* wasn't just staring back any more. Now it was walking and talking.

If the stakes were stereotypes then we were cash rich. If the cards were stacked against us what had we got to lose? Nothing we did or didn't do seemed to matter, so we did whatever we liked. We had become completely untouchable by virtue of our difference. I could have walked out in the garden with a bone through my nose and struck up a conversation with Mrs Parry and she would have been unable to comment, choked by her own prejudices and misconceptions. Beit-eel was rocking to the sound of the Troggs singing 'Wild Thing' the day we staged the ritual sacrifice of a rabbit for all the prying eyes. It was a scene straight out of *Zulu*. The rabbit smouldering over the campfire might have been Bea's fluffy toy but it didn't stop at least one of the neighbours phoning the RSPCA—damn, we must have been impressive. I suspect they phoned Social Services too but no one showed up that time. We were a coloured family at the end of the day.

Mr Jones Llanrwst's son got our version of The Supremes one Saturday morning as he unloaded the vegetable order from his father's lorry. We were backcombed to the hilt, dressed up in Ma's evening gowns and every inch of skin showing was boot-polished. If we could see ourselves now we might think it a kind of strange twist on the Black and White Minstrels. Even Al Jolson would have envied my oversized white lips. Jones Llanrwst's son might eventually have pitched his cap at Isabel but he had second thoughts that day.

It might have all been something and nothing until we started to venture out of the gate. The black people on the beach scene drew a substantial if somewhat bemused audience. We performed it just offside the Come-and-be-joyfuls, our voices pitched louder than normal so that our lines tremored above the hallelujahs. It was some invented African tribal language that had served us well on several occasions, this time punctuated with a few discernible sentences in heavily accented African English—"Leave the olive oil alone, Femi . . . how do you mean sunburned? You cannot get sunburned; your skin is tough like the elephant . . . the oil is for frying the meat. We shall eat coo-coo later. Collect some sticks, build a fire." What the hell was coo-coo? What did it matter? When they asked us to shut up or go away, we just gritted our teeth and started screeching hysterically like baboons. "If you light that fire I'm calling the police," one of them was saying all too seriously. "You can't do that in this country." That phrase seemed to be popping up just too often; a neighbour had shouted it out over the rabbit incident. They were little acts of resistance; small gestures of defiance from a very limited repertoire. How would we have known how to organise for resistance? We were far too isolated and in any case the pressure to conform kept a firm grip on any spontaneous acts of rebellion. We began to get high on the shock value of our pranks. Bravado drove us to shoplifting sprees. "Walk into a shop, pick something up and walk out," Evelyn instructed us. "Just keep calm, act natural—no one's bothered." Evelyn and Isabel waited outside chewing gum while I walked into the changing rooms of a shop on Mostyn Street, put on three garments under my own and walked out. I had a Mary Quant dress tucked into two pairs of Wranglers. When I reached the door I signalled the black power salute. None of the clothes actually fitted but it was the thrill that mattered, not the acquisition. Most of it ended up in the waste bins behind the Imperial Hotel. All's fair in love and war and this was war. Ma was away and nobody else cared or dared.

It may have been misplaced, misjudged and misguided but it felt good. We were on a roll and the forays got more outrageous.

Evelyn and Isabel had pockets full of money lifted straight out of the till at Woolies and we blew it at the fairground. Evelyn said they were all dopey in Woolies and if they couldn't keep track of their money they deserved what they got. We were riding high on the carousels, reeking of popcorn and candy floss and living on barley wine, Players No. 6 tipped and, just now and again, one of Isabel's omelettes. We were dreamers; unhinged, unhooked, just drifting.

Nineteen sixty-seven and Jimi's music burst through our psychological landscape like a flash of lightning. He wasn't a mirror image but he mirrored the rebellion that was stirring in all of us—"Purple haze all in my brain". I was totally shapeless, anchorless, careering on a roller coaster in the fairground under a kaleidoscope of lights, my bottom splitting through a pair of Evelyn's home-made psychedelic trousers. My hair was still hot combed straight as a die, but now I was wearing a headband like Hendrix. Hendrix was blaring from our front room, providing inspiration for madness. Our behaviour was bad and spiralling downwards. In an orgy of attention seeking we were using the only weapons we had—our exoticism and our charm—but it was filled with cynicism. We tantalised the fairground lads and the local boys who hung around the pier gates and the subterranean amusement arcade nearby. We took them to the edge, secretly mocking their vulnerability. It was just a game but it was dangerous. We were messing with Jim Crow in a way that could only spell trouble.

Like the year of 1944, when the GIs came to north Wales. There were billets of Americans right across the area; Denbigh, and Ruthin and Wrexham, a depot at Llannerch Hall near Trefnant, and a camp of them in the fields by Glan Conwy. Imagine it, scores of GIs, all pressed khaki, groomed hair and big toothy smiles in the fields outside Conway. "First the white ones came and then the black ones," Ma remembered. The girls were bowled over with them because local men had gone away to fight. They seemed to be everywhere. Handsome young men with names like Weinberger, Sekowski, and Lamarr. They filled the dance halls and pubs but racial segregation had travelled with them from America. Dance halls and pubs were designated white or black, never both. "Jim Crow for them, but we could go where we liked," Ma added. At that time young men must have met young girls briefly, very briefly, and babies were left behind, some of them brown like us, and they were tucked away in little villages, brought up as sisters or brothers of their real Ma without anyone telling them their story. Hidden stories. I suspect it was all very confusing for the black soldiers. They came from a society where they knew what they could do and what they couldn't do, where the rules were clear about where they could go and with whom. I doubt they were accustomed to the attentions of white women or the freedom to mix with them. It was playing with fire. There is a report from St Asaph at that time about a policeman being hurt while trying to prevent the admittance of black soldiers to a dance at the Plough Hotel. The two black soldiers were later court martialled at Liverpool for their part in the incident and sent home. Those few lines in the newspaper can only hint at the sad stories of Welsh Jim Crow.

*

Ma wrote home from Uganda,

> *Darling Cha, this is the first time I am writing to you. We*
> *have never been apart have we? There might be some trouble*
> *here. In Kampala most of the people are Indian and they have*
> *all the shops, cafes and cinemas, something like the English*
> *in Wales. The black people are quiet and don't do much, like*
> *the Welsh people. Their country is occupied but not conquered.*
> *It belongs to the African but he does nothing about it. I will*
> *be home soon.*
> *Love Ma.*

Things were changing everywhere. There was war on the streets in Nigeria and now Uganda was bubbling. Dad left Africa and took his new woman Toni, a part-English part-Scandinavian blonde-haired blue-eyed Tessa back to his home country. New project, new wife, sweet return. His searching might have been over but ours had just begun. *Other Leopards* was published, and *Icon and Image*, the outcome of a ten-year project on the art of Africa, was in the press. It was time for him to go home. An independent Guyana wooed him back. "What right have we not to return to build our country?" he argued. But he didn't mean *us*.

Ma's grief was fathomless and unending; her sense of dispossession profound. She came home as the summer was closing and lay down racked with rheumatism and mental anguish for what seemed an interminable period, enveloped in a cloud of cigarette smoke and worry. Slowly her strength sapped from her as if some parasite was draining her of life. It was miserable. She was only alive now in the memories of him. I couldn't carry the emotional weight of her. There seemed nowhere to go. I hated to be at school and I hated to be at home. Ma seemed odder than ever. The burden of her grief was too much, her analysis endless. She became locked into Dad's rejection of her and she couldn't find a way out. She must have been in a daze the evening she phoned the *Daily Post* and announced she was a Welsh woman with a black heart. It was around the time heart transplantation was making history and somehow the stories got confused. I knew they didn't understand her, neither did we. I suppose it was the culmination of a thousand small rejections; echoes from a purple past. She was a woman abandoned in a hostile environment in charge of five black girls. It was all going screwball. Ma, a Welsh woman fighting with her own people for a small space for us and we had become the enemy within.

It was easier to blame Ma for the break-up of the family and let Dad fade away in a romantic haze. He'd always been dispensable anyway. We'd managed the big things and the everyday things in his absence even if, like an absentee landlord, we regarded him with an ambivalent respect. It was easier to worship the memory of him. His name resonated through the house daily. Ma resurrected old conversations, passing judgements and comments on his behalf, talking about his work, analysing it, so that eventually his absence became more powerful than his presence. She kept him alive in her anger and her love. In bitter moments she would mutter, "Bloody men, te." We knew what that meant. We lived out our lives in a world where women made all the decisions and we knew not to expect too much from men. Eventually we would become Amazons. I don't know at what point Ivor Wynne realised that Dad wasn't coming back even for the summer but he continued to refer to us as though we had a father. I don't think my sister Bea understood he had left until she was a teenager. Perhaps we forgot to tell her.

I had banished him completely by the time I was sixteen. It was an inconvenience to think about the whole messy business. He had let us down. "Gone home," Ma said, taken another woman, abandoned the camp. I never saw or heard from him again for over twenty years. I froze him in a set of childhood memories that he could never alter.

Nothing physically changed about Beit-eel after he left. His paintings and the African artefacts were still there. The Ogboni *agbada* hung lifeless just as it had almost always done on the back of the bedroom door. Yet the family was cracking up like Britain. Africa had faded away and, for better or for worse, Wales was all we had. I resented both it and Ma with a passion.

Against all odds, I found myself sitting "O" level exams. I had written an excellent geography paper on the Nile Valley. I easily drew the map of Africa freehand. English Language was the last of the run and I was struggling for an essay topic, staring out the window hoping for inspiration. I knew everything depended on it, given that my profound language interference was bound to have messed up the comprehension question and the formal letter. With only ten minutes left I began writing a piece I called "Black Alice"—a wonderful unpremeditated diatribe on my entire schooling that flowed off my pen with a vengeance. It opened with a reiteration of Alice's conversation with the Mock Turtle on the question of education in which he tells Alice that he took a course in "Reeling and writing of course", and something about the different branches of arithmetic, "Ambition, Distraction, Uglification and Derision". It was a gift from the gods. Alice and her transformations helped me out again. "It's no use going back to yesterday because I was a different person then," Alice says at one point, and at another "I have the right to think, about as much as pigs have to fly." The quotes flooded back. What I didn't anticipate was that halfway through my tale Alice would turn black. Only this time she hadn't ingested anything, she hadn't passed through anything or fallen into a pool of tears, she just started returning slowly but surely to her natural state, having been completely faded under the light of a large silvery moon. She blushed black, she blushed back, like a Celt returned to his North African origins.

"And will we be required to sing Jerusalem?" Black Alice inquired of the White Knight.

"Undoubtedly," he replied with a slow guttural voice, like the words were being formed deep in his throat and the syllables were being softened as they rolled onto his lips.

"And will we be required to stand for the national anthem?" she asked, wondering to herself which one.

"There can be no question of that," the White Knight replied emphatically, "for all dutiful citizens in the state of Arcadia must show their allegiance to the Queen, they cannot face two ways, or speak with two tongues like a dragon." The "g" of dragon dragged itself across the White Knight's throat.

"A dragon," said Alice clearly. "And what do you know of dragons?"

I was happy with my efforts. As I walked out of school I felt I had won a small victory. It was a way of getting back at the teachers and all their ignorance; for all the times I was put in detention for not going in the showers with the pinkies, for all the innuendo and the covert abuse, for the miseducation, the uglification and the derision. I felt euphoric as I stepped away—call it gate fever—but it was more a sense that I had left some shit on the carpet. I remember around that time there was a song that went round and round hysterically like the fairground carousel that came every year, "They're coming to take you away ha, ha, they're coming to take you away". It went on until it reached a screaming ecstatic pitch that was both tortuous and pleasing. The whole Hendrix episode ended a bit like that song. They did come for us eventually. I suppose it was inevitable.

A place called Denbigh loomed large on the local horizon. It wasn't so much a place as a hospital, one of those towns dominated by association with the district's mental institution. Denbigh Hospital was an archaic place perched on a cold, windy hill, which closed not before time a few years ago with the coming of something called Care in the Community. It was all sloping corridors with green tiled walls. Corridors that all led uphill going nowhere; corridors and gloomy corners full of lingering people. It was a place full of lingering; a dead end. The end of the line.

It wasn't Ma who ended up there although she appeared to be headed that way. No, Ma was a survivor. Her sister, Ethel, had spent twenty years in Denbigh so Ma knew what it meant. Twenty years and her only sin was having a baby; a baby she was too sad to look after. Auntie Ethel was living proof that such places turn your head. She was constantly knitting; knitting something, knitting nothing, clinging onto a mis-shape, a few lines of stitches never becoming anything, like her life. NHS glasses and a set of false teeth were all they gave her but that wasn't all they had done to her. She was brought up in care and ended up in care. She had a way of hanging about that was institutional—a pleasant unobtrusive way of being just there and not there at all. A broken spirit.

Beit-eel was all in dark that day. The light seemed to have been fading but not Ma's grief. It was now summers and winters old but it still hung about like a cloudy day. It was one of those grey winter afternoons that closed in on me as I was walking home from school. Dr Arthur drew alongside me in his car; plucked me out from my cosy friend group. I could see the anxiety on his face and there was more than the usual stiffness in his stiff back. His eyes were grey and empty and his mouth was a thin straight line. I dropped my duffel bag and started running home, catching just the last part of his message as I set off at a gallop. "Your sister," he called, "it's a kind of illness."

She didn't look ill. She was bathing and saying nothing, silent tears rolling down her face. No words came out of her mouth although I fancied I could hear her screaming from within. She tried to laugh when she saw me but she couldn't. She looked sad and small and wounded. She was always so strong and adventurous but now something in her looked all broken up. She could have been any one of us. She was every one of us. Me, Janice, Evelyn, Isabel, Bea. "No one is going to take any of my girls away," Ma said.

Dr Arthur came back after tea. He seemed frightened of us

now that we were all congregated as one great bundle of pain, trying to stand between him and the wounds in the dim light. He sat on the Chesterfield settee and the arm dropped down, spilling him onto the floor. In that moment he lost any dignity he might have been clinging onto. Tight-lipped Dr Arthur was so ruffled he could hardly look anyone in the eye. Ma wouldn't agree to his demand. "The answer is no," she said. "Nobody is taking anyone from here. I've worked all my life for my girls and no one is going to take any one of them away from me. Make me the sacrificial head if you must. If you lock her up you will have to lock me up—you will lock all of us up—do you want that?" That was Ma, tribal. There was no individual about this. We were a tribe. Touch one, touch us all.

Ma was still going on when the ambulance arrived, at the same time as the second doctor. It seemed to be flashing its lights in the road for ages, its back doors open like a cavern. Nobody in our road came out that night. They must have known this was a family affair. No one was there for Ma except us. We unconsciously formed a barricade guarding our injured for hours and hours. Lobo lay amongst us battered and broken, the blood on the carpet. The Lobo in us all had been beaten down and quieted forever. We could have laughed or we could have cried; they'd have been the same things, the pain went so deep.

One of us did go, she had to, and we all went with her; that was our way. Things we had together were breaking apart, we knew that—all we could do was hold on as best we could but something big had snapped. The fighting was over. There was nothing but resignation and despair.

There were people lingering around the entrance of the hospital, all pale grey and white like Auntie Ethel, humming and mumbling and crying. We left her and a piece of all of us sitting alone in the corner of a cell and we promised, promised we would come back and get her out of the place. Then they locked the door with a huge key from the last century.

All the north Wales police talk with a guttural tone like the words are being formed deep in their throats, the syllables softened by sticky consonants as if rolling their "r's" and their "g's" will make the hard-edged English words into smooth waxy Welsh. I can imagine the police message now, all slow and deliberate and Welshy Welsh.

"Last seen entering a green Ford Anglia registration Roger Alpha Piper One Four Nine Charlie. A young coloured woman, answering to the name of Williams, abducted from the North Wales Hospital, Denbigh. Family members suspected. Wearing a blue cotton nightdress, no shoes and a stocking cap on her head. I repeat 'coloured'. Over." And the message coming back, "Coloured? What colour cap?"

I can imagine Ivor Wynne's newspaper headline although I never saw it. I can imagine what Mr Morris and Mrs Jones *fach* had to say on the matter although I never heard it. I can remember thinking as we all sat huddled in the back seat of Dave's psychedelic Ford Anglia, "If we'd had an ordinary car and a dad like everybody else they'd never have caught us."

One family all busted up.

Then suddenly Jimi was dead. I was seventeen, four months pregnant, working evenings in a greasy spoon café, surviving on black tea and cigarettes and waiting for the nausea to pass. All the summers seemed to be over. It was just one dark day after another and my horizon was shrinking. I lingered somewhere between serving mixed grills to overweight salesmen with greasy lips and wandering hands and spinning like a top, high on sweet cider on the dance floor in Paynes Corner House. I was careering off track and try as I might I just wasn't going to win. Ma stopped by the café where I was working on her way home from town one day with a remnant of pink velvet. "I'll help you cut out a wedding dress, Cha," she said.

Icon and Image

Jimi was dead and so was Africa, in my everyday world at least. The momentum of the Hendrix era could never have been maintained. There was no way of refuelling so I was always going to run out of steam. That's the thing about isolation. Africa became the same old huge, unexplainable encumbrance it had always been. I couldn't find a way to live with it so I put it in a picture-book bundle of memories.

In many ways I died too. I buried myself in August 1971 within the circle of druid stones in the Happy Valley. Well, that's how it felt. What a way to go—a sweet, salty kiss lingering on my lips, the seagulls laughing overhead, the smell of fish and chips floating on the breeze, Stan's organ music bellowing from the open doors of the Dolphin bar and the distant clack clack of the wooden deck-chairs being folded and stacked for the night. As I lay in my grassy grave my mind's eye could see the lads kicking the stay from under them one at a time, flattening them on their backs with the wood smacking the ground with a sound like gunshot. Six or so deckchair boys worked under the supervision of Bob Hughes for two-and-six an evening. I knew one of them: Jonesy. There was no one who could slap the chairs down with more speed than

Jonesy, he moved along a row of them felling them like a blast from a machine gun. Crowds of holidaymakers would gather to watch him. He was part of everything I knew and loved. I didn't want to move on. I honestly didn't. People my age all seemed to be going somewhere, away to college, away to work, away to get married; just leaving. There were loads of them hitching up the A55 to somewhere else. Janice, Evelyn and Isabel had all gone. The place might be becoming one big geriatric ghetto but I'd rather stay and face Stan Ryder's music. It felt safer. Better the devil you know. Better here than elsewhere.

So I did what you might call drop out or, should I say, drop in. I fell in with it all. Stopped fighting. It was a death; death by assimilation, death by concealment, death by contradiction, death by patterning myself on distorted images. Death by an over-whelming lack of direction. Buried. It wasn't what was there, but what wasn't there that did the damage. It wasn't what anyone did, it was what they didn't do.

Robbed of Jimi, the image thing loomed larger. Other images drifted in and filled the gap and I latched onto whatever was available. There's a photograph of me at twenty-something dressed in a candy pink mohair jumper, a set of pearls, a grey pleated skirt and American Tan tights. I could cry when I look at it, not because of the total incongruity of the garb but because of what it suggests about my thinking at the time, my inner self. Truth is, you just can't become something you have never seen or can't imagine. I was a lost spirit. Jimi had only been passing through and in any case he wasn't real life. He might just as well have been Dennis the Menace I suppose. Where was the "eternal presence of the ancestors" Dad spoke about? The available copyright? Where were all the icons and the images that might have given shape to my amorphous present?

During the Africa days, I would go with Dad on field trips; days and days of excavating, tagging, numbering, cataloguing and documenting evidence for his lifetime work on African art. We were digging out relics in the ancient provinces of Ifè and Benin, Ogbomosho, Osogbo, Abeokuta; in search of the sacred figures of these old communities. Dad was studying the technique of the blacksmiths and trying also to make sense of the images they produced and the meanings they held. Those were wonderful days. It could take hours of travel in the Land Rover across difficult terrain to reach a village where Dad was working. Sometimes we would travel in a convoy with other anthropologists and archaeologists like Ulli Beier and his wife Georgina and Robin Horton. The welcome we received was always magical. There would be food and there might be dancing. There would be demonstrations of the smelting process or a group of budding village archaeologists—young and old men alike—would lead us to a prime excavation site. Other times it was just a matter of examining artefacts and listening to the stories that went with them. We visited shrines where ancient effigies had stood undisturbed for generations. Sometimes the icons were so sacred Dad had to be satisfied with drawing them from a distance. He would sketch them into his journal as they stared silently back at him from their primeval worlds.

There's an African proverb that goes, "A thing is always itself and more than itself." It means that even inanimate objects have a life within them. That's the African way of thinking, the African physics of matter. These effigies were objects but at the same time much more than mere objects. They were symbols of worlds of meaning; sacred representations of ways of life long gone. They held within them tales of war and combat, tales of love, of fertility and prosperity and more. The craftsmen were the inspired artisans of the villages who were able to interpret stereotypes; templates which had been handed down to them through generations and generations in their reproduction of the icons.

We watched the blacksmiths work their magic and they in turn marvelled at mine. I showed them the magic of ice and they gasped in amazement. Grown men who had never seen ice, never mind touched and tasted it. "Eh eh," they said. "Eh eh," when they stared at the green eyes in my box of marbles. "Eh eh," at the picture box camera that they mistook for a gun. So each trip I would try and take some wonders from other worlds to share with them and they humoured me.

Dad and I travelled miles on those digs and covered ground that we lost elsewhere. His work made him passionate and whole. It was as if turning over African soil took him nearer to his true self. All the while Dad's Lobo was taking him closer to the answer to that nagging question, "What could prevail on a man to sell his brother into slavery?" Without this twist of history we would have been standing on our own African territory, him and me and all the others, whole and pure and African. We would never have been carried away. The digging took us closer and closer to the answer that stared back at him from every little metal figure and was buried in the fabric of every metal artefact. Iron. The iron bar was the key to the story that bound us all together.

Way back, from the beginning of the sixteenth century, there were great centres of iron smelting in West Africa, linking village to village and area to area in vast trade networks of buyers and sellers. It was an enormous and very sophisticated industry. The trade routes spanned Africa, bringing slow but permanent changes; developments that would transform the culture and the lives of the iron-using communities. In every village, even the smallest hamlet, there was a smith to fashion implements for farming, for hunting and for war. The smith was the linchpin between the community and the forest. The forest provided essential resources: meat, fuel, fruit and medicines in abundance. In order to take advantage of the forest, the villagers needed the metal tools and weapons that the smiths provided. The gods and the spirits of the forest also needed to be propitiated for the gifts they offered; nothing could be taken without something being given in return. And so an elaborate system of rituals was established to repay the gods for their gifts. In addition to tools, it became necessary for the villagers to have the paraphernalia of worship. They needed figurines, objects, icons to symbolise the deities to whom they made offerings. These sculptured forms also linked the living to the dead. Linked the people to their ancestors. It is not that the sculpture itself represented the ancestor but it became the medium of communication between the ancestor spirit and the people. These rituals changed the whole function of the metal. The smiths were no longer merely employed making functional objects but developed an art vital to ritual worship. They were now more artists than artisans. As their art developed, so did their status. The names of many became venerated in oral history.

The need for iron grew until it outstripped local supply. The great smelting centres couldn't meet the demand. Iron money was needed for dowries, iron gold for trade, iron for the deities, iron for tools, iron for weapons. Iron lust grew beyond the horizon of the village, beyond the network of villages until it opened up a trade in the voyage iron of Europe. First came odd little *peeces* of iron, *wedges* and *bits* carried along with other trade cargoes, from Brymbo, Bersham and Shotton. Eventually voyage iron became a major currency and the iron bar was developed as the standard. Iron bars as valuable as gold came from the iron capital of the world: Merthyr.

Perhaps the iron bar might have gone down in history as a simple fact of the industrial development of parts of Wales were it not for other world events. There was more than a twist of fate in the establishment of these great iron kingdoms and the dynasties they supported, for there was a new dimension to the iron hunger. It was the ingenious coupling of iron hunger with a sudden increase in the need for labour on the West Indian sugar plantations that sealed a terrible fate. As the sugar industry grew in the Caribbean so did the need for manpower and this could only ever mean one thing—the evolution of a malignant trade. The African iron hunger was fed and strengthened by the trade in human beings—thousands upon thousands transported to Barbados, Jamaica, Haiti, the Demerara—a great movement of human cargo to the Caribbean. Only by trading their fellow man could the Africans acquire the iron they needed so badly. Iron had become the backbone of industrial development in many areas of Britain; in Wales in particular, the iron masters grew wealthier and wealthier, ploughing back the profits of spices and sugar and slaves to make more and more iron bars and then manacles, fetters, neck collars, chains, branding irons, thumb-screws . . . those rusty remnants turning into artefacts on the sites of slave factories and fortresses. This iron and steel was the organised complement to the man-hunts in West Africa, the crux of the triangular trade. There was copper and brass too from Parys Mountain and the Mona mines in Anglesey that sheathed the slave ships and supplied them with plates and pots and drinking vessels. On the dig with Dad we held the core of this terrible history in our hands. It explained us. All mixed up and intertwined in connections that I never knew.

I look at those African objects today, the icons and the images, and ponder my relationship to them. I wonder about the spirits within. I wonder why Dad spoke about the eternal presence of the ancestors. I can't extricate myself from them and their magic. I'm not sure I can mark out the boundary between us.

ICON AND IMAGE

I've seen Africa
I've seen "it"
in the Africa shop on Liverpool dock.
The one next to the slave museum.
Three hundred years down the ancestral trail
I stand;

object and subject, it and other
me and mine
here to pick over something
in this shop, on Liverpool dock, this shrine
where the Fante, Ashantie and Ebo collide
with my twentieth-century mind.
Ritually silent, expression denied
in ebony figures the beings reside.
The historical signature, the coded motif.
Behind mask, masquerade
and mirrors of imagination
I stand
face to face with
Trinket or artefact? Icon? Image?
Me?
And mine
to capture and reinvent
with time.
I've seen Africa
I've seen "it"
in that shop on Liverpool dock.
There's one in Betws-y-Coed too.

That's my Africa. A whole mixed-up jumble of things. A body map. An ancient echo. A reminder of something that might have been. An explanation. One of my conversations with Wales. Just there and always there waiting for me to make sense of it all.

That's my Africa. The Africa in the mind of Wales.

GUYANA

I goin' away

Where is the land of mud? If the reader will kindly turn to the
map of South America, and look at the tract of land on the
northeast coast lying between the rivers Orinoco and Amazon,
his question will be answered. There he will find a stretch of
country called Guiana, British, Dutch and French Guianas side
by side. British Guiana is the country that is spoken of as the
'Land of Mud'. The part most thickly inhabited is nothing more
than a vast 'fluvio-marine-alluvium' as scholars call it — which
simply means mud from the rivers and the ocean, washed up by
the tides, and baked by the sun into a mighty bank, some two
hundred miles in length, from five to thirty-five miles in breadth,
and one hundred feet thick. On this mud bank live considerably
over a quarter of a million people of almost every nationality
under the sun. This strange country has the honour and distinc-
tion of being the oldest of our British Colonies; and the only little
bit of the British Empire in that vast and wonderful Continent
of South America; besides it is one of our earliest and most suc-
cessful mission fields.

(Rev. Alfred Hardy,
Life and Adventure in the Land of Mud, 1913.)

Going away. Going back. Return. Going home. Both sides of the same coin. The guy with the locks has woken up, stretched out his Africa and he answers me. "I'm going back in truth. Well, I ain't lived in the Caribbean since I was a kid but I've decided to go back," he says. "I'm going to try and make something of it in St Kitts. That's where I started out, you know? My name's Parry Sinclair by the way." He smiled and offered his hand. "They call me Paris. Paris, and it's just sort of stuck. I'm going to grow tomatoes. At least, that's the plan. You know all the tomatoes in St Kitts are imported? Yup. And cost a fortune too. Anyhow, I've been reading up a lot about hydroponics, growing tomatoes in water instead of in soil, you know? So I put me lickle bit of money into that. I had an accident at work, see, and damaged me back. Got some compensation so I thought I'd chance my luck and have a new start. I'm tired of Slough. I want me boy to have a better start than me."

"You haven't been back since you were a kid?" My tone gives away some misgivings about his plan.

"Oh I've been for a visit to check it out but I haven't lived there, no. Left when I was three. Me and me mum. She's dead now. I've got an uncle there though. I've sent over a lot of stuff by boat already and we're going to work the business up together."

"Were you a farmer in England?"

"Nah, not at all. Didn't even have a garden. Lived in a high rise. It's a new start I tell you. What about you, are you going back?"

"Sort of," I say, thinking about my first journey. Why do I always find this a difficult question?

"You know Jamaicans have a word for our kind, the returnees.

They call us Frosties," he laughs.

"Frosties?"

"Yep," he says, getting to his feet. "Frosties. Fancy a beer?"

"Why Frosties?" I call after him.

The *Windrush*, the *S.S. Empire*, *S.S. Trooper*, *Reina Del Pacifico*, *Marine Merlin*; ships full of pilgrims, pioneers and hope of a better life left the Caribbean and none more an icon than the *Windrush*. In our collective memory all the individual passages across the Atlantic become one great *Windrush* exodus; one composite moment of exile that defines our presence in Britain as if we all had someone on that particular boat. That's how Paris and I come together. When we look at that small clip of BBC footage of the *Windrush* arriving in Britain we are looking at our root generation and we're bound together with the shared history of that first-generation exile. In fact the movement was longer and slower and much more diverse than we have come to imagine both before and after those four hundred and ninety-two men and one woman descended from the *Windrush* onto Tilbury docks in the summer of 1948.

It's hard to imagine how amongst our generation we can encapsulate the collective experience. Paris and I are sitting here but we don't have a boat or any mass movement to reference us; there's no single port of exit or entry, no date or event that at once serves to bind our stories together. We are the dribs and drabs of the story with nothing so all embracing as the *Windrush* landmark. Perhaps it lies in these Piarco moments. Maybe Piarco Airport in Trinidad, the funnel in and out of the Caribbean, will be a marker on our map. I sit and wonder how many of these travelling souls recognise the import of the moments as they sip their beer and worry about the size of their hand luggage.

A newspaper clip from 23 June 1948 reads:

> *What were they thinking these 492 men from Jamaica and Trinidad, as the* Empire Windrush *slid upstream between the shores of Kent and Essex? Standing by the rail, high above the landing stage at Tilbury, one of them looked over the unlovely town to the grey-green fields beyond and said "If this is England I like it." It was curiously touching to walk along the landing stage in the grey light of early morning and see against the white walls of the ship row upon row of dark, pensive faces looking down upon England, most of them for the first time.*

"If this is England, I like it," he said. I didn't know Dad's boat story until recently. He sailed out of the Caribbean on the *Marine Merlin*, a ship carrying mainly German soldiers leaving a base in Argentina. He was the first person from his country to win a British Council scholarship to study in the motherland. Artists and writers from all over the Caribbean were sponsored in this way and together they formed a small but significant movement of their own quite different from the *Windrush* migrants. He had longed for this moving away like many others of his age. He wanted to break both physically and mentally from the small-town life of Georgetown. This was his claustrophobia to which there could be no return. I guess the home we return to is never the home we leave. The baggage we take back with us alters it forever.

Dad sailed on that same sea of hope and optimism that buoyed all those boats of exile. It was 1946 when his paintings were first noticed by a British Colonial Office official and he left his job as a clerk in the government offices opposite Booker McConnell for a round trip that would take twenty years. He was *goin' away*, shedding his small-boy world and his small-boy skin as he moved. And so he began a most natural exile to the motherland that others would follow. From their individual stories a pattern of shared experiences emerges; through their conversations, their writing, in letters and poems and in paintings so that generations later we could know them.

He didn't know that then, just as the likes of Paris and I can't imagine how we will come to be collectively anthologised. It was only when Dad was gathered up into the belly of the *Merlin* that he began to know himself as a *West Indian*. Later there would be more collective labels—*immigrants*, *coloured people*, *black people* and much later *ethnic minorities*. In some ways these labels themselves mark out epochs of the shared experience. Yet until that moment he had never met chaps from Trinidad, Antigua and all those small island places. It wasn't until that boat journey that my father had even heard a Bajan or a Jamaican speak. But in the thirty-three days on board, he shared their mood and their aspirations and their dreams of England in a kind of contagious hopefulness that hopped and danced about amongst the young travellers, infecting them and filling the ignorant spaces in their knowledge of England. "Sonny" was twenty-three when he first left Guyana; a smooth skin, low-cut hair, smart boy of twenty-three. The newspapers called him *Denis Williams, the painter*.

I never understood Dad as an exile. He didn't speak that way about his homeland. "We weren't looking back, we were looking forward," he told me. "We weren't rummaging in our histories, we were escaping them."

I touch down on the Georgetown of 1946, the Garden City, that he left behind. The Promenade Gardens where the militia band plays and the League of Coloured People hold their annual fairs. The Victorian Botanic Gardens where lily ponds conceal dozing manatees, oblivious to the children and their nannies who come to stroll at five o'clock—the time of the day when the white ibis return to litter the green and the parrots come home in pairs. A city of gardens. A city of tree-lined avenues and wide grassy verges shaded by a canopy of flower-bearing trees where the kiskadee sings. A city cooled by the gentle flowing water in the canals draining into the Demerara. A city of elegant white-painted wooden buildings with dusty red zinc roofs, a legacy of Dutch and British architecture. The Parliament building, constructed in 1832, the Tudor-style Law Courts guarded by a statue of Queen Victoria and St George's Cathedral, reputed to be the world's tallest wooden building, stand as testament to a long colonial history. On Main Street is the exclusive Park Hotel reserved only for the sahibs and, close by, the bustle of Booker McConnell's department store selling imported goods of all kinds—books from England, pictures of the Thames, dolls, chocolates, face powder, ice apples. In the early evening when the sea breeze picks up, families come out to promenade and play ball games on the sea wall. Every Saturday afternoon the militia band plays on the seafront bandstand. On Easter Mondays their tunes will be accompanied by the buzzing sound of a thousand kites dancing on the skyline between Kingston and the Conversation Tree.

It is that familiar world that would become fossilised through being turned over and over in talk and remembering. You hear about the "I goin' home" stories of these exiles when the "I" turns up to find Stabroek Market is half the size of that in his imaginings, or that Dr Gomes and Aunt Eloise have long since passed away. You hear the disappointment that the dollar is just not worth a dollar any more and you wonder how they can all have been so wonderfully fooled by their dreams and their imaginings. That's the thing about exiles. They tend to carry pockets full of still photographs but no moving pictures. Frozen crystallised memories.

My first encounter with this exiled class was at Rosemary's party in London. I was in my thirties by the time I came face to face with a whole seam of experience missing in my life. It was perhaps always assumed by others that it was there and somehow I had managed to let that assumption ride. Then, like all untruths, eventually you come to believe in them yourself. Yet the truth was, I was history-less, an unclaimed orphan of some "elsewhere" place of which I had no first-hand or even second-hand knowledge. I hadn't seen my father for over twenty years and I had no contact with his generation. I didn't know them. Dad had left in the middle of the Africa story and it just didn't occur to me that one arm of the great triangle remained to be drawn.

That was the beginning of the grief. Years had rolled by and there were other things to occupy me: university life, marriage, children and work and I had done all of this in a vast white wilderness. I knew a picture-book Caribbean but nothing of Guyana and perhaps in some respects, therefore, very little about my father. I could have turned to that first-generation literature. Writers like Wilson Harris, Jan Carew, Derek Walcott, Sam Selvon.

V. S. Naipaul had provided a rich account *but I wasn't looking*. I guess sometimes you just don't know what it is that you are missing.

Like the *Windrush* imagining, my movement away wasn't one event but more like a small slow trickle of events that I have now made into one. First there was a letter out of the blue from my father, then a gift from a friend—a book called *Life and Adventure in the Land of Mud*. And there was my husband Malcolm, all pushing me along to one outcome; a return or an exile, I am not sure what I should call it.

Dad's letter read:

> *Darling Cha Cha, I've recently done the very best painting of my whole career so far which (symbolically) I call El Dorado, a private symbol for the discovery of a new world, after a 16th Century legend of a fabulous city of gold in Guyana. Here is no city of gold, of course, but I do still think of our natural riches as many. The forest, the noble river Mazaruni which seems almost sacred, our passionate sunsets. Deep stuff here for writing and painting. You must come.*

Clare sent me the book with a note:

> *11th April 1984. Dear Charlotte,*
> *I finally remembered this book for you. I found it in a second hand shop. I hope you enjoy it. The author is so pompous in parts*

which gives you a good idea of his missionary background but he gives a beautiful picture of Guiana. He must have been there about a hundred years ago since it says he returned in 1893. Perhaps one day you will return? Clare x

Then Malcolm called me on the phone. He'd seen a job in Guyana advertised in the *Guardian*. "Shall I try for it? I think we should. Let's just pack up everything and go. The girls are getting big now and they'll be fine at school in Wales. C'mon, Charlie, let's give it a try . . . it'll be great. Two years at first and then who knows. You should see your dad's country."

Slowly it all fitted together and we were going. If the Möbius strip was taking me home, it was through a very curious route. Like Dad's encounter with Africa, which was so much more problematic as a black man, history seemed to be repeating itself. Now I was thrust officially into the role of British expatriate wife but going away to the country of my origins.

It was the practice of the Overseas Development Administration at that time to send all employees and their partners taking up an overseas posting for a week of orientation at Farnham Castle. A week of luxury amidst beautiful surroundings. I can't imagine this still happens; beside anything else I can't imagine the taxpayer footing the bill for it. We were part of a course entitled "Latin America, the Caribbean and the Pacific Islands". It was May, we were full of fun, and we talked only about the move, about giving up our jobs and about spending time with Denis.

Somehow the standard orientation package didn't quite fit the bill.

Everybody else at Farnham, both staff and participants, were very white and very English and I suddenly felt very black and very Welsh. Between three-course meals and bottles of wine we sat through lectures on travellers' health, lectures about getting on with the locals, about the flora and fauna and about managing money. A guy with a beard and sandals called Tony from Stafford University did the American occupation of the Caribbean. A woman called Hilary put us into a focus group and showed us a video called *Expatriate Wives* which seemed to be about nothing more than playing bridge and supporting your husband at social events. She told us to keep up to date with current affairs by listening to the World Service and she shared some recipes with us. There was a session on tropical attire and equipment. The list of what-to-takes and what-not-to-takes wasn't too dissimilar from a list I found in a book about travel to the Dark Continent written seventy years before, directing travellers to Walters and Co of Oxford. The 1918 list of essentials read:

2 Khaki drill tunics
Two pairs of Bedford cord breeches
Tropical weight dress coat
Blue flannel blazer
3 pairs of white flannel trousers
Jaeger cholera belt
2 pairs Fox's tropical puttees
2 pairs of mosquito boots
Pair of bush boots
folding green canvas chair with leg rests
2 sporting guns and all accessories

I only needed to make a few small additions—a pair of sandals like Tony's, a floppy green cotton hat like Tony's for wearing on open boats and a watch like Tony's that could tell the time in five countries at once.

We first met Rosemary at Farnham. She had been invited to participate because curiously the course organisers thought it might be useful for us to meet a "real Guyanese". We talked over dinner about the course and what we had learned. "This is sheer nonsense," she said finally. "You'll come and stay the weekend with me at my home in London. I'll tell you all you need to know about Guyana." And so it was that three weeks later I travelled down to London alone because Malcolm had already departed for Guyana.

Rosemary had planned a whole weekend of activities culminating in a party at her home on the Saturday night. As part of what she called my immersion, she had bought tickets for a Guyanese evening on the Friday night, held at a community centre somewhere across the other side of London. I suspected this would be as near to the real thing as I would get this side of the Atlantic. The institutional fluorescent strip lit up the brown-face smiles of the ladies dishing out the fried chicken and rice onto paper plates that folded under the weight and turned translucent grey with grease. The atmosphere in the place was almost spiritual like a Jehovah's Witness convention. The greeting and meeting was endless. The pieces of conversation rose into the air like bees, the buzz of voices connecting the congregation's histories into one living community.

I guessed the backbone of this event was church people, the kind of people who raised money to repair the Georgetown hospital or fund the Palms old people's home on Brickdam. These were the people at the other end of the barrel economy, the people who had responded in their own way to the shortages and hardships of the Burnham regime back home by sending barrels full of tinned food and cut-price clothes from the end of the season sales. All those Guyanese homes in Brixton and Hackney and Haringey with a barrel in the corner slowly being filled up for the passage home. A whole industry of support. *Windrush* people, ordinary working people, hard-working people preserving home and contributing to both sides of the Atlantic. These were the people whose mommy or Auntie Shirley *com tuh visit* had tried in return to carry bottles of rum and green mangoes and any small piece of home in the bottom of their Burnham bags. The same Auntie Shirley who stayed back to look after Alicia or Babs or Winston or Charles until we *can sen fuh dem*. I was learning about a missed inheritance.

Since I was a child I had not seen this number of black people together and all Guyanese by birth or ancestry. I had nothing with which to negotiate this event. I sat in an oasis of detachment, miserable and then happy by turns. Rosemary moved about the room and the bee trail hovered over her like she was an orchid. She called up characters and street names from twenty-five years before and they were met with a chorus of recognition. I watched her swell. I guessed that in these rejuvenating downtown excursions she reconfirmed her Guyanese-ness. She was alive in this passing and catching of comments. This Rosemary seemed vivid, rooted and whole. What must have been a huge class divide between her and the woman serving the chicken disappeared.

I took it all in. Every now and again some small thing, some small spark of recognition reached into my being and found home. The texture of a woman's hair as she leaned across me at the buffet table. I wanted to touch it in reassurance. The girl with the square shoulders held me for long moments and I studied the rounded protrusion of her bottom, her posture and her walk. She was a familiar stranger. Each fragment of shared origins and beginnings chipped away at me and carved pain and joy simultaneously. There were parts of my splintered self in this crowd. I ached for what I was missing and for what I had missed. This loss of contact had left a whole dimension of me dormant, undernourished and dying. I submerged my confused feelings. I think I denied them to myself.

On the Saturday afternoon before the party in Rosemary's house we went to Brixton market to buy in the foodstuffs and the flowers. Rosemary bought an Afro wig for fun. I was a first timer to this small West Indian outpost and I think it showed. I saw shops and stalls full of West Indian vegetables I couldn't recognise and a black guy was serving. I saw a counter stacked high with tins of ackee and bottles of hot pepper sauce and a jar full of mauby bark and a black man was serving. A black woman sold me cherries. I saw a drum seller, a cloth seller and a black woman making clothes with African cloth. I found a shop selling all kinds of hair preparations. As I entered, the man behind the counter asked me, "Natural or treated hair?" and I just stared at him. On display were hair preparations and accessories I had never seen and never even heard of: jerry curl, pressing oil, curl activator, relaxer, revitaliser, hair food, hair wax, pomade, Afro-wigs, extensions, nylon hair, plaits, wide toothed combs and hot combs.

The names of all the products made a poem in my head: *Black Beauty*, *Soft and Lovely*, *Hairlox*, *Black and White*. Stacked on the top shelves I could see black porno videos. I picked up some incense sticks called "Black Love" and wondered how black love might differ from white love. Where had I been?

In the adjoining hairdressing salon they were hot-combing a client's hair in full view of the window and dressing it into a style from a picture of a white girl! I was stunned by the way in which the emblems of such shame for me were being brandished with a certain nonchalance. I stood, staring in amazement until two black girls started talking about me. Rosemary and her cousin Rachel said I was acting like a *"neva see com fo' see"*.

Back at the house, Rosemary had prepared a trestle table of remembrance, at its centre a harvest of Caribbean fruits: pineapple, papaya, different types of bananas, mangoes, carambola—fruits I didn't recognise at that time, piled high into a mountain like Roraima. Yellow and orange lilies hovered close by like graceful birds. She had cooked up a feast of memories. Plantain chips like yellow roulette discs tinkling over the sides of perspex bowls, fried chicken, cook-up rice, pepperpot—food that provoked the yesterdays' talk, full of meanings and associations lost to me. Here was a small piece of Guyana chewed over in an elegant house on the Thames embankment. I had nothing to connect it with. But this was a sweet baptism.

Rosemary must have left the same British Guiana as Dad, perhaps some ten or so years later. One night she danced with a charming young British Army officer who had been posted to Georgetown and later married him. "A good marriage," her mommy had said. She told me this later as she was explaining a thing or two about Guyanese life. "Light skinned should only marry light skinned and white even better. That's how it was." Rosemary married very white. Her husband's credentials couldn't have been more authentic. I wanted to understand this marriage but the Major General withdrew to his quarters and the party weekend went on largely without him. I thought about a man raised in Evelyn Waugh's England. That same Evelyn Waugh who whilst a student at Oxford had drawn cartoons of his own chosen seven deadly sins which listed the fourth deadly sin as "the hideous habit of marrying Negroes". That same Evelyn Waugh who in the 1930s trekked ninety-two days across British Guiana, all khaki and colonial.[35]

Rosemary was hardly a Negro. She was vaguely brown with *good* hair and a good accent. "I'm ashamed to say now," she said, pulling off her Afro wig in the bedroom mirror and arranging her large soft breasts into the small space of her blue evening dress, "but we thought ourselves so much better than the black family who lived by us; they were a nigger-yard family living in the small wooden backhouse." A group of us were gathered in her bedroom as the crowds on the riverbank below dispersed from the afternoon boat race. Oxford had won. Alone and together the girls lapsed into Creolese. They were laughing and slapping their thighs at my ignorance of the culture.

"Yuh know how tuh wine?" Rosemary asked me. More laughing and testing me out. I had no idea what she meant.

I wondered how she managed such a schizophrenic existence.

[35] *Ninety-Two Days* by Evelyn Waugh (Penguin Travel Library, 1934).

Rosemary represented a particular tier of London Guyanese—those who like my father had come on scholarships and sponsorships of the British government, as writers and painters and lawyers, doctors and engineers. Amongst them were a host of sugar people—"Booker people" they called themselves. And people like Rosemary who had made "good" marriages. These people weren't boxers and sailors and entertainers thrown together in the hugger-mugger of London backstreets. They hadn't been London street sweepers or bus drivers or cleaners in an NHS hospital. They were something different.

As we sipped champagne on the roof garden under Heathrow airspace I think I espied for the first time black middle-class Britain wearing a gown sequinned with paradoxes. They wore a mantle of contradictions with their very British outlook, their privileged lifestyle and their forays into convenient bits of Caribbean-ness. They existed under a part of British airspace a million miles from the *Windrush* people. How had these people survived in the motherland? *Had* they survived it? Why had they put up with its ambivalence and hostility? Why had they invested so much of themselves in this country? Why hadn't they returned? When Denis and Katie Alice fled towards Africa these people had stayed and taken on the work of transforming Britain. And Britain had transformed them, for better or for worse.

Looking back, this Rosemary event was a kind of middle passage for me, like Dad on the *Marine Merlin* and Ma on the *Prome*. It was one of those transitional moments like the boarding of boats with some new and imposed collective status—slave, West Indian, migrant, émigré, evacuee, refugee, expatriate . . . Frostie.

Neva see com fo' see

ON THE TIMEHRI ROAD

I comin', I goin'
I comin' back, I goin' away
along the Timehri road
out and in,
pulsing through the small mouth airport
and the long thin choke road into Georgetown,
then out again.
Rasta boy gives me a stay-awhile smile
but I movin' to taxi man tales
movin' like the people trails shuffle the Timehri road,
on the left and on the right.
Movin' like the girl's arm flapping for transportation
Like the jhandi flags flutter in the hot air fan of the night
   breeze
movin' in and out of town village by village.
Coconut palm leaves drum out a rhythm on zinc rooftops.
Moments of yellow light hold my eye
along the black Timehri road

and the bottom house business goes on, snatches of life
revealed now between empty pine lady stalls
and hushed banana groves,
bar and rum shop jaws open loud to the Timehri road.
Then taxi man shouts "damn fool"
and his voice and horn carry on the wake
of the minibus race against time, in and out of town
and flows off across the Demerara waves running close by
Timehri road
to town or out,
so close; the smell of earth
and the taste of peaty bush and brown water hint at the vast
interior
teasing and calling me back,
the black water gliding by the Timehri road
in and out of town.
I comin', I goin'
to the whispers of the sugar cane fields
and the cloy of ferment rising at the edge of town sweet,
heady sugar rum Demerara
Intoxicating, Inebriating
Sucking you in and blowing you out gently, like breath,
I goin' away, I comin' back.

One heat-filled day climbs upon another. I thought I might
remember tropical heat but there is something different about
Guyana. It smells and it tastes different. If countries have smells
then Guyana smells like a great big greenhouse: peat, mud and

swamp all held in under a moody grey sky. The space really belongs to the hugeness of the rainforest in a way that makes people only incidental to it. You feel sort of pushed out to the sea fringes. But I like the way the heat sets the design of the day. People get up before the sun strengthens when it's easier to think and move around. It's not a siesta country and there are no collective afternoon dreams like the Africa days. Everything keeps turning, sometimes slowly, but like a heartbeat, never still.

Yet my father still slept in the afternoons. He seemed unable to give up the tropical habit. In the late fading light of afternoon I would find him on the veranda drinking tea sweetened with heavy Demerara sugar. He would always get out his best china that he had bought in Venezuela, adding a formality reminiscent of the afternoon tea ceremonies we had in Africa. We both thought so. Memory and reminiscing are the stuff of return. A smell, a vista, a voice, can all trigger distilled memories. And in time all the borrowed memories come up for inspection; the type of memory that you claim because you have heard someone else's account of it so many times—memories of holidays and events and rituals that you never really experienced. These trick memories are soon exposed but they too are part of the project of return.

I didn't have such a memory bank. I didn't know Guyana, I had only the potential of some imported memories from childhood days in Africa. I knew how a pineapple grew. I recognised the six o'clock flower. I'd tasted papaya. I would be able to recall small things like the ant trails and the cockroaches and the rains and the feeling of reprieve that went with the afternoon tea ceremony. Yet they nevertheless held the surprise of rediscovery. At the heart of it all there was Denis. I had assumed so much on the basis of so little. Our shared life amounted in reality to just months and yet the years that had passed were seamless. Had he ever left? He smelled the same after twenty years of separation and I reconnected with him in the same way as we had left off, father to child. Father to good child.

At first we would sit on his veranda lost in the past and complacent in our easy relationship. We kept it safe; like printed words in a book, we re-read the lines over and over again and agreed them. I told him about the family. He asked after Ma and each sister in turn. I guess we had implicitly agreed to keep all the sad stories buried and deeper still the complicated ones. I didn't want to confront him, there didn't seem to be any point. I was happy to be with him and it was easy because we kept things much as they had always been.

Now he had three families. A Guyanese wife and child replaced Toni and their five children like Toni had replaced Ma and the five of us. He spoke about us all in separate epochs. There was the Africa project and the discovery of himself with Ma. There was his post-independence return to his own land with Toni the English nurse and now there was a return to his true self, to his soil and to his ancestry with Jenny. He made it sound so tidy and logical. It wasn't an excuse or an explanation, it was a description. There wasn't a hint of regret or pain in his story. Life seemed strangely compartmentalised; was I a part of his past or a part of his present? I didn't know. The story was interesting but stripped of emotion for me.

It was his physical self that brought back the initial reconnection.

The fact that he was so intimately recognisable seemed oddly remarkable. Is this a fact of long estrangements? You need something to cling onto immediately and the visual aspects are the most accessible. I re-examined him minutely—the browns of his skin, its lights and shading, the set of his teeth, the small pulse at his temple and the perfect line of his lips. His every movement could be traced along a series of beautiful muscle lines. His gestures were always so graceful. I re-noted all his mannerisms, the way he crossed his legs high on his thigh, the way he pointed his finger as if he was giving a lecture, the pursing of his lips while he thought something over. He hadn't changed at all yet I didn't recognise anything of myself in him. I didn't feel that heavy emotional resonance with him as I did with Ma, just recognition and familiarity. A fossilised landscape.

My father lived on the outskirts of the city close to the National Theatre and the Botanic Gardens. There was a peaceful elegance about the area; large houses with spacious lush gardens clinging to a sense of a past Georgetown whilst everywhere about them was evidence of change. Denis clung meticulously to his rituals. Monday to Saturday he got up at four in the morning and wrote until seven, showered and put on a freshly ironed shirt that Gloria the housemaid hung up for him the previous evening. After breakfasting on a little toast and tea, he would reverse his twenty-year-old red Datsun out from under the house and drive to the Museum of Anthropology on Main Street where he worked. At one o'clock he would return home for lunch and a siesta. At four in the afternoon he would be on the veranda looking out over his shady garden. It was a quiet orderly life.

I never saw him go out of his garden on foot. Beyond his gate, across the plank bridge over the trench that surrounds his house there was another life to see. There is a small, corrugated zinc shop on the corner where the road meets Mandela Avenue. Occasionally, drained of energy by the heat, I might stop to buy a Coke or a Banks and a packet of biscuits before reaching his veranda; take a five sitting on the bottom shelf of the two-tier bench. Like any corner shop anywhere, there is a continuous trade in small items like soap, matches and kerosene. Young jobless boys might be hanging around there, maybe an old guy or two taking a beer, a child sent on an errand for his mommy. The minibus stops at this corner and spills out a handful of office workers, clean, smart young men and women, too proud to admit to their version of the poverty that blankets this society. I hung about the place taking in the life. Beyond the shop is Lodge, an estate of poor housing. Small, hot, concrete houses, ill-designed for the climate with windows that never close like empty eye sockets. Blindeye houses that see everything. There were many places like this around Georgetown. A life I could barely imagine and never know.

Dad was poor too in many respects. There wasn't much money around in the country and public servants had seen their incomes shrink with inflation to a level where it was almost impossible to survive without help from relatives outside. The Burnham era had left a deep scar on the country's economy—low wages, food shortages, and high crime. Occasionally Dad would give a lecture abroad or write an article for a journal which provided him with a small foreign currency income, just enough to sustain the new family. He neither had money nor did he covet any. His work shaped his life and sustenance and comfort were secondary. The house was crumbling around them. The rains came through the tin roof in a dozen or more places, collected in plastic ice cream containers and used as drinking water when the water in the pipe failed. In his bedroom, amongst an impressive collection of paintings by Aubrey Williams and Philip Moore, hung an original Turner landscape left over from colonial days. He seemed not to care that it might have been worth a fortune if it could be caught before the penetrating humidity lifted the paint off the canvas. There was a library of books that no robber bothered with. The books smelled mouldy and so did the clothes in the wardrobe. When the robbers did break in, which they did almost as often as the rain, they took his iron or his transistor radio, small things that he would have difficulty replacing.

Dad didn't socialise, not because of poverty but out of choice. Like Ma, he had no small talk. Nevertheless, one of a small court of Georgetown intellectuals might call on him in the late afternoon and they would be welcomed; Miss Dolphin, Frank and Billy Pilgrim, the Prime Minister, Mrs Burnham and on occasion Forbes Burnham himself would pass by when he was alive.

Georgetown is a small face-to-face society and these people represented a powerful if not particularly privileged black elite who kept a very tenuous grip on the country. They discussed the future of the country, its politics, the artists and the writers. They were a vestige of a British colonial past. A slowly withering elite, all with their very British education like Dad, struggling to define a sense of post-colonial Guyana. They seemed to me to represent a gentle meandering stream, flowing alongside rapids and currents on the streets, currents spurred by racial politics, poverty, crime and despair. I wondered when they had last walked out on the road. There was a deceptive tranquillity about my father's house but not much sign of Lobo.

Out on the road I felt the chaotic current running through the city. A lorry had spun off the road, spilled its contents and pulled down the power lines. Half the city would be without electricity for days. Sections of the bridge across the Demerara River had broken loose and floated away. A child knocked down in the street by a speeding minibus bled to death in front of a growing crowd of people helpless to change her fate because no ambulance came. I picked up an elderly woman lying on the pavement on Lamaha Street. Passers-by were stepping over her. She had waited all day at the public hospital to see a doctor but to no avail. She was too weak to walk home, she had given up. "All meh chil'ren outside," she said to me as I lifted her tiny body into the car. It is difficult to swim against this current once you get caught up in it. Its whirlpools are as strong as the mighty Essequibo River and no set of contingency plans can counter this torrent. Life runs along channels of uncertainty sometimes forming big gaping pools of unpredictability and calamity like the potholes in the road. I see it clearly now.

But I was lulled by the graceful façade of colonial buildings; the wooden palaces placed square onto tree-lined avenues and streets laid out house lot upon house lot in straight lines. This symmetrical grid is Georgetown's fragile order, the only obvious sign of the taming of the constant threat of the sea on one side, the naked bush and the vast rivers of the interior on the other and the steady process of decay within it. Any of these could swallow it whole at any time, or swallow me whole. I breathed in this precariousness unconsciously and clung on to the few certainties I carried with me, ignorantly confident in my sense of self.

Was this really the city of my father's childhood? A city I could only ever have visited in some shadowy glimpse of his reminiscences. His mother was a seamstress and as a child he would accompany her to the grand houses in Kingston on the far side of town, where she would measure up the expatriate white ladies for dresses. Wooden palaces with highly polished purpleheart floors, the functional beauty of Demerara shutters and the soft tints of coloured light painted by the stained glass of the front windows. Palaces where the lady in exile had surrounded herself with the emblems of home, the symbols of her culture—mahogany furniture, velvet-covered chaise longue, Victorian clock, jardinières, china tea-set, bone-handled cutlery, and the picture view of the Thames. The kind of small touches his mother imitated in her own home with imported reproductions bought in Stabroek Market. This was a Georgetown society overlaid with the inheritance of Victorian mores and values. I caught sight of this place in a photograph album at Auntie Eileen's. Photographs of young black men in 1930s suits and felt hats captured by the lens of a box camera on Stabroek Square. Girls with hairstyles and dresses that would not have been out of place on Llandudno promenade at the time. "It was so beautiful then," Auntie Eileen recalled. "We played gramophone records and went to dances and parties dressed in the latest fashions. When we couldn't get shoes we crocheted them and had the cobbler make the soles." They painted such a wonderfully romantic picture. It was the same still-life portrait the people at Rosemary's party conjured up. A memory of home that no one seemed willing to alter. Yet it was a colourless picture until I had seen it for myself. I was yet to discover the life of the place for myself. Everything awaited my discovery whilst I sat on the veranda with Dad.

I suppose I expected him to open the door to Guyana for me. I had assumed he would be my way into the place. On the veranda I was listening to the tone of his voice but not the words. I noticed he spoke with no real authority for me any more. That was gone. How could he after all this time? He could not significantly alter our circumstances. I admired his intelligence and the structure of his argument. His articulation was pure poetry. He could turn his mind to almost any subject. He had a way of musing on matters as if he was giving a lecture to a world audience. It allowed him to avoid the ordinary and the everyday. It allowed him to avoid the uncomfortable, the emotion, the mistakes and the regrets. He was unassailable, unchallengeable and dogmatic but extremely charming. I knew I loved him as I always had from somewhere very deep inside. I had to go back over and over to view him but I realise only now what we had lost.

"He's spent his life turning over old bones," Ma had said and I could still see the Dad of the African digs, excavating history, trying to make sense of himself. Perhaps that mental colonisation he pitched himself against goes just too deep. Perhaps the academic enterprise in which he was steeped was just too European. He had rejected the West but not the Western. He refused aid monies and research funding from the West. He refused Western publishers for his material. He refused to collaborate with Western academics. They called him arrogant; maybe because they didn't understand he was rebuffing Lionel in his search for Lobo. But I couldn't help thinking Lobo still eluded him or more to the point that he just couldn't see the Lobo that was all about us.

I would come back to his veranda time and time again until I began to find the experience somehow empty. There was a hole in my consciousness that these meetings didn't seem to fill. As the comfortable afternoons turned over on the veranda, I became restless. I found it hard to share my father's concerns. I was being held in the quiet retreat of his enclave. I searched his mind for a sense of Georgetown, of Guyana, yet what he offered didn't satisfy. I would present him with my outsider observations and musings for correction or amendment like lessons in reading the cultural scripts of Guyana. There were stories there, but not the story I wanted.

In weeks to come I would cut adrift from these conversations on his veranda. The cool afternoon tea meetings with an address on the culture and society of Guyana would be lost on me. His Guyana wasn't mine. He belonged to a fading elite whose concerns seemed quaintly out of tune with the harsh reality of life in Georgetown; the terrible poverty all around, the almost daily power outages, the lack of medical facilities, fuel shortages and battered infrastructure. His was a distant Georgetown, a beautiful place that sponsored him on a journey of exile.

Expat Life

My anxiety about the immigration desk at Timehri Airport always builds up as I walk across the tarmac from the plane and into the arrivals hall. I remember that first time. It was eleven o'clock at night local time and three in the morning according to my body clock. I'd been travelling for twenty-three hours with no sleep. Around two hundred of us waiting in one long, weary and sweaty line for our passports to be stamped. Finally my turn came and out of ignorance or just sheer tiredness, I didn't wait for the signal from the immigration officer to step over the red line to approach the desk. I laid my passport down in front of him. He looked the other way, swinging backwards on his high stool and talking quietly out of the corner of his mouth to a nearby colleague. Long minutes passed. "Why are you being so rude?" I asked. No answer and no attempt to pick my passport up from the desk. "Officer, I've a good mind to report you to your superior. What's your name?" "Mr Johnson, ma'am," he replied politely without looking at me, before getting up and walking away. The long line of passengers behind me sucked teeth and cussed me up. I felt suitably humbled by the time he returned some fifteen minutes later. I couldn't get used to the idea that the customer is not king and the process of giving service to someone else must not even vaguely appear like serving. All of that is just too colonial.

The last thing a fish notices is the water in which it swims. I hadn't given much thought to the water in which I swam until I was out of it. Like a fish out of water, even the tiniest of cultural norms became magnified now that I was the outsider.

I wanted to send a telemessage to Ma. I had assumed, not unreasonably I thought at the time, that there would be a pen available in the post office. But there wasn't so I crossed Main Street to Guyana Stores. It took me twenty minutes to buy one. The shelves throughout the store were sparsely stocked. In the stationery department I found the haphazard collection of items sobering. Three copies of *What's Cooking in Guyana* and a single copy of *Lesbianism Made Simple* occupied a whole shelf in the books and magazine section. There was a selection of tired-looking imported Christmas cards bearing the words "Felix Navidad" curling at the edges, envelopes whose sticky wouldn't stick any more, boxes and boxes of pencils from China. The assistant glanced across at me with her don't-bother-me eyes and continued her chat with her colleagues; engrossed in her own concerns, indifferent to the idea of customers. Just as I was about to give up she nodded her head and raised her eyebrows upward. I took this as the signal and pointed to the pens. The biros, all identical, were stored under glass; all thirty or so of them laid out in neat rows. "Which yuh wan?" she asked without looking at it or me, moving slowly towards the counter, still faced toward her friends. The apparent indifference coupled with a directness of speech was difficult to get used to. "Any one please," I said, trying to engage her with deference, struggling with her lack of eye contact. "Two or one?" she asked with an exasperated sigh. I felt castigated for my indecisiveness. The pen was passed to a second assistant who very slowly placed it in a bag and sealed it with sellotape. "How much is it please?" I asked, the same deferential tone in my voice. Without speaking or looking at me, she gestured with a nod of her head to a third sales assistant standing behind a till.

I guessed it wasn't rudeness but I couldn't make sense of it for some time. I suppose a lot of eye contact is quite unnecessary. After all why not preserve it for those closest to you? I've heard it said that this custom has its origins in slavery, in the need to avert the eyes from the colonial master but I don't care for that explanation. Sustained eye contact is something quite Western I believe. In Europe, eye contact is a way of assessing another, of judging or determining mastery. I remember Dad saying African art doesn't have all that stare-at-you portraiture like in Europe. I suspect the gaze in Guyana is reserved for some much more intimate expression. In Guyana Stores the transaction is neither reliant on smiling or on eye contact. It's not unfriendly; they just don't really look at you eye to eye. I never quite got used to it.

Back in the post office a small crowd was gathered to make overseas phone calls and send telegrams. They wisely seemed to have set aside half a day or so. The crowd had formed three lines; one led to a desk where customers picked up telegram forms, a second to a desk where the forms would be processed, and a third queue had formed to use the phones. I took my place in line one. However, some criteria other than "next in line" were operating, orchestrated by a very slow-moving black girl behind the desk who had not said more than two or three words and didn't look up. For example, persons would occasionally walk in off the street, go to the front of the queue and be served immediately. And she seemed to be sending people to the back of the queue indiscriminately, rejecting forms for some small detail or other or just totally ignoring them. I was so hot and exasperated by the time I eventually got to the counter I stupidly asked her if she made it her business to be unhelpful. "And why did you send that old woman to the back of the queue?" I added. "She's been waiting over an hour already!" She said nothing. She just got up, picked up her handbag and went off for a very long toilet break. When she returned she announced that the desk was closed for lunch. I asked if I might see her supervisor and she passed me a form to fill out. I'll never learn.

We lived in a cream and red house on Delhi Street. We moved there from a traditional wooden house on Lamaha Street because of the security problem. The Lamaha house had wooden jalousies and a long deck-style veranda that skirted the whole house and proved very handy for the burglars. In the Georgetown style both houses were built on stilts, a constant reminder of the potential of the sea to reclaim the borrowed coast. There was a happy community around the house. Rati cooked and cleaned, Fred the guard slept under the house when the sun got hot and an older East Indian man called Gardener sometimes did the garden. A friendly black boy called Winston, who worked for a Portuguese gold miner next door, became accustomed to doing some fetching and carrying chores for us and to *liming* away an afternoon here and there with Fred, on the rare occasions he was awake. Winston dreamed of owning a gold dredge and Rati dreamed of buying a small place of her own one day so that she could bring her two boys down from Essequibo. Fred dreamed of Rati but she would have none of it. The door to her little pink and red palace in the bottom house was firmly locked.

I'm not comfortable with servants. That's easy to say but there must be a certain ambivalence between black woman as mistress and black woman as servant. I felt it even if Rati didn't. I'm sure I would have felt it even more if Rati had been black and not Indian. History was just too close. More by accident than design on our part, the people who worked in our house were all of East Indian descent. My father was rather dismissive of this "Indian set-up" as he called it, and rarely paid us a visit. He thought we ought to have black people working in the house just like he thought we should only shop or do business with black people. The divide between Indo and Afro-Guyanese seemed to go deep. All along the East Coast you could pass through segregated Indian and black villages. The parallel communities mingled but in so many ways didn't mix. Even though I had no direct experience of either racial group in Britain, it seemed to me at an intellectual level at least that Black Britain meant all of us who weren't white and that this term alone somehow united us. But the racial politics of Guyana were very different.

Our first maid, Doreen, was a black woman. I learned a lot from Doreen's silence about mistress and maid, about mulatto and black woman. We had inherited Doreen along with the Lamaha house from a black family who had migrated to Canada. When we moved to Delhi Street we took Doreen with us. She understood Malcolm; their respective roles were clearly defined—white man, black maid is an old formula—and I guess also she understood me more than I did her for a good long while. Doreen would make potatoes and peas and rice and meat for lunch and English custard for afters. Then another day she might make plantain and potatoes and steamed bora and fried chicken and rice. She cooked like there was an army of people to feed in the house. I had to tell her to stop, "before we explode like the black pods on the frangipani tree". She didn't laugh. She just put a cut-eye look on me and was as silent as ever. "Back home we just eat a bit of bread and cheese at lunchtime, Doreen," I told her as she was walking out of the room, taking her time, hearing but not listening. How could I know that my change of menu was to deprive her of her only meal of the day—Fred and Gardener too, and heavens knows who else back at Doreen's home in Lodge? In a city where thousands only have a drink of brown tea at midday I should have been more tuned in. Doreen caught the minibus before seven each morning. She *took a drop* to the corner of Duncan Street and walked a dusty flip-flop walk along Sheriff Street and into Prashad Nagar. She was a large, heavy woman, with a rolling, slow and deliberate walk, and by the time she reached our corner she was wearing a tiara of milky sweaty beads and a matching diamanté necklace. Doreen was a *big woman*, meaning she was older and mature. Doreen was a black woman and she didn't take orders from any half-Negro. "Mm mm, mistress, not dis African," she muttered under her breath one day when I confronted her about the map of Guyana she had created by pouring neat bleach onto Mal's blue work trousers. She left and so we came to have Rati, aka Shanti.

In Africa we'd always had men servants. Joseph had been both our servant and our nanny. It was an easy relationship because we were children and Joseph was not in our command. He fed us, bathed us, played and told us stories. He was a black man, an ordinary man in the way Dad never was. Dad was too self-important to be ordinary. Looking back I realise Joseph's ordinary black self was a threat to my father, to who and what he had become: a black British colonial in another British colony. So the relationship between them was always tense and sparky. My discomfort with Rati was not of the same order. Rather the opposite, because as much as Rati distanced herself from me respectfully, I tried to find every kind of social leveller I could to minimise the mistress/servant divide. After all she was a woman, a mother and importantly an Indian in a country where Indians and blacks have a troubled history. But my efforts were to no avail. Maybe I just didn't understand the rules. Rati saw her service as a pleasure and a gift and my reluctance to accept it only wounded her. Gradually I learned to manage my respective place but intermittently I would lapse. I would loiter about in her spaces probing her in my search for Guyana, demanding that she interpret this world for me. She did her best but she was, after all, a country girl. Things could get very mixed up.

"Are you coming with me to market today, Rati?"

"Is okay, Mistress."

"Is it alright to wear shorts to go to market, Rati?" I ask, having put on my shorts.

"Is what yuh does like, Mistress . . . yuh can wear sharts."

"Are you wearing shorts too, Rati?"

"Nah, Mistress, meh neva wear sharts to market. Meh put on meh nice dress."

Guyana. Where shorts are *sharts* and shirts are *shorts*. I learned a lot from Rati.

Expatriate life is both something new to Georgetown and yet something very old. Guyana has known hundreds of years of the white explorer, white missionaries, white planters, white administrators. However, the Burnham years following independence in 1966 had all but closed the door to the West and a white face became a relatively scarce thing. But after 1986 with a change of political leadership and a kind of perestroika in the new politics, aid workers, consultants and technical advisors were flooding back in. We were part of a new expatriate class. We were still, nevertheless, a conspicuous and somewhat marginal minority and the attitude towards British intervention was very much changed. Anti-colonialism hung in the air and inevitably the new relationships were built with the echo of the past.

Mal and I fell in with other expatriate workers, British, Canadians, Americans, Dutch and whoever else appeared in the expat bubble. It was the most natural thing to do in some ways. It wasn't easy to find Guyanese people of my age with whom I had a lot in common. The massive migration of people of my age group from Guyana during the 1960s and 70s had left a whole tier of the society missing. The thirty- and forty-somethings, the educated and the skilled, seemed to have left for Canada and the United States, leaving behind a society of very young people and very old people. I like to think of that as the reason, but I suppose the truth is that I felt more and more British every day; whatever that was. I didn't know how to be anything else. I clearly wasn't one of the locals and if identity is a collective experience then the only available identity was British. For a while it was a charmed if not particularly comfortable life of cocktail parties, bridge circles and weekends in the bush in a convoy of Land Rovers with the likes of Tony from Stafford. It wasn't difficult to idle away days and weeks. People came in and out and joined and rejoined the exclusive club—the English and Australian cricket teams, British and European dignitaries whom we would never rub shoulders with back home. We mingled like we were all from the same background. We were frequent guests at High Commission functions and state events. At a luncheon, the British High Commissioner asked, "Are you glad to be back, Charlotte?"

"Well I'm happy to be here but I've never been to Guyana before," I replied.

"Oh I do beg your pardon. I thought you were from here?"

"I am—well, I like to think I am," I said and walked off as confused as he was.

But it was the *Hash* that gave the first real hint of the discomfort of this odd status. The Hash is a peculiarly British expatriate activity that occurs in countries all over the world. The story goes that some British army officers in Malaya first started it after the second world war and it spread. It's a weekly fun run of four or five miles following a paper trail set by the Hares that ends with the runners gathering for a meal and some drinks. Ostensibly it is quite a harmless way of taking some exercise and meeting people, and Mal and I made it a part of our weekly calendar of social events. For a small fee to cover the cost of drinks, as many as fifty expats would turn up and join in the revelry. I soon got over the embarrassment of running with a white-legged, red-faced crowd through the streets of Georgetown or through the country villages to the sound of the bugle call and the rituals and ceremonial songs that went with the after-run drinking.

We are the hares, we are true blue
We are piss pots through and through
We are piss pots so they say
And we'll never get to heaven in a long long day!
Get it down down down down . . .

Gradually a few young Guyanese women locals joined the Hash too. They spent their time vying for the attention of the single white guys. I didn't blame them. Life in Georgetown was tough and the expats brought with them access to some luxury and the dream of getting out. But I came to resent with a passion the men who dated them. I found it ugly, as ugly as the guys themselves. But more than that, it was an affront. It wounded me in a way I couldn't articulate and it disturbed my ease with Malcolm. We were taking a drink after one of the runs when a couple of guys joined us. They were consultants out on a short-term contract. They directed their conversation to Mal, male to male, white person to white person, sharing their experiences of local culture, places to go and things to do. I wasn't really paying too much attention to the exchange until one of them glanced at me and asked Mal, "Wife or girlfriend?" I got up and walked off with my cheeks burning with embarrassment. Mal's gentle correction reached my ears but the damage was done. We both knew too well the assumption beneath the question; I was Malcolm's very own little piece of the colony, his local arrangement or at best the product of one of his previous overseas adventures. They didn't need to address us as a couple because to them we weren't a couple, more like a man and his property. It was nothing to these guys; most had a wife back at home and a little piece of ass half their age hanging onto them for dear life in every port of call. It was everything to me. It was like I had a part in this story that I must accept. I wanted to feel anger. I wanted a furrow in my brow like Dennis the Menace but I could only feel shame and embarrassment and then the hurt that came with the recognition of my defenceless-ness; that same shame that I had always felt back home when the contract of politeness was breached by a racist comment. A shame based on some misguided sense of responsibility that I can only describe as the inconvenience of my difference. It was as if all would have been okay or everything would have been nice and not spoiled at all if only I wasn't black. That's what racism had done to me. It had silenced something in me. It had made me compliant and accepting in the way that any vic-tim becomes compliant. It had made me responsible for my difference.

The life began to feel more and more like ill-fitting shoes until it gave me blisters. At the Queen's birthday party celebration a group of seven Peat Marwick management consultants engaged to work on Mal's project turned out identically dressed in blue blazers and stone-coloured flannels like they'd taken advice straight out of Walton and Co. Tropical Outfitters. Mal picked a row with them over something and nothing and called them a "bunch of bloody English twats" and then refused to sing the British national anthem. It was getting a little out of hand. He was struggling too. His Welshness was showing in a way I hadn't noticed before.

There was a life on the streets and I skirted the edge of it, watching and observing it, but not being any part of what was going on. Delhi Street was a retreat but I was bored, plain bored. Bored with the small chat, the backbiting, the pretence and the emptiness of the whole expat existence. It was as if I had been taking part in some grand British parade, marching along slightly out of step so the rest of the world seemed cranky. I remember getting home from the post office. Fred was having his customary closed-eye afternoon. I reckon he could say, "Nah Mistress, meh nah sleep," without waking up. We might have been robbed blind and Fred would be none the wiser. I walked past him unobserved, grateful for the peace of the house. I had written a poem on the telegram that I sent to Ma while I was waiting for the clerk at the post office to end her protest. I knew Ma would understand.

EXPAT LIFE

Expat Life
is crap for a wife
A wistful partnership built on strife
like chaining yourself to a dream

Tagging along
in an empty space
where there is no place
for a mind
that would rather stay behind
and think
not drink
on miles and miles of terrazzo tiles
in a cocktail dress from the Sixties
Filling time with good deeds
reluctantly received
by bemused faces
who amicably watch the appendaged soul
with little control of her mind
Not their kind
an outsider
So what?
There's hashing
and dashing
to coffee and gin
in an empty circle of
tapestry ladies with macramé faces
A caucus of hands that play bridge
and have places to "do"
not see and live!
Smoking and drinking and thinking
Who are you? And who are you?
And what does your husband do

when he's not by the pool with you?
And the parties for smarties
when you attach your soul
to his arm and smile
No harm in doing your bit
for a grand or two
The clatter of chatter
mesmerising you
Someone else's wife? Oh dear
You too?
It's a ticket to oblivion
Your identity displaced
For life in a waiting room
you don't even need a face.

Parallel Lives

It was about a year before I realised that the main characters in my dreams had changed colour from white to black. I awoke from a kind of sweaty half-sleep, dreaming about our home back in Wales. I'd seen a woman coming down the stairs. I couldn't see who she was—that didn't matter—but I could see that she was black. It was the simple juxtaposition of the ordinariness of home with the normality of her blackness that took me aback. To see the two together was not ordinary for me and yet by a trick of my brain I saw in one moment that black life was very ordinary and not as extraordinary as it had been patterned deep in my consciousness. It's the same sensation people struggle with when they hear an Asian man speaking with a heavy Scottish accent, or see a guy with dreadlocks riding with the hunt or a black ballerina in a tutu. Lying dormant in my unconscious were two unhappy realities: that I saw black life as something other than ordinary and that I had little ability to imagine it. I would be reading a book, any book, and interpret all the characters as white. The words *man*, *woman*, *crowd*, *handsome*, *pretty* had come to mean white. Even words like *ordinary*, *normal* and *everyday* meant white life. I couldn't conjure up anything else without effort.

When Dad first came to Britain he was shocked to see white people doing menial jobs, sweeping the roads or cleaning toilets, when in the colonies they were always in the top jobs. When I went to see the bank manager in Georgetown she was black, the librarian, the minister, the lawyer and the hockey team, they were all black. I had been so accustomed to people in professional positions being white that it was initially difficult to adjust my thinking. I had to stop seeing it all as different. I had to stop staring. My observation was obsessive and thorough, and through this observation I discovered aspects of myself that I had never before recognised, having always been the only black face. I learned that my thinking about black people was distorted and corrupt, that deference to white people's whiteness lurked in me like a cancer, and that second-class citizenship was my inheritance in a way that these people just didn't accept. Their post-colonial temperament reminded me of my mother.

Around that time I began working for an aid agency on Carmichael Street, turning aid money into small-scale welfare projects. There was a project for feeding street children, school meals for the children in a primary school in Mahaica, money for the Red Thread women's co-operative, a healthcare clinic in Region One to equip and so on. The work suited me. I wanted to be part of putting back into Guyana what colonialism had taken out and, as a newly reclaimed Guyanese national, I thought I was well placed. I shared an office with a girl called Olive and an English volunteer called Mrs Shackleton who, with her husband, was planning to drive from Guyana to New York in a 1962 Vauxhall at the end of their two-year stint. Well into their sixties, the couple had retired after a long expatriate career and become VSOs. He was a hydraulics engineer, I recall, working on the sea defences, and she was a professional do-gooder and a character. I liked her and I loved every moment of Olive.

Olive was shiny black and skinny with legs like pencils that had no definition for calves or thighs. Her overlarge glasses gave her a gawky look like Popeye's girlfriend, her namesake. She was a clean-living, slow-moving, slow-working Guyanese in the style of so many public servants. The agency was entirely staffed by these slow-fingered beauties, with their ritualised bureaucratic behaviour and their quaint Shakespearean English. Miss Vigilance, Miss Benfield, Miss David, and Miss Cadwalader, Miss Gwen Llewelyn. Where did these Welsh names come from? And there was the new girl Alicia, sassy and not quite of the same mould, who slapped her thighs and threw back her head when she laughed; very often at me and my ignorance. They made an art of doing nothing and it was beautiful to watch. Sometimes the beauties were sick and didn't come to work, sometimes they had difficulty with transportation but most days they came to work for a rest. There were male colleagues too, chaps who spoke in the same old English and used words like "behove" and "tarry" and phrases like "Whilst on my sojourns on the west coast . . ." I loved to listen to them. When they weren't in meetings or speaking to me, they spoke Creolese which by and large meant I didn't understand them.

Olive and I became friends but only in the way that white people can with black people. We couldn't go for lunch or out anywhere because I had money and she didn't. I would be too anxious to offer to pay and she would be too proud to accept. Our inequalities were too many and too obvious. I took her back home to Delhi Street once for curry and roti and she told me that her entire house where she lived with her mother and two brothers, was the size of our kitchen. She had nobody *outside*. No barrels came to Olive's house. I knew she had days when she drank only tea. Many public servants were as hungry as the street kids only they couldn't show it. "*Yuh can't look de bah if yuh is de bah,*" she told me. I carried a lot of white guilt around in my head and it got in the way. But Olive did invite me to her church and arrived early to collect me one Sunday morning.

Olive was a member of the Assemblies of God Church. She told me she didn't dance because dancing in Guyana was too "*disgostin*" and that church people didn't do that. I guessed Alicia did dance. Olive's Sunday best outfit was gorgeous. White gloves, white shoes and a full-skirted floral dress with a wide white belt and just-for-today white translucent stockings. I felt dowdy by the side of her. She glowed amongst her church friends. It was an important day for her bringing an outsider as guest to church. Nobody stared but everyone saw. Ladies in straw Sunday hats and floral dresses, thin little girls in white and yellow and pink nylon party dresses like puffball fairies, with short white socks and patent shoes and their hair immaculately divided and decorated with multicoloured bobbles and ribbons. And the young men in sharp suits and Omo-white shirts escorting in the old timers. These were black people looking and feeling good despite everything. Despite the water shortages, the blackouts and the lack of food; despite the expense and the difficulty of getting transportation, they were out in force.

The importance of these congregations was not lost on me. It was Olive who had shown me one of the oldest black people's churches in Guyana in the region known as Berbice. The colony of Berbice was an area of some of the earliest and most bloody slave uprisings in Guyana. In 1762, plantation after plantation had fallen into the hands of rebellious slaves who pillaged and burned their masters' houses, set sugar and rum stores on fire and killed so many whites that the survivors were forced to flee in boats. The slaves held the colony for almost a year. But the plantations were eventually reclaimed and the subsequent repression of the rebels was merciless. The beatings, the killings and the withdrawal of any privileges meant that any further rebellion would always be a risky business. So other strategies were deployed, like acts of defiance and sabotage, practising the strange rituals of *obeah* and running away. The dense forest areas nearby and the network of rivers made an ideal setting for runaways, and Amerindians with their superior knowledge of the forest had to be employed to seek them out. Some runaway slaves managed to establish more or less permanent communities and set up their own churches. I didn't know that much about slave life. I had spent sombre moments in the slave museum on Liverpool dock immersed in the disgraceful story of the mass movement of Africans. I knew about the centuries of injustice that flowed from the human trade, I knew the Wilberforce story but little about the everyday experiences of slavery, about their own record of that history and about their resistance or about their link with the missionaries. But in Berbice, on soil where this had been played out, I experienced an entry into the memory.

Olive and I had been on a field trip to New Amsterdam and after the work was complete she took me to see the slave church. It was a plain structure, built by slaves for slaves, and had been in constant use throughout its two-hundred-year history. It was churches like this that became so central to the abolition of slavery, and paradoxically it was missionaries who were the linchpin to the freedom of slaves. Olive was telling about the marvel of Christianity and how it brought education to the slaves and a reprieve from the arduous work on the sugar plantations. She explained how Sunday was the only day of the week they had the right not to work and the right to go to church. The Sunday concession was the first battle the missionaries won over the plantocracy and a crucial one in an ironic confrontation that would eventually work for the freedom of the slaves.

I stood in the old church and thought about the slave memory with its own web of rituals and traditions and religions that had been plundered and brought together under this one roof. I thought about their *jumbi* and *obeah* that had travelled with them from their tribal villages. The slaves weren't Africans at all except in the eyes of the missionaries and the planters and the Europeans who were fast inventing Africa. They had come from many different places and many different tribes and spoke several different languages when they found themselves lumped together as African slaves learning scripture and hymns and mission stories in churches like these. I thought about what the church came to mean to the slaves, how they made it their own and what it provided for them. It was one of the few ways in which they could hold on to themselves as human beings. The church provided the hope of equality and freedom for them, but more to the point, it provided the only legitimate place they could assemble. The church was a meeting place where their solidarity grew and rumours and news travelled from one plantation to another, making them one class, one force and of one mind: to overthrow the planter. It is a paradox that the church pew was both the seat of colonisation of the slave mind and the seat of revolution. The very act of bringing the slaves together for worship gave them opportunity to resist the plantocracy.

The alliance between missionary and slave was always going to be full of contradictions. The aspirations of Christianity could never sit comfortably with the facts of slavery. In the chapels and meeting halls in Wales abolitionist pamphlets and lectures gave account of the horrific trade and pleaded with the sensibilities of the congregation to lobby for change. I thought about Wales, "the Land of Bibles", and the missionaries and their intimate connection with the colonial enterprise on the mission fields. It's true to say the Bible and the colonial mission went hand in hand, until inevitably the alliance became untenable.

There is a famous missionary story from the British colony of Demerara—now part of Georgetown—about the start of a rebellion that goes down in history as one of the most significant. Twelve thousand slaves took up arms against their masters. One missionary, the Reverend John Smith, was to pay a heavy price for his assumed role in sparking the event. John Smith had arrived in Guyana in 1817 and, like all missionaries, attempted to manage the fine line between gaining the trust of the slaves and appearing not to co-operate with the slave masters and their concerns. In fact the planters were distrustful of the missionaries and there was always to be a tension between them. The missionaries gave the slaves a sense of themselves as human beings whilst the planters treated them as less than human. John Smith was known to be controversial in his style. He encouraged slaves to congregate by arranging extra Bible meetings for them. He encouraged them to be ministers and teachers themselves and he encouraged them to establish a black church of their own. In small but significant ways Smith took up the mantle of the slaves against their masters and his humane treatment of them brought him into continual conflict with the slave masters.

The crisis arose in 1823 in the year of the formation of the Anti-Slavery Society. A resolution was presented to the House of Commons in Britain by Sir T. Fowell Buxton which read: "The state of slavery is repugnant to the principles of the British Constitution and the Christian Religion, and that it ought to be abolished gradually throughout the British colonies, with as much expedition as may be found consistent with the due regard to the well being of all the parties concerned." Following this, measures of reform were proposed to the colonial authorities. In Berbice the proposals were publicly read and explained within the slave communities and the reception was by and large peaceful. However the slave owners in the Demerara were outraged and unwisely tried to conceal the proposals from the slaves. But the slaves heard rumours that they were to be released and the false news moved from whispers to statements of fact and travelled along the East Coast like wildfire. The slaves were convinced that it had been decreed that they be freed and that this was being

Sugar and Slate

withheld from them. They refused to work and were punished. An official notice was issued that they were not allowed to attend any place of worship without permission of their masters. As the anger grew, slave leaders across the plantations planned a dreadful and bloody uprising. The story goes that the Reverend was accused of purposely misinforming the slaves to stir up a rebellion; that it was he who leaked the information and encouraged their protest. He was tried and sentenced to death by hanging. There is no doubt that his sentence would have been carried out had he not died in custody of illness caused by the poor conditions in the Georgetown gaol. His name goes down in history as the Demerara martyr.

The strength of this missionary connection with slavery was always bound to bring Wales into view for me. There is something about standing on these sites of struggle that locates you in a huge historical picture. I stood in the slave church as a confused descendant of two intertwined histories. I tried to disassociate myself from the white history to survive the moments but I felt the misery of it all, a recognition of an uncomfortable past. Why do we go back to these places? Is it to retrieve this pain? It wasn't simply a recollection; I wasn't just thinking about the slaves and their predicament. I was somehow re-enacting the history and locating myself in it. It's a particular type of remembering; an all-consuming experience that comes in the moment of retracing the steps of our forefathers. It is as if you enter the coded stereotype of the memory, the imprint of it on the physical site, and replay the past as part of the present. As you stand in the sacred spaces the past is recreated, ritualised, made real and enduring.

All of the meanings and traditions, the stories and the symbols are inherited in those moments. Perhaps that's what Dad meant when he spoke about the "eternal presence of the ancestors".

Much as I hoped for that now familiar spiritual awakening it wasn't honestly mine—not immediately at any rate. I was full of reverence for the place but the spontaneous emotion I felt didn't spring from echoes of that awful past. I was living and breathing in something else. I hoped for the stereotype but it evaded me. Another memory was all about me, a memory of unresolved conflict. It came as a loud thunderous and most dreadful argument, a row full of ambivalence, a row full of love and hate, a row filled with fear and yet with the knowledge of peace, a row that recognised belonging and rejection, possession and dispossession, that twisted and turned like a tornado sweeping across the fragile wooden structure of the church and shaking it on its foundations. A huge momentous Katie Alice-Denis row with screaming and bellowing and I stood powerless, a miserable child unable to affect or change the reality.

Perhaps those African Americans feel free enough to go to the slave forts in Ghana and retrace the steps of their forefathers but it only filled me with discomfort. My connection with the slaves was so disturbed, so corrupted, so uncomfortable, I felt a fraud to it. I yearned for the purity of Olive's connection to the past. I held her hand hoping to acquire what I had lost and I wept.

I was lost again in my own thoughts of that day when Olive's minister started up the song accompanied by a drummer and a couple of amateur guitarists. Both they and the minister's voice were so powerfully amplified that I imagined the whole community of Kitty would be part of the Sunday service. "Brudders an sistuhs" the minister bellowed out between the lines of the song. "How great thou art, how great thou art."

Whatever back kitchen you were cooking in, or bottom house business you had to do today, it had better stop. Even the dogs scavenging in the trench would prick up their ears to this song. The congregational voice was high pitched and halting, a slow, pained, collective voice roamed the words. I swallowed hard. What a privilege to be deep in the bosom of this black people congregation and feel part of them. I melted into the oneness of it.

Ever heard the way black people sing the word "Jesus"? The word rang out with such love and such rhythm. There was ecstasy in the expression of every syllable. "Jeeeess-us". I was away, mesmerised. Heaven could not be better. Then the minister's voice rose over us in a trembling pitch, sometimes whole—"Brudders an sistuhs"; sometimes broken up, "Bru-dders an sis-tuhs", "Brudders an sistuhs". Brudders and sistuhs sat down in their seats and I was with them. I would have done anything they did at that moment. Someone called out "Hallelujah" and the minister answered with his staccato voice.

"Hallelujah brudders an sistuhs. Jesus, Ah say Je-ee-sus, AH SAY JEEEE-SUS loves you." There was no height or depth his voice couldn't find that morning. There was no one's soul that would be left without examination. We would be left in no doubt as to what a sinner was, what it was to betray another. We would be left in no doubt that if we wanted salvation we must "Follow de Laard, follow de Laard, Ah say what?" "Follow de Laard.

Hallelujah. Ay-men" the congregation replied as one; arms waving, heads shaking, eyes rolling, straw hats wobbling.

Then the minister suddenly called out. "New brudders an sistuhs wid us today . . . you new brudders an sistuhs, please stand op. Stand right op, don' be shy." With the rather too enthusiastic assistance of Olive, I stood up, alone under the gaze of five hundred pairs of eyes.

"What yuh name is, ssssist-uh?"

"Charlotte."

"Carla? *Carla?*"

"No, Charlotte."

"Sharla? *Sharla?*"

Please God make me invisible. "No, CHARLOTTE. You know, like Charlotte Street in Lacytown."

The whole congregation relayed my name to him and he replied gratefully, "Oh oh oh . . . Chaaar-lat like deh Chaaar-lat Street. Deh Laard has blessed yuh tuh-day, ssssis-tuh," the microphone turned up so high that he had begun to sound quite drunk.

"An where yuh's from, Sharla?"

"Wales," I shouted back, cheeks burning with embarrassment.

"Oh oh oh, dat's Wales in England, rite?" the congregation relaying his words to me even though they were still on full amplification.

"No," I replied, "Wales in the UK."

"Oh oh oh, Wales in duh Yookay. Mmmm. Yoooo-kay. Mmmm. Dat's in England, rite?"

"Yes, UK in England," I said with the sermon about betrayal fresh in my mind.

193

But we were all happy with that and I was blessed and warmly welcomed. "De Laard Jeeesus welcomes our sistuh from Wales in London," the minister hummed. When I answered the question "How yuh likes Guyana?" the whole congregation roared with laughter, there was literal rolling in the aisles at I don't know what until finally I was allowed to sit down in my own piece of heaven and die.

Olive seemed happy with my performance. She talked about it for days at work whenever she thought I was out of hearing. Was it something I said? Why was Alicia laughing so much?

I tried hard to befriend Olive. She was ever polite and always friendly but ultimately regarded me with the cautious mistrust that existed between Negro woman and "coloured", between insider and outsider. We were different although I didn't want us to be. I knew that my great-great-grandmother had the experience of slavery like hers, and I thought of the generations of Negro women who were my ancestry. Somewhere we were joined at the root.

As the days in the office rolled on, I learned quickly about how to work in the face-to-face culture of Georgetown. If you wanted something done there was no point waiting, no point phoning, no point writing a letter or a memo that could lie on someone's desk for months; you just had to do it yourself or go directly to the person who could. "*Aks*" as they said, *aks* firmly and directly, with not a hint of the please and thank-yous and *still* nothing might get done. Then try again and again. Nothing works first time, not in Guyana. It seemed you could get anything or nothing depending on whom you knew. It didn't bother me. I liked the way things came about, sort of unplanned. I fell in with the routine of the working day; getting about like everyone else and finding myself in places I would not normally have had access to. All of this prompted new dreams and my new consciousness. I felt I was getting in, getting somewhere, getting on instead of just standing in a waiting room—getting real, getting black. I soon sussed the beggars outside Guyana Stores were richer than the public servants and when they called out to me for a *"lil' help mistress"* I rationalised that I didn't have to respond any more. When I went to buy provisions, the women in the market called me "darling". I was getting used to the etiquette of buying and selling, to the street language and kidding myself that I might just be breaking through.

A team of American consultants came to work in the agency. I was consumed with anger as these white interlopers with their "development" language picked over our work like overseers and dated the girls from the office. There were more and more of them appearing in the country every day as overseas aid continued to pour in. The New Colonials came in their four-by-four Toyota trucks brandishing all the symbols of their forefathers' exploitations now reinvented in their Coca-Cola mentality, their designer "jungle-explorer" garb and their voyeuristic fascination with the natives and their culture. Armed with Camel cigarettes, their talk of "outside" and their hard currency, they took their pick of Georgetown's young women. They incensed me with their insensitivity and their patronage. I took to distancing myself from anything white; from anything that reminded me of the place of my kind in this country's slave history, from the skin privilege and the colour hierarchies that so clearly marked out this country. I expressed it in my contempt for these New Colonials.

But there were frequent reminders that I was so intimately and inextricably wedded to them and that history had placed me in an ambivalent position.

"Hey sistuh, wha' yuh do wid Bab'lon?" a Rasta man asked of me as I strolled arm in arm with Mal along the sea wall one evening. "Why yuh's slavin' on dis white mudderskunt?" This incidental but charged confrontation struck home. "Married . . . to he?" an immigration officer at Timehri Airport had exclaimed. "Yuh don' know dat's all jus' colonial rubbish?" What Mal and I had taken for granted was now so publicly called in to question. I began to doubt all that had been so secure. I wondered if our love could escape the nonsense of race despite our protestations.

My distancing from "white" ways of being took on urgency but there was nowhere to go with the feelings. Even Betty Shackleton's volunteerism began to grate on me. I was confused. Aid, help, exploitation, colonialism all melded into one and I had no idea whose side I was on. Both my public and my private lives had gone topsy-turvy. The streams of life that rarely mingled just intermittently touched at the edges uncomfortably. I loved what I saw. It fascinated me. I watched and I listened moving between the parallel worlds. But my worlds were getting scrambled.

I had been in Kitty police station for two hours when the sergeant came to take my statement, and two hours before that standing on the road waiting for the constable to mark out the scene of the accident. But then, so had all the people on the minibus that had ploughed into the offside of the Land Rover I was driving to work. Nothing moves fast in Guyana. It was three o'clock hot hot and I struggled to keep my thoughts straight. So what was I doing driving a Union Jack stamped British High Commission Land Rover through Kitty? Who was I anyway? Not a diplomat?

"Then who are you and where do you come from?" The desk sergeant was asking the questions but the eyes of the minibus occupants seated expectantly off-stage silently made the demand. I had immediately offered to pay for the damage but that was too simple. Maybe I should have realised that I first needed to be called publicly to account. I was the only one who could not mentally conjure up the road markings and signs long faded or broken since colonial days. My plea of "How was I expected to know it wasn't my right of way?" was met with a hum of disbelief from the crowd because EVERYBODY knows you must give way at the end of David Street, unless of course, they are from "outside".

"So yuh's a mix, rite?" This official term to describe my origins was already being written onto the report form. There may be all kinds of "mix" in Guyana—"dougla" or "boffiano"[36] or any other variation but clearly in this oldest of old pigmentocracies, this mix denoted the "superior" union of black with white. This status meant most definitely that I would offer paternalistically to pay for all damage, that the minibus driver would concede, but that the black sergeant would find as many ways as he could to

---

[36] "Dougla" is Indian/African mixed and "boffiano" or its correct form "boviander" is a mix of Amerindian and African.

remind me that this was now a black people's country and I shouldn't dare assume any of those colonial privileges.

The Kitty incident badly dented my identity and added to a growing number of bruises that damaged my still fragile sense of self. Like any true mulatto I was straddling parallel lives. One of Malcolm X's *house niggers* caught up in scrupulously imitating the master's ways; over-identified, assimilated, content to access white privilege yet trying to live myself black. There were the New Colonials unashamedly brandishing their difference and there was the local, and I was negotiating my access to both. I was caught in the schizophrenia of wining and dining in the master's house when it suited me whilst milling around on the edges watching something I saw as black life. It was as if I was hanging onto Lionel for dear life because he was all I knew, but flirting with someone called Lobo.

Tekkin' a walk

Both *The Stabroek* and *The Chronicle* were carrying advertisements for "summer clothes" and talk on the road implied that there was a thing called "summer" when really it was the beginning of the dry season. "Place hat baad, man . . ." had replaced "Morning, morning" as the standard greeting. My older sister Evelyn came to stay. We met her at Timehri Airport and as she came through the barriers, she still had that tied-back hair, thick-stockinged, flat-shoed look about her like she'd stepped straight onto the plane from teaching Four B. A lifetime of teaching in a large Scottish comprehensive showed on her face. But there was more as well. I could tell she was troubled.

Malcolm had invited three or four of his expat friends to the dinner party we had to welcome her the next night. A Dutch engineer with yellowing crossed-over front teeth casually remarked over his fifth Banks that he was seeing a girl less than half his age. Evelyn opened up on him immediately. "Seems to me any sad old white fart can come out here and pick up someone's daughter just out of school." The uncomfortable silence and averting of eyes downwards hinted that he wasn't the only sad old white fart at the dinner table to have a *sweet ting on deh side*. Mal tried in vain to change the subject but Evelyn was on a roll, mocking him with questions that mercilessly exposed his stupidity. "She's nineteen huh? And you're what? Fifty-seven? Is it your good looks that attract her do you think? Has she seen you with all your clothes off?" She was funnier than I had known her for some time and clearly looking for trouble like the day she caught shit-man in her gaze. I didn't know her marriage was cracking up. I didn't know mine was. These things can just creep up on you.

We decided to take a trip out of town. I had learned from a friend that the very next day a couple of supply trucks were heading out to a foreign-owned gold-mining camp on the Essequibo. A quick phone call to the company's office in town secured us a ride in and a bed at the camp for as long as we wanted to stay. And so we set off, following first the highway to Linden and from there, the burned earth trail that runs through the bush and across wide empty savannah all the way to Lethem on the Brazilian border. Evelyn and I sat in one corner of the canvas-backed Bedford truck with six or seven black men; young, strong-looking fellows dressed in raggy-assed shorts and little else. They were sprawled out across sacks of rice, sugar and spare parts, desperate to snatch a few more hours of sleep despite the occasional bone-jarring pothole that put blue bruises on my backside for days after. No one spoke or appeared to pay any attention to us, but the occasional half-open-eye glance that did pass our way hovered between mild curiosity and complete indifference. We were moving miles from anything called home, physically and spiritually, and as we did so Evelyn and I drew closer together. Eventually she began to open up. Her story was confusing. She had a good husband, lovely girls, a comfortable life in Scotland, but she didn't want any of it any more. "How can anyone be married to the same guy for twenty years?" she asked. "Why not?" I replied, automatically defending my own position. "But why . . . ?" she pressed me. I left her question hanging. Something wasn't right but she couldn't quite put her finger on it. Her story unsettled me. After our family broke up she had become obsessive about order in her life and now she seemed to be so disordered. Like the Jimi Hendrix summer, life seemed to be somehow careering out of control.

At five o'clock in the morning the Linden highway was empty but for mud-covered bush trucks coming out from the interior and the occasional minibus plying the Linden to Georgetown route. Occasional clearings appeared at the side of the road. At weekends these made stopping-off places for picnickers and bathers escaping the heat of the city. But the creeks were fast drying out and the pools had shrunk to half their size. A piece of red cloth tied to a bamboo stick—barely visible unless you know it's there—is all that marks the narrow trail which leads to the Amerindian village of St Cuthbert's; a trail now well used by a steady flow of watchers and seekers, eager to find a little piece of the "real" Guyana. I'd been there myself with a group of High Commission staff for a game of cricket. I fielded for the British and was secretly delighted when we were soundly beaten.

Linden is a dusty town. And bloody hot. That's all you can say. A bloody hot inland town coated with a grey film of bauxite and thirty thousand or so people unwittingly breathing it in. That is, everyone except the expat managers who live at the top of the hill while the dust settles at the bottom. This now ailing industry used to ship bauxite to the world: to West Africa, maybe even to the aluminium factory in Dolgarrog where Uncle Walter worked, his voice hoarse from too much pipe tobacco and swapping stories of last night's boozy leg-over above the constant drone of machinery. Dolgarrog is a one-horse town built around aluminium and Linden has that same feel. On the outskirts of town we stopped at a roadside shop that sold liquor, ground provisions and a few groceries. It was about seven-thirty in the morning and the men ordered Banks beer. I asked the sleepy-eyed Negro boy behind the counter if he could make a cup of tea. "Coffee-tea? cocoa-tea? bush-tea? tea-tea? milk-tea? Wha' yuh wan, Auntie?" I settled for tea-tea because it sounded less complicated. It was strong and bitter and my stomach burned with acid. Our fellow travellers talked in an indiscernible hum between themselves over a second beer as if we weren't there while we stood at the shop entrance stretching the stiffness out from our joints. Twenty minutes later it was time to leave; the men taking turns to piss up against the side of the truck in full view of Evelyn and me before climbing back in to resume their sleeping positions. Leaving Linden we crossed the bridge over the Demerara and picked up the trail that links Guyana to northern Brazil. Only passable in the dry season, the trail is fast becoming an important trade route—some say a drug route—between the Brazilian state of Roraima and the north-east coast of South America. Our journey was taking us along just forty miles of it, cutting off down a small track to the staging near Rockstone and the small company boat which would take us and the cargo up the Essequibo to the camp.

The supplies were loaded into an open fifteen-foot wooden

boat with a little gap left for us up front between the boxes and sacks. The captain and his mate sat either side of the engine and a young, fine-boned Amerindian man called Curtis joined Evelyn and me in our little space for two. He had travelled almost unnoticed with us from Georgetown where he had been hospitalised for malaria. He sat beside us in our confined space, self-contained and peaceful. He didn't acknowledge us with any words but he had a nice smile and soft, gentle eyes that constantly scanned the riverbanks. The captain, Jinxy, a flamboyant red-skinned character, sensing a captive and slightly intimidated audience, humoured us with plenty of *gaff*. "Under deh water is Masakuruman, deh river spirit," he ventured. "He like a big big snake, duh biggest Comoudi[37] yuh eva see—like a giant, he waiting fo' yuh. Any time Masakuruman can com tek yuh. Yuh neva know when." Jinxy rocked the boat as if Masakuruman was bumping his head underneath it and the Amerindian smiled knowingly to himself.

Story upon story followed. About tragedies on the water, each one more harrowing than the last. Like the annual boat race at Bartica when every year "deh water tek someone". He spoke about grown men being pulled down to their death by silent currents, about fish—pirai—that could pick a man's bones clean in minutes. He tried us out with one about a man who had fallen overboard just a few days before. "Man na drown, engine mash up he arm bad bad maan, he lose out so much of he blood he jus fall down and die in deh boat fo' him can save. Deh whole boat

[37] Anaconda.

red man, meh tell yuh . . . red!" The blood story sank into the water as legend with lots of others. "Do you ever wear life jack-ets?" I asked hopefully. The captain and his mate laughed simultaneously. The mate pointed to a torn and stained orange-coloured heap below his seat. Nobody bothered to reach for one.

The Essequibo River is massive and fast flowing. I've heard it said that there are islands in its mouth the size of Barbados. It cuts through the jungle like the M6 through Birmingham and Jinxy steered and manoeuvred like he knew every inch of it; every turn in the narrow deep channel, every rocky outcrop, every fallen tree floating downstream. He twisted and turned the high prow effortlessly. Doubtless he could have done this at night with just the light of the moon and probably often did. Our boat skimmed and bounced across the brown water, hugging the mangrove bank until we eventually took a turning into a slower-moving creek. Jinxy's stories ceased and the engine lowered its voice. The forest closed above our heads and the big country sucked us in. The coffee-tea water of the Essequibo turned to wine, the rich bur-gundy of the creek. New sounds: the urgent high-pitched screech of macaw and parrot and the unmistakable "cling clang, cling clang" of the bell bird contrasting with the constant cicada click. Occasional flashes of colour through the dappled half light of the forest: the neon blue of a large butterfly, bright purple epiphytes nestling high in the fork of a tree branch, orange-coloured fruit of the bulletwood tree. Where the sun was able to force a way through the canopy, the glassy water mirrored the forest bank leaf for leaf. Several times we passed Amerindian families in canoes making their way on the silent water from one village to the next and we waved enthusiastically to be greeted in return by equally friendly waves and wide grins. Humbled in the mighty cathedral of forest I felt gradually and inevitably severed from the web of little threads that bound me to my familiar. I let them sever willingly. One by one they trailed off into the water. Down on the river bed somewhere beyond the eddies and swirls, Masakuruman stirred.

It was still early when we arrived at the camp. We were helped ashore by the camp medic who introduced himself to us as Stanton. He led the way to our quarters pointing out various landmarks as we walked. The camp stood in a large clearing in the forest, the creek forming one boundary. Nearest to the landing were the mess hall and kitchen. Under a lean-to roof of corrugated zinc sheet, large aluminium pots bubbled away on open fires. We walked along the path past a suite of portable offices of the type seen on construction sites all over the world. The workers' sleeping quarters stood at the back of the clearing against the wall of forest, and at the most elevated point in the clearing, slightly off to the left side, stood the guest house where we would sleep. It was a simple structure; just a raised wooden platform about thirty feet by thirty feet with a zinc sheet roof and mosquito-meshed sides. It was the only totally see-through building on the site. Inside were four mosquito tunnel bunks and three or four single beds with nets hoisted above. We were to share the accommodation with Stanton and some Canadian surveyors who were out working in the forest. Someone had attempted to give us some privacy by slinging a line between the beds with a pegged sheet acting as a curtain. There was a fridge full of drinks, a table and some chairs that suggested a hint of luxury in what was obviously a very harsh environment. Mining operations in the interior, like logging camps, run a hard regime. Long, dangerous working days that start at dawn and finish when the last light fades from the sky. And wet. Inside the forest it's always wet. Dad told me the forest is black and he wasn't wrong. That green you see from the sky is deceptive. That green is sunny side up. The picture-book images of rainforest with its lush greens and filtered light are about as distant from the reality as Mowgli himself. Inside, the rainforest is black black dark, dense and wet. Malaria is endemic and inevitable and diarrhoea rife. Normally a six- or eight-week working stretch is followed by four or five days out in Georgetown, for those who choose to take them. Four or five days spent completely blitzed in Demico House before being poured back on the truck pissed and broke; explosive compensation to make up for the brutality of bush life.

Stanton took us on the back of a four-wheel bush buggy to view the operation. We followed the trail that led off past the sleeping quarters into the bush until we found the men working at the front line, clearing the virgin forest. It looked like a mock-up model you might see on a table in the corner of the geography class with various stages of the process separately labelled—"slashing and burning the primary forest", "lumber-jacks at work", "a skidder", "a bulldozer" and so on. The men and the equipment looked dwarfed alongside the trees; some of them, like the purpleheart, hundreds of years old, their stems straight as arrows reaching up to the canopy ninety feet above. A man picking a splinter out of his finger stood alongside a felled tree that I swear must have been seven feet across its fluted base. The noise of chainsaws and heavy equipment was deafening, the ground a constant tremble from falling trees. The smell of woodsmoke overlaying the familiar earthy smell of vegetation. Some way further we came to the white cyanide lake essential to gold extraction. Stanton talked about a phase three of the operation— the regeneration of the forest that the Canadians had promised, when the cyanide lakes would be decommissioned and the forest replanted. He seemed to believe it. Maybe it would happen but it was hard to imagine how. I mean, just how do you dispose of millions of gallons of cyanide? How do you replace indigenous tree species that take hundreds of years to reach maturity? He argued us out of our protests. "Companies like this bring jobs and wealth for the country," he said. "Guyana is rich in minerals but we can't afford to access them without outside help. Plus, this government does nothing for the Amerindians. At least now they have a chance to improve their lifestyle," he claimed. He smiled as he talked in a way that suggested he'd met the environmentalist lobby before. I liked his smile.

Stanton was a well-spoken guy of about my own age, with a smile that caught me off my guard. He was reserved yet friendly, like the perfect host. Despite the muddy, wet, dirty surroundings, he looked immaculate. Nothing dries in the rainforest, the occasional sunny spells never quite get the dampness out of your clothes until everything is tainted with a dank, musty smell, even your skin. I can smell that sweet, sickly fermenting odour now— it's a smell that you wash away and then rub back into your skin with your towel. But Stanton's khakis looked like they had just been starched and ironed. His hair was cut on his head, he was clean-shaven and there wasn't a bead of sweat on him. Mr Kool. I was dripping sweat from head to foot. My cotton shirt was sticking to my back and I felt the strength sapping out of me. I wondered how anyone could do a day's work in these temperatures. Stanton on the other hand had an air of complete control over the environment. It wasn't dominating him in the way it dominated me. His confidence showed in his relaxed posture and his calm. He didn't need to say too much. He was a natural guide, a bridge to the magnificence of the place. I silently studied the back of his neck as we drove back to camp. He fascinated me.

There is no evening in Guyana. The sun drops out of the sky at speed and night falls like a blanket at six o'clock. Then the mosquitoes come out fighting. We knew we had to be washed, creamed up with repellent and covered up by then if we wanted to survive the insect onslaught. The canvas bush shower and pit latrine were at the edge of the clearing, fifty yards or so from the guest house. After dark it would be unwise to use these facilities; only the main areas of the camp and the path that connected them were lit for a few hours by generator. Evelyn and I took turns to shower, screened from the camp but naked to the open eyes of the forest. Refreshed, I stood for a moment, arms and legs akimbo, enjoying the sensuality of wearing nothing but my boots to protect my feet from jiggers; inviting the invisible forest watchers to check to see if I was clean. If that's the meaning of close to nature, it felt wonderful. There is a twisted logic in the pleasure of small deprivations. Being pushed back into the simplicities of hardship and survival has a sweet resonance with so much we have lost.

The two Canadian surveyors with whom we were sharing the guest house weren't Canadian at all; they were Quebecois. Every day they walked with a small team of men into the forest, leaving at dawn and returning at sundown. They had been doing this solidly for four months when we arrived at the camp. They had no radio, no television, no newspapers. No news whatsoever of the outside world, save that brought in by word of mouth. A calendar hung from a nail hammered into the side of the locker that separated their bunks, days passed crossed out in heavy red felt tip pen. One was a red-haired, red-faced guy in his fifties and the other much younger, pale like he'd been kept in a dark room for years. The older guy had clearly lost the plot altogether. He was edgy and irritable with us from the word go and in no small measure seemed quite paranoid. Perhaps there is a name for this syndrome—bush fever or something. He reckoned someone made holes in his mosquito tunnel every day while he was out. He reckoned the *Chinee-man* cook was hocching in his food. He insisted it was Tuesday when it definitely wasn't. He thought the work gang was the stupidest bunch of idiots that could ever have been brought together and had obviously been recruited directly from the lunatic asylum in New Amsterdam. And judging from his reaction to us, he clearly didn't like women. His younger colleague on the other hand was more humorous and seemed to welcome our company.

That first night we talked about snake bite for a while. Stanton showed us some of the antivenin in the fridge, though it sounded next to useless in most cases. The thing about antivenin is that you have to have seen the snake—better still got a piece of it—if the medic is to know which one to use. Also, the camp was just too far away from back-up medical care so treatment probably only prolonged what might otherwise be a quick and efficient death. Stanton told us that in his experience most people die of shock before they make it back to camp let alone to hospital in Georgetown.

The Quebecois didn't ask for news from the outside world. They had nothing to relate it to. And they didn't want to talk about home. If they had families, they were very far away. They didn't want to talk about films or books so we asked about the forest and life on the camp and the red-haired guy had plenty of opportunity to air his discontent. "Ferking 'ard and dangereuse," he said. "Ot, muddy, yoo-mid as ferk and nothing to do but eat, sleep and work. Ah 'ave eatern every cheekern part zere is to eat. Cheekern for breakfast, lunch and dinner. When ze supplies arrive, first we 'ave ze cheekern baked, and slowly we work our way through all ze rest—cheekern neck soup, cheekern liver soup, cheekern every-ferking-thing soup. Ah 'ate cheekern."

I don't know if it was the arrogance of the older man that provoked Evelyn or whether she was looking for some fun. Maybe she was cross with them for their invasion of the forest or maybe we had all had too much D'Aguiar's vodka by the time she asked, "Why Quebec? What's all the fuss about Quebec anyway—you all speak English there, don't you, so why do you want to be separate from Canada? I can't see why if you want to be French you just don't go and live in France."

"And do you want to go back and live in Afrique?" Red Hair fired back.

"Don't be so stupid, that's not the same thing; we're not African, we're . . . well anyway, language and skin colour aren't the same thing at all, we can't change our skin but you can change your language."

"And we are not French, we are Quebecois! We 'ave a rat to speak our own language, not ze language of North America, and we 'ave ze rat to speak it on our own terry-tory."

"Don't you start on about fucking territory when you've just walked in from burning that forest. Anyway it's more than that," Evelyn rolled on, "It's about privilege and power and keeping people out of your special little kingdom."

The mixture of alcohol and politics was explosive. The language war was something too close to home for me to just pass off. I could feel the anger welling. "What about Wales, where I live?" I threw in. "You can't be Welsh unless you can speak the bloody language. It's ridiculous. At one time in history a whole generation were robbed of the language. At another, a whole generation of us were discouraged from using it. When we were growing up, speaking Welsh wasn't the way to get on—a good English accent and a good English education was. And now we're seen as outsiders in our own country because we can't speak Welsh." I was angry with the politics of Wales. It felt like a double whammy—damned if you do and damned if you don't. There seemed to be no way to be Welsh unless it was apologising for not speaking Welsh, one of those Not-identities again. There was infighting and squabbling over who was Welsh and who wasn't and it seemed fewer and fewer people could make the claim. Despite Ma, despite everything, I realised I didn't feel in any way claimed by Wales. The threads that linked me were fast being severed. I was angry with the Quebecois for the luxury of their position. I envied them.

"You don't 'ave to learn French to live in Quebec but you won't get very far if you don't and zat is rat. We don't want to be dominated by North American culture," the quieter one said. We knew he was right but by now the appeal of the banter had overtaken us all. We had not exchanged any niceties. We knew nothing about them and they knew nothing about us and we were engaged in a frenzied row in which Red Hair stood up and banged his fist on the table. Stanton, who was silent in all this, jumped to his feet to protect us. Things had gone far enough. Evelyn grabbed some bottled water from the fridge and we walked out into the black to clean our teeth, find a place to pee and let the guys cool off. Stanton went off to do a check of the site.

The guest cabin was a box of misty light as the Quebecois crawled into their mosquito-free coffins. They were only speaking French by now. It was a strangely clear night as the rainy season reluctantly gave way. A big moon rolled across the sky above the purple-black line of the forest roof. In Guyanese folklore all manner of spirits dwell amongst the forest fauna and haunt the night forest. There are nights when you can see Ning Ning, a sparkling vision of lights, flashing fountains of scintillating shapeless patterns across your eyes, like seeing stars from a blow to the head. And there is Old Higue who travels like a ball of fire across the night sky seeking out children to suck their blood and leave them ailing. For her nocturnal devilry Old Higue may change her skin many times, transforming herself like a shapeshifter into an animal, a bird, a tree. And then there is Moongazer, that figure of destiny, as in African mythology. A shadowy, luminous chalk-white figure you meet specifically at crossroads.

Feeling vulnerable, I lowered my bare bum for a pee, thinking about snake bites and wondering if it was still practice to suck the poison from the wound and if so, who would I ask to do it, when suddenly Evelyn screamed—a great, loud, choking scream. I jumped up mid-wee, convinced she must have been bitten by a startled bushmaster snake. "It's vodka!" she screeched. "Fucking vodka!" The shock of ice-cold vodka mixed with frothy tooth-paste hitting the back of her throat had sent her into an involuntary paroxysm. Do people in Guyana use water bottles for vodka or vodka bottles for water? Same difference, she'd been caught out fair and square. I washed the wee off my legs with the remains of the vodka. Our laughter echoed across the compound. I reckon the Quebecois thought we were laughing at them.

Back inside the lit cabin we assumed ourselves to be unob-served as we climbed into our beds, although someone knew when to switch off the generator. When we awoke in the morning Stanton had silently been and gone. But I had seen him. I watched him for long moments by the light of the moon.

I don't know how long I had been in my bed. I was hot and drenched with sweat, listening to the occasional zing of a mos-quito passing by my ear. I looked out through the mesh to the forest. It was like a living, breathing wall, exhaling a soft, melodious chorus of night beetles and frogs. The feel of the forest makes up for its harshness. The sense of its sheer scale, its power and magnificence against my diminutive self was overwhelming. I felt a deep symmetry with its colours and its contours. Masakuruman swallowed me into the depths of the brown rivers; the living, breathing wall leaned closer. He touched a sense in me that had never before been touched.

I watched Stanton undress and sit in his shorts on the side of his bed. His shoulders were strong and broad, the colour of bloodwood. I was taken back to those moments watching Dad lying on his bed through the louvres all that time ago—the forbidden viewing. I had been looking at Ma, thinking about only her at the time. She and I were one. She was my focus that day and only inadvertently had I taken Dad into the scene. I had hardly dared look at him but his nakedness was stored in the corner of my mind. Now I recalled the scene and all its anxiety, guilt and excitement. I called up the tension of the moment. Those same feelings gripped me. In my whole life I had never had access to a black man as a sexual being. I had never viewed a black man as an object of desire in this way. I had no experience of such intimacy and those quiet moments became an intimacy. Ignorance and stereotype tainted any image I had previously conjured up about the black man and now here was Stanton representing something so close and very natural like the forest. I led him into my imagination.

Nothing of Stanton blocked the sensations of the forest. The sounds resonated through me. I saw Stanton as the way in, an experience I was craving, the only way to feel the place fully, the only true way to be part of it. I wanted to feel that closeness to Guyana. I wanted to be filled with the sensations of it. Stanton was the bridge into the forest, but it was a bridge I couldn't cross.

I felt released but not free. Masakuruman might be severing the ties but his work was not complete. I was twenty years in a strong and loving relationship with Mal. Twenty years in a happy relationship, the very core of which was now being questioned. That's the thing about interracial marriages. I think they have a fundamental asymmetry, a political asymmetry more than anything. They are subject to the vagaries of the political context in a way other marriages are not. Things in the wider environment reverberate through them. Ma and Dad lying on the bed—two continents back to back—a domestic scene where elements of colonialism, exploitation, conflict and trust were continually called up for inspection. "You know I love him," I had said to Evelyn earlier, "but when you get down to the heart of the black thing I wonder if he will ever, ever really understand it all, ever really know what it's like, ever really see that it's not just the him and the me in it all. Is the difference just too deep?"

These feelings and thoughts flashed through me, not in disparate sequences but as one inexplicable feeling. If I had been able to speak about it I could not have conveyed the intensity of that moment. If I had dreamed it—dreamed about the touch of his skin, his shape fitting mine in a wild and careless moment—it would only have taken away from what I experienced, from the absolute unadulterated passion of the moment. Nothing of that scene was consummated. Nothing reciprocated. Stanton moved in his own world, oblivious to the encounter. It was something and nothing, yet I sensed a deep fissure opening up in my relationship with Mal with no ordinary reasons to explain it. I hadn't fallen out of love with Mal. In those few moments I saw it all but I couldn't

verbalise what I had seen. I don't even think it was a fully con-
scious thought. It was a feeling not a thought. A passing shudder
resonating across every muscle in my body. But it left a crack. My
breath rose and fell with the pulse of the forest. I felt its depth and
its density. I felt devoured by it, overpowered, then it was gone.

That night, miles and miles from anywhere, we slept side by
side with some very angry Quebecois. That night I thought one
of them might just strangle us in our sleep. That night after the
tinny reggae music from the mess hall gave way to the sounds of
the insects I saw the lights of the little boats bringing women
noiselessly into the camp from across the river. That night Evelyn
knew she would leave her husband. That night I knew I had met
Moongazer.

Sometime the next day I met up with Curtis, the young skinny-
framed Amerindian who had travelled up with us. He was on light
duties until his health was fully restored. We sat on the mess-hall
step overlooking the creek. I think he mistook my hangover for
sadness and decided I was in need of some cerebral therapy. As
we sat, he wrote out a poem. I don't know if it was his own work
or something he had memorised from somewhere, but this is it
just as he wrote it down:

> *Is anyone happy because you passed his way?*
> *Does anyone remember that you spoke to them today?*
> *Can you say, tonight, in parting with the day that's slipping fast*
> *That you helped a single brother of the many you passed*
> *Is a single heart rejoicing over what you did or said?*
> *Does the man whose hopes were fading*

Tekkin' a walk

Now with courage look ahead?
Did you leave a trail of kindness
Or a scar of discontent?
As you close your eyes in slumber
Do you think that God will say
"You have earned one more tomorrow
by the work you did today."

We didn't speak with the Quebecois again. They left for work before we got up and in our remaining evenings we found a number of diversions to avoid any further confrontation. We were ships that had passed in the night and Curtis's poem made me ponder our encounter. On the morning Evelyn and I were leaving we couldn't resist writing on the Quebecois's calendar "Who am I? Why am I here? Where am I going?" . . . in French.

Goin' for X amount

IF YOU'RE GOING TO WEAR SANDALS
GO HOME

Has the world gone mad or what?
Did you lose your head or what?
Is my chalk like cheese to Guyanese?
If you're going to wear sandals go home.
And if you don't know who's who or what's what
Who you are or why, then that's okay.
If the familiar seems unfamiliar then stay
But if you're going to wear sandals go home.

I'd been in the forest. I wanted to go native, to make the place my own. But belonging can't just be plucked off a tree like a juicy mango. History and attachment don't just flow into your body like the deep breaths of warm air blowing across the black creek waters; that part of your identity can't automatically fit you like the "I love Guyana" teeshirt you can buy anywhere on Main Street. Still, I tried.

We took Evelyn to the airport. Coming back along the Timehri road into town I somehow knew there was no going back to the life I had made for myself in Georgetown. Mal was talking but I wasn't listening; his voice and the noise of the big white Land Rover had become one monotonous drone. The holes that were opening up in my own terra firma were as conspicuous as the gaping potholes in the road. We were riding high but I wanted to get down and walk. I wanted to smell the soil of my father's country. I suppose this was something of what Dad went through in Africa. In his book, Lionel carried "the mark of the slave, the expatriate African, the distorted blue copy, the misplaced person, the sham". I hadn't read the pages then but they ring in my ears now that I am thinking back. But in other ways things were different. In Africa you are no one without your tribe—you can't be located without that reference. But the Caribbean was created and is recreated as a huge mix of races and cultures, a congregation of the dislocated and the dispossessed. The heritage is so Creolised that it's easy to be fooled into thinking you can just blend in. If I could have stopped to think about all this it might have fallen into place but at the time I was just rolling on, moving with no real direction. If I were back in that Land Rover now I might shout out of the window, "If this is the land of my ancestors where the hell are you?" Thinking back, I was looking in all the wrong places.

I can hear mega mega watts of music blaring with *MASSIVE* distortion. Someone invited us to a wild end-of-year jump-up called "Academic Freedom" on the university campus at Turkeyen. A long trail of minibuses race three and four abreast along the East Coast Road vying for punters along the way. "*Goin' for X amount*" they say—going for the maXimum amount of passengers. Horns beeping like sirens, each cab a moving disco of reggae and soca; cutting in and weaving to avoid colliding with the cows and horses on the unlit road. "Mash it up, mash, mash!" the conductor shouts, half-in half-out of the window, looking ahead for custom. The driver's foot is mashed down to the boards. Inside the packed minibus the frenzy is mounting by the minute. As we slow for the turn people are flooding in like the tide over the sea wall, dancing their way onto the campus. There are small boys on customised bikes doing bike dancing, wheels and handlebars festooned with glow-in-the-dark tape. Young affluent dudes in four-by-fours with giant XL wheels and blacked-out windows spinning up clouds of red dust honk their way between the crowds. Our neighbour, the Portuguese gold miner, is one of them. His *I've-made-it* emblems are heavily on display; heavy gold chains and bracelets, Ray-Ban sunglasses, Hawaiian-style *short* open to the waist, looking like a downsized Elvis Presley. A king in a downsized kingdom. He's part of the Hollywood contingent that grows by the day, the Americanisation of Guyana. You gotta have 'em: imported goods, pseudo-American accents and lifestyles borrowed from the telly. In this version of *The Empire Strikes Back* the drug barons and the gold miners rule.

The VSOs spill out of their "*cork-ball*", a clapped out old minibus they have hired for the evening. There is a "Jesus Loves You" sticker peeling off on the back window. "Wicked . . . !" one of them exclaims, as he dances his way into the throng. He is a thin guy with John Lennon glasses, white man dreads and cut-off denim *sharts*.

Around the dance area, stalls are stacked high with crates of

Banks beer, Malta, rum and fizzies. There are towers of imported Heineken beer for the Hollywood contingent. Or how about an IPR—*Instant Panty Remover*—for seventy dollars. For the uninitiated, that's vodka with coconut water. Guaranteed to work, they say. Food smells come in waves; curry and roti, fried fish, channa, hamburgers and hot dogs. A battery of chickens is being barbecued on forty-five gallon drums cut in half lengthways. It's all pure temptation. We are swimming on a tide of Banks beers and music. It's dance where you stand—a jump-up; the music pounding out from a dozen or so giant black speakers each one the size of a refrigerator. The band have taken the stage; the Mingles Sound Machine. All the songs they perform seem dedicated to the bottom. *"Grease up ya bumpah, grease up ya bumpah,"* and the bumpahs and the batties begin to wind and grind, moving to the rhythm. *"Deh bumpah, deh bumpah, deh big fat bumpah."*

The bottoms on display are a study in themselves. There are big and comfortable ones designed for rolling and swaying to the slow beat. There are batties only just about held in by *battie riders* hot pants, flimsy saddles on firm little haunches, designed more with a faster beat in mind. But the best by far are those that can tremble and ripple and shake, stop tight, ripple again, first one buttock then the other in an ongoing dialogue with the music. The type of bumpah that seems to possess a life all of its own. A mahogany goddess with one of these dance-alone bumpahs poured into a bright orange minidress steals the show. She has long ago flipped off her sandals and the white of her soles forms a rim on her feet like pink silk ballet slippers. She's like midnight: enchanting, mesmerising and secret.

We're going to *wine* all night. That means wine to the music, nothing to do with drink; or *backball*—legitimately grinding your bumpah or battie, whichever you are endowed with, into the groin of your dance partner. "*Ain't suppose tuh mean nuttin,*" I learn. The place is pulsating like one living, moving beast, gyrating rhythmically under the pearly eye of the moon.

Now John Lennon is up and dancing his white-boy dance around the mahogany goddess. He remonstrates with his colleagues over his dancing shoulder in a broad Yorkshire-cum-Guyanese accent, "Come on, don't be boring, maaan . . . come and dance." His naivete, his over-exuberance, his VSO-ness are almost as captivating to watch as the goddess herself. He presses himself against her buttocks as she bends forwards and places her hands almost flat on the floor in front of her. Her backside moves rhythmically and sexually across his crotch, up down, round and round. She glances at him coolly over her shoulder. John Lennon has died and gone to white-boy heaven. The lead singer has spotted him from the stage and wants the audience to share the spectacle. "Yuh eva see ah Jamaican dance?" he asks. The crowd respond with a collective "Naaaah!" and the on-stage girly show give us a demo. Then he purrs, "Yuh eva see ah African man dance?" and we are treated to an incredible drum solo and the stage-show responds with a wild round of jumping and dancing in a frenzy of colour. He asks the crowd in a near whisper, "Yuh eva see ah English man dance?" His question is greeted by one almighty whoop from the crowd. It seems everyone except Lennon knows what's coming. He is swept up from his spot and crowd-surfed onto the stage. Lennon is wearing a calypso shirt and a pair of sandals and is using a pair of white lolly sticks for legs.

Responding to his five minutes of fame, his arms are flailing and his hips are swinging like a stick insect on ecstasy. Suddenly a woman dressed in a tasselled bra-top and the smallest pair of *battie riders* I have ever seen in my life emerges from the crowd and joins him on stage. She pulls him in close and places his hands onto her buttocks. She jumps up and wraps her legs around his waist and buries his face in her beautiful voluminous chocolate breasts. This has got to be a set-up. She eats him alive like a black widow spider and the crowd love every minute of it. People are bent double with laughter. Girls are slapping their thighs and falling over. They are roaring in unison for more. "*Deh English man, deh English man.*" Last week he could have been sitting in his living room in Bingley watching *Coronation Street* with his mum. Now he's on a mission like his forefathers. But nobody minds tonight; he is welcomed tongue in cheek.

The music binds us all in a universal language and it never stops. There are no gaps or pauses. The place vibrates with sexual overtones. The primordial smell of burning meat with woodsmoke and sweat is aboriginal. I've lost Mal in the crowd somewhere. I am dancing with a guy in a Kangol hat and white socks; three other girls and me. I don't know if he's considered cool, I have no way of reading the social script. The who's who of it is lost on me. I just love it. My head is drumming with the riot. I am submerged in the crowd. I feel myself shedding old skin. I am touching home. I LOVE GUYANA!! We are all wooed. Lennon has tasted the breasts of freedom and he can never go back.

We've been talking tomatoes when I decide to probe Paris with one of my favourite questions. "Do you think we can ever really return?

I mean, can we go back? Should we?" He stares at me blankly for a while. It's been a long day and I'm sure my questions are too demanding. There is something about the intensity of being caught up in a bubble of time, locked away from everything and everywhere. You make relationships quickly under these sorts of circumstances. It's always easier to share bits of our life with a complete stranger. I read somewhere before about the luxury of an intimate disclosure to a stranger.

I had learned that Paris never knew his father. I know that he had lived with his grandmother as a little boy and that she told him to eat rice and peas every day and he would live a healthy, long life. His mum came to Britain in the late fifties and worked as a nurse. She saved up and sent for Paris in 1963. She died when he was still a young boy and he was fostered by a white couple, Auntie Eunice and Uncle Colin. Uncle Colin had taught him to play the trumpet. I had learned that he always knew one day he would go back to the Caribbean. But I don't know what it is that spurred him to return or why.

"Yes and no," Paris begins, "but that's not the heart of the matter. You know it's *how* you go, that's the point."

"How d'you mean?"

"Well, look at me. There was something itching away at me. Something, couldn't say what. Started as a lickle irritation inside me and then grew and grew 'til it got to be like a ache. I had things turning round in me head, sort of jumping out at me here and there, lickle pieces of things that I couldn't put anywhere and I wanted to sort them out, give them some sense. Put them together like a jigsaw, I suppose you could say. D'you know what I mean?"

"Yeh."

"It's the trumpet started me moving though. Uncle Colin taught me the trumpet so that I could go with him and play in the town band. Got me marching in the streets like a regular little chocolate soldier, blowing away at me trumpet for me life." Paris stopped to give way to a huge laugh. "You know the kinda tunes town band plays. Tarara bumdeyay, Tarara bumdeyay, and so on. I telling you, I was out for every ceremony: every bank holiday, Remembrance Sunday, Christmas, the whole lot. Me and Uncle Colin, cheeks like hamsters, blowing away on our trumpets. People just loved me man. Me lickle black face was a real crowd puller. It was great; great until I started listening to our kinda music. You know Duke Ellington, Louis Armstrong, Harry Beckett, Wynton Marsalis—real music. I mean *serious* music. Jazz has gotta be the best music in the world. It takes you somewhere man. Somewhere higher than all of us. That's the education. And they just called me back in. 'Times up, we reeling you back in boy,' they were saying to me. 'Right back to where you belong.' Liberated me. Taught me how to be who I am."

"So it's not the tomato farm calling you home?"

"Nah, that's me home," he says pointing at a trumpet case below the chair. "That right there takes me home anytime I want."

"I got you all wrong, Paris. You know the Africa thing on your tee shirt and your hair?"

"Not wrong, that's all about me too. Africa's in there too, somewhere deep. You know, like a fusion. Another story but with the same ending."

"Home?"

"Yep, home—just another way back."

LENNON'S GUYANA-MAN RAP
(rap style)

Maan, I got no real intention
to give up all pretension
to this life of my invention
where I find identification
I hear you say

> *Get real*
> *Experience what you feel*
> *Dream on*
> *For your time in Guyana*
> *Is very nearly gone*

I've been through my induction
Had every introduction
Here I feel some vilification
For my trials and tribulation
I hear you say

> *Get real*
> *Experience what you feel*
> *Dream on*
> *Maan, yo time in Guyana*
> *Is very nearly gone*

I need constant inebriation

Every kind of degradation
Maan I love the jubilation
De hustle and de motion
Wha' yuh seh?

      Get real . . . etc.

Gotta find some satisfaction
Go with my gut reaction
Don' give me no restriction
Dis place is my addiction
No maan

      Get real . . . etc.

Make all yuh smart prediction
Don't touch my resolution
Ain't really no solution
Dis place give me inspiration
Don' she

      Get real . . . etc.

No maan

      Get real (repeated more and more softly)

You don' say.

The Jumbie Parade

He did the unforgivable. He did something unforgettable. First he fell in love with the country, the freedom and the anonymity it provided him. He became historyless. He celebrated his exile by banishing his past.

Everyday life was difficult but he loved that too. There were power cuts that lasted for days, food shortages, water shortages, shortages of almost everything. Things worked and then they didn't. People got sick and died, people got shot and people bled to death in road accidents while no ambulance came. Things got stolen and lost. "Expect nothing," he said, "then you won't be disappointed. Whatever the problem, there's always a way round it and when you work it out you know you are alive." He thrived on the unpredictable, he came alive with the uncertain and the unexpected and there was plenty of it in Georgetown. He swallowed great gulps of it.

He drove every inch of the city. He knew every street name. At night you would find him in Palm Court or Headquarters or eating *cook-up* on the road outside the Library. *The Library*, what a great name for a nightclub. "I passed by the Library on my way home," or "I've been on the road," he would say. When he walked into a bar, any bar, there would be someone there who knew him. "*Hey, Malcolm!*" they would shout out. They knew just enough of him and what they didn't know he chose to forget. He would drive into the interior in the Land Rover and stay for days, sleeping in a hammock, hunting wild meat, laughing and drinking with the chaps, living in their stories. He loved it all, until the only thing left for him to do was to fall in love with the girl; first with the places she could show him and the stories she could give him and then with all that was her. And at last he felt himself in the bosom of the place; close to its heart. At last he felt to be within it; intimate and exclusive.

I think about that first spell in Guyana and wonder why things turned out that way. I suppose it was a baptism by fire. Somehow if I could survive it I might just return. It's as though Guyana always tests me to my limits—each time it spits me out I get closer and closer to it. I remember being delayed for fourteen hours of unwelcome contemplation passing through Piarco that first time trying to escape from it all and swearing I would *never* return to the damn place.

The crash in Kitty was the beginning of the end. A few days after that I was browsing in Guyana Stores when I was in another head-on collision. Jackie stopped me with a contrived puzzled look on her face.

"Hey, Charlie, we not seein' yuh," she said. "We tought yuh gone outa town, gone in deh interior." She wanted an explanation. "We all wunnerin wha' happenin wid Malcolm an deh gyurl an all?"

What girl?

What did he mean, "It just happened . . ."? Is this life so beyond his control? "Who told you?" he asked.

I have lain on my bed too long, exhausted and shapeless under a fog of mosquito net. Too long, trying to bring order to my life, tired by my inner story. A type of order goes on in the yard downstairs seemingly oblivious to my unhappiness. I can hear Gardener's bare feet shuffling on the concrete below the house as he carries buckets of water to the okra and calalloo. Rati is cooking. She is humming her Indian tunes, melodies that blend with the smell of each lil' *mecha mecha*[38] added to the pot . . . geera, masala. She always cooks food with a song story. She will try to tempt me back to reality soon with an offer of soup blended with a story of love, betrayal and repair and then will come her remonstrations. She'll get the comfort words all wrong. "Is nuttin Mistress," she sighs. "You is still Mr Malcolm's wife." In her matter-of-fact way she will tell how everybody in Guyana "have deh same story". Then she goes back to the beginning of the sentence and says the same things again, this time with a few more sighs and some large blinks, her head tilted to one side. I switch on the radio to blot her out and listen to *Death Announcements and Messages*.

"This is a message for John Pereira also known as Tall Boy, working somewhere in the interior in the north-west. Travel today, your mother is dead." I imagine the cruel news passing from person to person, deeper and deeper into the interior until finally the message finds Tall Boy. Now he must try against the

---

[38] "Seasoning". Possibly of Indian origin or a word that Rati made up.

odds to make his way back to Georgetown while his mother lies on ice, melting ice, her body rapidly bloating in the relentless heat. I remember waiting two hours with a schoolroom full of children for Father Christmas to arrive at Sandhills Mission. I just happened to be passing through the village on a boating day out on the creek with a couple of friends. We were somehow mistaken for the advance party and ushered onto the stage at the front of the schoolroom. We passed the time by telling the kids something about our Christmas in Britain and singing a few carols. The children knew the words better than we did. There was a fidgeting sense that we were only filling in until the main attraction arrived. I heard the news coming in a relay across the village. It began as a faint echo and became increasingly audible and more incredulous as it got closer until the final message bearer burst into the room and shouted, "FATHER CHRISTMAS . . . HE DUN FALL OFF DEH BOAT! FATHER CHRISTMAS . . . HE IN DEH WATER!" We rushed down to the stelling along with the entire village population to witness the last scenes of the drama—a half-drowned Father Christmas, being dragged face-down from the creek clutching his empty wet sack in one hand and sorry grey wig in the other. His trousers had come down and were now trailing behind him, attached to his legs only where they tucked into his wellies. He had on little purple briefs that had almost disappeared into the crack of his big behind. The children squealed with delight as they dived into the water to retrieve their brightly wrapped Christmas presents that were now floating off downstream. Only in Guyana. I rehearsed the parts of the scene that I had missed. A tinny reggae version of "Jingle Bells" blaring from a portable cassette player as the speedboat approaches, and black Father Christmas, gold-framed Ray-Bans glinting in the sun, standing proudly on the bow with his sack of presents on his back. The speedboat swerving to miss some over-exuberant children rowing out towards them in a canoe. Then the speedboat hitting the end of the stelling and Father Christmas being pitched through the sky in slow motion to land head first in the creek. I imagined that evening's *Death Announcements* on the radio:

> *This is a death announcement. Clifton Beverney, also known as Daddy Christmas, husband of . . . father to . . . drowned today in the Madewini Creek.*

One afternoon I learned that Winston had drowned. Rati told me while she was mopping the floor. It was his very first day in his new job on the gold dredge and all that he had ever spoken about and longed for. Soon after his eighteenth birthday he had finally been allowed to go. "Winston fall over deh side and deh water tek he jus like dat. He gone, Mistress. Dem boys neva even hear he call out." I felt everything was out of control.

What did Malcolm mean, "You'll never be Guyanese"?

My hair is dead. Dead straight. Was it Tuesday I was walking past Nalini's Salon and called in for the complete relax treatment? I can't remember. Nalini did it herself. It was the challenge I think. Hairlox double-strength relaxer with Dream conditioner. Maybe she left it on too long. I didn't care. I came out transformed, with strange un-belonging, wig-like hair. Black Barbie hair. Looking "like Diana Ross on deh cover of *Ebony* magazine,"

Nalini said. Yet when I looked in the mirror I saw Diana Ross in the film *Lady Sings the Blues* after she comes out of the asylum. My face had shrunk to show off new black-blue rings round my eyes. I bought a pair of shades and a Kangol hat on Regent Street.

What did he mean, "You're not black enough"? What did he mean *black*?

Rati's soup smells good but I don't want to eat it. These are wasting days, wasting away days. I feel too numb to warm to food or comfort, too wounded to eat. A trail of ants finds its way from somewhere, somewhere I can't see from my bed, marking an orderly line through my chaos. Their map is drawn by a mango smell, traces left from another time Rati tried to tempt me with food. I have been out on the road for days. I have walked the entire city looking and searching. At first I just went out in my *shorts*, out of the gate, out onto Delhi Street, past Big G's bar and the dead dog that has been slowly dissolving into the tarmac by the Conversation Tree and onto the sea wall.

Sections of pain come and go. This story burns a hole in my head. Hours turn to days out on the road, days of searching and watching and infiltrating hostile territory. Days anchorless and adrift until I know I can't stay, I can't go back, and I can't find home so I just lie down and the fan turns and Rati sings and I am held together only by the present moment.

I seek out pain on the streets, demanding something. I defy anyone to challenge my right to move about where I want to in the city. I walk through parts of town I know I shouldn't walk. Places where faded matchstick houses teeter precariously on their stilts as if one sharp exhalation of breath might just blow them away. What kind of garden city is this? The trenches are clogged with filth and stagnant water. I am angry. This place owes me. I can only keep walking; there is nothing for me to do except walk. In Tiger Bay red-eyed, oily-sharts men, beggars, old timers high on rum, or rasta men stoned on *sensi* see steel in my eyes. They throw out "*Sss Sss*" sounds at me as I pass by. "*Com sistuh, stop a while huh?*" But I keep on walking. America Street where on the pavement, bright green iguanas destined for the cook-pot, heads erect, their legs trussed across their backs, watch the passers-by with the same detached contempt I too feel inside. On Regent Street a solid block of music falls out of Matt's Record Bar, so loud it draws me in. A group of East Indian boys are asking to hear Chutney music, the multicultural mix of Indian style overlaid on the steady ragga beat. Racial mix. A black girl with a golden smile floats in, her hair straightened and turned in rusty coils. Her gold front teeth are inlaid in gold with the four suits of the pack of cards. Heavy golden discs hang from her ears and she wears a chain and rings made of ounces of Guyana gold which shine against the shiny black of her skin. As poor as the country is, *nah skont gun rob she*; she is untouchable. Her stonewashed jeans can barely accommodate her large, rounded, protruding bumpah that moves to the music as if it is connected to her spine by only a swivel. A golden swivel. "Play dis," she instructs the Indian boy behind the counter. A heavy dusting of white talcum powder extends downwards from her neck between her breasts and tells her world something I might never know. What kind of black woman is this? I watch only her. She doesn't need to give me the cut eye. She knows I am inferior. She belongs.

On Stabroek Square the minibus touts try to scoop me up into already overfilled vehicles bearing names like *Sweet Jesus* and *New Orizon*. The thin cotton of my shirt sticks to my back. I burn from the inside out, the deep fire inside me like an unexploded bomb waiting to shaboom and take the lot of them with me. At going-home time I watch the working girls in their neat tailored cotton suits: the girls from Guyana Stores, from Fogarty's, from the government offices on Main Street, take their slow, graceful walk towards the minibus stands and select their carriage. The drivers beep their horns and make as if they are pulling off, to fool them into thinking there would be no waiting. The minibuses are jam-packed, the conductor re-arranging the internal contents to accommodate the shape of each new passenger. "Fat boy . . . go up duh back nah? Move to duh back, mek some room for Moms and duh Chinee lady."

"Yuhs Putagee?"[39] one of the touts asked. "Espagnol? Rasta? Wha' yuh really are, gyurl?" I am no particular category but they will have their own name for me: English Lady, Reds . . . I'm not black in Georgetown.

I follow the girls into the minibus and sit close to them examining their nails, smelling the sweetness of them; a hint of the thick coconut smell similar to that which rises off the yellow gorse hills in May back in Wales. Their skins are soft caramel, mocha, nut brown, chestnut, grape black. Their high cheekbones and sculptured features give them a haughty look. Not a hair is out of place; styled, stretched, coiled and curled. Neat. Laughing girls with

[39] Portuguese.

white teeth and secret smiles and stories. The lilt of their voices, their private language, identifies them as authentic. They are what make the place. They throw back their heads and laugh, loud, natural laughter and I long for their special knowledge, to be part of their wholeness. I am curious about them because I am curious about her. I despise all of them because I despise her. I despise their small-town dreams and their aspirations. I despise them for wanting to leave for the States, for Canada, for England, for wanting a white boyfriend, for wanting to be Whitney Houston. I despise them for the compromises they will make. I despise the fact that they betray the closeness of each other for the closeness of a man. These minibus rides will be the closest I will ever get to any of them. I search them with my eyes for some answer to my predicament. My loathing is irrational but real. I am angry at the black that they are and at the same time angry at my alienation from it. I feel rejected and betrayed by every one of them.

"Who said life was fair anyway?" he asked.

I don't seek sanctuary in my father's house, although part of me wants to go there. It is difficult to find solace with him for the moment, the stories are too close. I relive Ma's story. I feel her hurt within mine. Dad left Beit-eel and Wales and all that we were seemed to be not good enough. There was a new country and a new woman, an English woman, and that must be better. We were discarded without a chance to speak or defend what we had. That's how it seemed. We were left with Ma's hurting and we could never mend it. Only he could do that. They say there is no colour in love. That's stupid. There damn well is. It may lie dormant at the heart of the relationship but it's there. It's there in all the times you are asked, "Why did you marry a black girl?" "Why did you marry a white man?" Old grief torments me. I am angry with Mal. He has forced me to confront the fact of this question. I feel intimately betrayed by a white man and by a sister, not simply by my husband and a woman. Together they cast me as white. I will not find him yet to ask him why. I can't ask, I don't want to hear the answer. I want to be alone, alone and invisible. I am taking this city by stealth, invading the territory of my betrayers, sitting close to them on the bus like the enemy within. Angry with father and fatherland that rejected me.

Night is closing in but I get no peace. It will take weeks of roaming to close the wounds. How could he rob me of myself in this way? How could he rob me of my inheritance? Why had he spoiled what was rightfully mine? My nights on the road were bad. Lonely lost nights, dizzy drunk nights, nights when I tasted the dirt on the pavement and cared nothing. To cover up the bloody scars on my knees I bought a pair of long trousers from a stall on Regent Street, next door to a shop that sold real teeth. I must have looked like Genevieve, the mad woman with the doll. When the shop fronts are pulled down, the stalls packed up and the lights switched on in the bars, new characters come out onto the streets. Car wash boys outside the Palm Court, smackheads begging for dollars, hookers who will go with anyone in their car to the sea wall for a small piece. Fat-cat businessmen taking a Heineken on the way home from work. I took a room at Trio La Chalet. *La* Chalet not *Le* Chalet, in Guyana. It cost barely two pounds a night for a sparsely furnished wooden room. There was no mosquito net, no sheets, no towel. Just a bed and a window that opened onto the lights and noise of Camp Street and the high prison walls opposite. The shower rooms were shared. A VSO woman, new to the country and white as alabaster, offered me a towel without question. It was her second night in Georgetown. I didn't speak to her, she looked too much like Ma. I was numb and empty of anything but anger. I spent days and nights in La Chalet until he came to collect me one evening under cover of dark. He waited downstairs like a white pimp behind the wheel of his Land Rover. There was so much damage. A chill of secrets settled between us. Lies lay on the bedcover, on the back seat of the car, in the bank account waiting to be discovered. These weren't adventures, I saw them as conquests and colonising. Did he have to have his very own black slave?

Why did he say I should go home, that I didn't belong here? "There's nothing for you here now," he said gently. "Go back to what you know. It will help you." When I finally went to the veranda, Dad said much the same. "You have a symmetry with Wales you won't find here, Cha. Your mother fought for it. She had the authority to define you within that country. She shaped you there. Go back and find your own Wales, Cha. Go home."

I go back to Delhi Street and lie down. Rati tries her best, she knows it's not easy for me to go upstairs to my bed. She invites me into her little pink palace under the house. "Meh sarry Mistress," she says. "Don't tek on so. Com lie here a while." And so I lie on her bed while she is preparing to cook crab and calalloo for supper. I hear her in the yard singing and going about her business. I've never been in her little space before. It's as neat as she is.

*

238

There are pictures of a very brown Jesus pinned to the wall, a birthday card I sent to her a while back and one my daughter sent to me, which she has retrieved from the waste bin. They both have a design of pink roses. There is a row of empty tampon boxes on the shelf that she has also retrieved for some purpose. A paper napkin covers her bedside table where she has arranged a few pots of nail polish; a touch of luxury. The room smells of her diligence. I watch her from my resting place. She is sitting on the steps with the crabs in a large bucket clambering and dragging each other down. She takes them out one by one, gives them a sharp crack with the back of a big knife and then pulls them apart limb by limb ready for the cook pot.

I fall asleep under the spell of her song. Afterwards I go upstairs. Then I go home.

WALES

Sugar and Slate

Return. Up against history and memories; back on home ground, homeland, motherland. Back to Zion. There are lots of reasons why I might call Wales home. Home, the place you know, the place that knows you, the place you leave, the place to which you return, that place filled with memories and dreams, a place of ties and connections, that special hearth. I love Wales but there's a twist in the dragon's tail.

"There are roots and roots," Suzanne was saying as the *Red Dragon* rattled along the north Wales coast. She'd taken the time to come and welcome me home. "Ever see any of our kind go searching out their white roots?" she laughed. "I don't know why all this stuff is bothering you. Dewks, just live your life, Charlie. It's not where you come from that matters, it's where you're going," she added. I looked out of the train window in the direction we were going—iron grey sea, mercury sky, miles of rippled mudflats and the familiar scribble of holiday caravans like English graffiti daubed on the sea defences of Wales. My eye followed the artwork: pastel pictures of seaside towns, Flint, Prestatyn, Rhyl, Towyn, Abergele, Colwyn Bay. I was moving towards somewhere I called home with no obvious sense of symmetry. It didn't really make too much sense any more. The colours were all wrong.

I came back to Wales, quietly questioning, still searching for home. I'd left Llandudno but I was returning to Wales, if it was possible. Yet Wales seemed to be speaking with a forked tongue. The choirs might have been singing of a welcome in the hillsides, but I didn't feel that welcomed.

They say that in crisis you see truths. I was angry, angry with Wales for rejecting me. It was Wales that had betrayed me, let me down, cut me off. The anger had spawned initially from a private betrayal but somewhere over the Atlantic it had become far more than that. It had become something political. I'd been displaced, involuntarily exiled. I felt homeless, rootless, dislocated, effectively a refugee from an untenable set of circumstances. Mal was only the medium of that deeper rejection; the relationship a cosy cover thrown over a bed of contradictions. That's what I mean about interracial marriages being political. It's as though your private world mirrors disturbances and tensions in the public world and your inner struggles reverberate outwards like ripples on a pond. It wasn't just him and me. He was Welsh and white, I was black. We were innocents in a story that was so much bigger than both of us. It occurred to me that if I wasn't going to be claimed by either country then I would have to do the claiming myself. It would be up to me, and if I was going to adopt the country that seemed so reluctant to adopt me, I had to make some sense of myself within it. I had to find some kind of foothold without Mal or Ma to mediate it for me as they had done all along. I had to go back to the beginning and write the story again.

I was glad Suzanne was there to meet me on that homecoming. Her connection to Wales always seemed so much more secure than mine and now even more so, but yet she shared the same deep ambivalence to the place. It's difficult to feel belonging when nothing tells you that you belong. There was nothing about Wales giving even the slightest hint that I might be a recognised part of it. We both knew that alienation. I couldn't remember thinking much more than, "Well, I grew up here so I must belong." I thought Suzanne was lucky. She's Cardiff black and that's at least a recognised, albeit tiny, patch of Wales shaded with a little colour. She knew people who looked and thought like her. She belonged to something called a black community. She had history on her side.

"You're not so bothered about the roots business, Suzanne, because you've got roots," I said. "Africans have been in Cardiff for a hundred and fifty years at least. You don't need to go checking out your ancestors, they're right there on your doorstep explaining you."

"Ah, but how long d'yave to be around before you get counted in?" she muttered, almost to herself.

"But you're not exactly invisible are you, Suzanne?" We both laughed; laughed at our predicament and ourselves.

"Huh, that's what you think. I might be as Welsh as the rest of them but it don't feel like that." Suzanne's accent itself is a passport. There's something about the south Walian way of speaking that seems to bind them all. It's not the same in the north. I was thinking a lot about Wales—not just my small bit of it—and the whole seemed to matter more now than ever. My home town, the place I know, the place that knows me, was a temporary sanctuary. I needed somehow to reconcile myself to Wales if I was to find my way back home.

Poor old mixed-up Wales, somehow as mixed up as I was; confused about where it had been, what it was and where it was going, rapidly re-writing history to make sense of itself as some kind of monolithic whole and it just wasn't working. I love its contours and its contradictions. There is the north, "*Welsh Wales*" they call it, and a very different south, connected only in name. We in the north probably have more ties with people in Liverpool and Chester and those in the south to the south-west of England, if you look at it from the perspective of a train ride. Then there are the industrial towns; great ugly scratches of poverty and deprivation, deserted mining towns and a rural heartland desperately clinging to a past that has long gone. There are the seaside towns like Llandudno turning into geriatric ghettos, attracting retired settlers from the Midlands, Lancashire, Yorkshire, Manchester. In the place but certainly not of it. The Welsh and the English, the Welsh-speaking and the English-speaking, the proper Welsh and the not so proper Welsh, the insiders and the outsiders, the Italians, the Poles, the Irish, the Asians and the Africans and the likes of us, all fighting amongst ourselves for the right to call ourselves Welsh and most of us losing out to some very particular idea about who belongs and who doesn't. How would we ever make sense of it?

"You're lucky, Suzanne. There are lots of people just like you in Cardiff. You've grown up with them. You're Welsh alright. I envy you that," I said.

"You've got that one wrong for a start. I belong to a lil' bit of Cardiff, not Wales at all. Wales, what's that?" she asked looking out the window of the train at the north Wales coast as if she was in a foreign country. "I don't know why you live up 'ere; it's all grass and sheep, isn't it?" Sometimes I think she is right.

Wales. I can easily summon it up as a series of picture postcards—the same scene, a different season and so a completely different scenery—the landscape changes like a kaleidoscope. I love it. There can be few places more magnificent in the architecture of the landscape, in the drama and magic of the scenery, in the range of vistas it offers, seascapes, rolling hills, craggy horizons, its rivers and its lakes. There are few places with such a sensitive complexion that rises and ebbs in a thousand hues to complement different days, different lights, different times of year. I could never ever tire of those visions of Wales. I wanted to be part of the landscape, to be in view. When I got back from Guyana all the colours seemed sharper and the lines more defined and angular like someone had edged the scenes with a charcoal pencil. Even the greys were not simply grey but cast in infinite variations: stone, pebble, mercury, pewter, chrome, dust, steel. The air felt thin and cool on my nostrils. I could breathe properly, huge great big gulps of air like I was trying to get the life of the place within me.

I arrived back to find Wales was itself in an angry mood. Twenty years of Welsh-language politics had risen from a simmer to a boil. The conflict about housing had shifted to jobs. Whilst English-owned holiday homes weren't being burned down any more, the battles were being played out behind closed doors in

County Hall and on the front line in the public offices and in the schools. I went back to lecturing at the university and continued to dangle uncomfortably between the English/Welsh animosities. It was an old battle that I had been caught up in before during my own student days. At that time there had been a moment of student activism of the type we hadn't seen in Britain since the sixties, only Britain didn't seem particularly interested. I suppose it's fair to say Britain was distracted. Toxteth and Brixton had been set alight as race politics moved onto the streets. It all seemed very far away, too far away for me to identify with it.

It's hard to believe that the first major race riots in Britain were in Wales. The Cardiff riot in 1919 was one of the fiercest racial outbreaks in history. Hundreds of people took to the streets in a melee of racial violence. Black people were attacked in the streets and in their homes by lynch mobs led by soldiers who had been drafted in to quell the violence. Ugly crowds rampaged through the streets rooting out black men, damned for working and damned for having relationships with local women. The disturbance led to the laying off and repatriation of hundreds of African and West Indian sailors who were blamed for trying to defend themselves. Suzanne's grandfather was one of them.

What a lot of people don't know is that the Cardiff riots triggered an upsurge in black consciousness in the West Indies and a major insurrection against British colonialism all over the Caribbean. It began when some Trinidadians who had been caught up in the conflict returned home. Within days they started rioting against white sailors in Port of Spain. The conflict grew and became a major dock strike that almost brought the Empire to its knees within days. Soldiers in Belize began an uprising against the white British, and in Jamaica, seamen were out fighting hand to hand with British sailors. There was so much unrest all over the West Indies that the Colonial Office was forced to take steps to protect British subjects in the region. The protests had links with struggles in America and spread across continents in the Pan Africanist movement. At home the memories of the Cardiff race riots were etched into black consciousness and became the touchstone for black people fighting against the colour bar in Britain during the twenties and thirties. None of this was part of our course at university. We were sitting in warm lecture rooms listening to lectures about Marx and the class war whilst out in the quadrangle Welsh-speaking students were painting anti-English slogans and noisily protesting about English oppression of the Welsh.

Language politics filled the air. I remember experiencing the sense that things were changing but that I wasn't included in the battle. I couldn't empathise with it at all because for the great mass of us the agitation was unexplained, decontextualised, something to do with a history in which there were only two sides—Welsh or English—and for those of us who didn't sit comfortably on either, there was no role at all. This great movement for Wales wasn't taking us all along with it. On the contrary, out of necessity or neglect it was fast excluding us. To be Welsh meant Welsh-speaking and English was portrayed as one great monolithic block of badness. The Welsh were the Negro slaves and the English the plantation owners; it was as simple as black and white and yet not so simple at all.

When I eventually got round to looking in the front of the

family Bible I found that John William Hughes, my grandfather, had written the names of his parents in a beautiful sweeping hand on the inside cover.

Margaret Hughes of Quarry View Stores, Bethesda. Born 1844, died June 29th 1909. Buried July 3rd 1909 aged 65 years

William Hughes of Quarry View Stores, Bethesda. Born 1831, died October 22nd 1910. Buried October 25th 1910 aged 69

My ancestors were Bethesda people. Bethesda, a forgotten place, an empty spiritless place which like so many Welsh villages has been stripped of its function and its industry and struggles to maintain an identity in the face of incomers. A place of empty pubs and chapels and vacant stares. I knew Bethesda, its parallel cultures and its tribal wars, not that we particularly fitted anywhere in its spectrum of animosities. Hatred of the outsider might be the oxygen of the place but that meant the English. Colour didn't come into it or so they said. Uncle Walter lived out his dream in the King's Arms on the high street. Somewhere along the line he had managed to convince Auntie Enid and son Simon that he could make a go of it and took over the last pub as you leave town or the first as you go in depending on how you look at it. Ma spent her weekends there serving a small number of dour-looking locals who sat in the right hand bar, while the English, largely lifelong students and ageing hippies, sat in the bar to the left of the main door. Simon and Bea and me watched *Double Your Money* in a small dark room upstairs while Auntie Enid desperately tried to recoup some of hers in the bars below. It was a desperate, bottom of the world experience even then. If Uncle Walter hadn't steadily drunk away the profits, pissed them all literally down the kitchen sink and slowly driven away all the punters with his foul temper, we might still be sitting there some Sundays, looking down on the empty high street watching nothing happen.

The Bethesda of the ancestors was a very different place. I conjure up Margaret and William Hughes, the great-grandparents in the Bethesda of their time when the slate quarries were thriving and the business and the talk in their grocery shop was lively. I have a photograph of them taken out front of the shop, William in his white apron, handlebar moustache and flat cap. Behind them a cornucopia of goods on display: buckets, brushes, brooms, pots and pans, tins of biscuits, quarrymen's tea, rice, tins of salmon, sugar from the Demerara. Shelves with ornaments and crockery and fine things for the "lazy" wives of Bethesda. They were called lazy, although in truth they were probably just unoccupied, bored women. On the Bethesda horizon loomed the famous Penrhyn quarries, one of the two largest slate quarries in the whole world. Bethesda was a town built on the prosperity of slate; slate that covered miles of roof in the industrial heartlands of England and beyond. A place where the vision and the vista of everyone was dominated by slate workings. The menfolk, quarrying, splitting and dressing slate, and the women washing the slate doorsteps of the rows and rows of slate-topped cottages.

I see that purple place; a place of cramped terraced cottages, a place of so many chapels and public houses where temperance and sobriety and Old Testament morality stood back to back with drunkenness, revelry, scandal and gossip. A town where the inhabitants lived their lives entirely through the Welsh language with only a few having just a chance knowledge of *yr iaith fain*.[40] English was almost exclusively the language of the overseer and the landowner; the language of the slate masters who ran the Penrhyn empire from their mock castle. A town steeped in Welshness in play, prayer and productivity, where the only points on the compass were the chapel, the quarry and home. I see a town angry about low wages and debt; angry about injustices and damp and disease and death. And a town that resisted over and over again the incursions of the English power system into the heart and mind of the place. The people with little more than their language and their culture to subvert the system that wrought sweat and blood and profit out of them and corrupted the relationships between man and man. Perhaps the English have forgotten about all this, but the legacy shapes Wales. History matters. History had come to matter.

Like lots of Welsh people of their time Margaret and William had emigrated to America looking for better fortune. When news came that the Bethesda quarries were thriving they had returned home and used what small profit they had made to start their grocery business. My grandfather John William Hughes was just ten when the family returned from Wisconsin. By the time he inherited the family business, the fortunes of the Bethesda township

---

[40] Literally, "the thin language", a pejorative description of the English language, implying its inferiority to Welsh.

had changed. A strike at the Penrhyn quarries that lasted three long years, the longest strike in living history, struck to the heart of the community and threw the town into a slump from which it never recovered. The business quickly fell into difficulty. His wife Mary took ill and died and the family was pauperised. In the front of the family Bible, John William wrote:

Mary Elisabeth Hughes born November 14th 1890 died May 17th 1923 aged 33, buried May 19th 1923

Mary was mother to eight children, three died as babies and five were left living. When she died, John William could no longer cope. There was nothing else to do but to put the three youngest children into the orphanage at Bontnewydd. The two eldest children went into domestic service in Liverpool. Only now do I hear Ma's story of Bontnewydd; a story about the crushing of her spirit and her struggle for freedom, a story about the history of her people. A story that left an ache in her that she couldn't shake off, an ache of rejection that grew to consume her.

Annwyl Margaret Hughes
Annwyl William Hughes
What are the slate memories to me?
How will we meet and what shall we discuss? Will you
    know me?
Will you look for me in the stillness of the mountains above
Coetmor?

Or down on Ogwen bank where a blade of silver water
　slices the
meadow
And pours into open fields, across the valley,
between rusting hills,
Will you see me on the lane where the crackle of slate chips
below foot
announces the slate sculptures,
the hand made mountains
appendaged onto the purple hills,
a plateau to the black forests above.
Will you look for me?

I am compelled to go back in time and meet up with the ancestors in the shadow of a great slateocracy, compelled to visit my
history. I walk with them across a hundred years in the grounds
of Penrhyn Castle from where Richard Pennant, the first Lord
Penrhyn, ran an empire built on his profits from land ownership
and a massive industrial wealth. He was ranked as one of the
wealthiest men in the whole of Britain. Some claim he owned fifty
thousand acres of land in Wales. His most lucrative enterprise by
far, however, was slate. Lord Penrhyn owned not one, but two of
the largest slate quarries in the world. The two and a half thousand
men he employed in Bethesda alone produced for him an income
far exceeding any that he gained from his land ownership. He was
a slate baron and Bethesda was his baronial kingdom. The raw
material of his profits was the quarrymen themselves. He couldn't
exploit the slate rock himself; only the quarrymen held mastery

over the skills of their industry. He would never know the trade in the way that they did. But he could exploit the workers who quarried the slate, their labour and their lives, if not their thoughts. He had command over every aspect of their miserable existence; he graded, judged and split their ranks just like they did the slate. They were the black slaves to his white supremacy, the real Welsh to his Anglo-Welshness.

Penrhyn Castle looms on my own horizon now, a monument to my double historical heritage. The twist for me is that this whole empire would not have been possible at all had it not been for the huge fortune Richard Pennant made from what he called his *West India interests*. It was the cruelly driven slaves; men, women and children who toiled and sweated for the huge sugar profits that built the industries in Wales. Out of the profits of slave labour in one Empire, he built another on near-slave labour. The plantocracy sponsored the slateocracy in an intimate web of relationships where sugar and slate were the commodities and brute force and exploited labour were the building blocks of the Welsh Empire. My slate memories and my sugar memories are forged together. In the chapels on the high street of Bethesda the people turned over the pages of the abolitionist pamphlets and found the quarryman and the slave were like one in their resistance of the oppressor. The shared plight of the factory slaves at home and the plantation slaves elsewhere had an echo right across Wales with the quarrymen, the iron smelters, the black-faced miners: all knew what it meant to be robbed, beaten down, have their language, their culture, name and place stolen from them—what it was to be enslaved.

The story goes that Richard Pennant called his two nieces Sugar and Slate, in recognition of his sweet successes. It is whispered that Richard Pennant was Welsh. I wonder if he will be claimed as Welsh when we rewrite the history and the hidden histories? Poor Wales, if only we could remember our mixed-up roots, that the us and the them of the matter can never be so simple.

Dear Margaret, dear William Hughes, *Annwyl Margaret ac William*. We meet with the legacy of these two intertwined histories and struggles over freedom and identity and in my split memory we speak the same language. So are we really all comrades under the skin? It's a curious thought. Perhaps we are in many ways. Paul Robeson in the film *The Proud Valley* isn't a Welsh folk hero for nothing. He played the part of a black man who comes to live in south Wales. When he is refused a job in the mines because of his colour the coal miners protest, "But aren't we all the same colour underground?" It's a sort of civil rights film for Wales, even if the common enemy has become English and not British imperialism. Yet maybe we have woven the connection rather too deep into the mythology of Wales.

There was Ma, the Welsh woman with the black heart, her savage spirit, her passion and her fight for justice coursing through her veins. There may be a feeling that the nigger man and the Welshman are one, or that the Welshman is a black man at heart but there still isn't any recognition of the black man who is Welsh or the Welshman who is black. Is it all just imagining? I remember one of Ivor Wynne's stories about the black Celts. He claims a genetic marker has left its trace. "How can you identify them?" I asked him. "Well, they've got black penises," he replied, "that's how we know about their North African antecedents." We will have to wait for DNA to prove or disprove Ivor's thesis.

If I were to meet up with the ancestors I'd want to know more than the story of sugar and slate. I'd want to examine Ma and her people more clearly, and think about all the ins and outs of this cultural inheritance that I am burdened with. I'd want to write myself into the story as best I could. All of this became my preoccupation; part of my reconciliation, part of my reclamation of what I had lost, part of rooting myself.

I love Wales but I suppose there will always be a twist in the dragon's tail for me. I can feel a passion for the country stemming from Margaret and William. They explain in part why I am interested in things Welsh, why I am fascinated by the history and life of the place. Why I feel pride in its achievements, why I feel wounded by the insults and mocking of the Welsh and things Welsh; why, when the Red Dragon pulls its way over the border into Wales, I feel that faint sense of homecoming. Yet at the same time the ancestors can't ground me physically. They offer a vantage point from which to claim a place in what the country will become, but physically I am distanced from them. It always feels such an unsure foothold, like standing on shifting sand. Somehow, I do know Margaret and William well, but they don't know me. I wonder if this country will ever imagine me when it imagines what it is to be Welsh.

I began to imagine Wales as my own. It wasn't the same Wales as before though. My vision wasn't anything to do with the Welsh Dragon and its tongues. It wasn't to do with the Wales of my childhood, nice as that was in so many ways, or the Wales of the Tourist Board with its ladies in tall black hats, rugby players and choirs. It was to do with the twist in the dragon's tail.

When Auntie Maggie died we walked up onto the hills above Bethesda to bury her at Coetmor, the burial ground of my grandparents and my great-grandparents. It was such a fine day and the black slate awakened blue in the summer light. We made a small gathering at the graveside. On the sloping bank above us, three gardeners stood like three Welsh knights of Llywelyn; their protective visors raised and their grass strimmers paused, tilted downwards like lances. Ma stood with her two remaining sisters, five already buried and returned to their history, their soil. I stood with mine, dressed in black, and saw in those warriors' faces hundreds of years of Welsh, and whilst it beckoned me it gave me no clear signal, no history, no genealogy and no explanation. I wasn't yet sure if this could be my burial place.

As the Red Dragon pulled out of Chester station and crossed the border on its journey towards Holyhead, I might as well have shed my skin. Colour didn't exist in Wales. It dawned on me that there were literal geographic spaces in Britain where it was legitimate to be black and where it was legitimate to speak about race and there were great white spaces where it was outlawed. Race was just an ugly rumour spreading into Wales from across the border. That's what I began to notice more than ever on my return. That the idea of black Welsh wasn't really lodged in the cultural consciousness or in fact in the cultural memory. It was one of those sickening pieces of cultural amnesia that had conveniently managed to disassociate the Welsh from any implication in the facts of black history and in doing so rendered us with an invisible present.

The idea of a pure Welsh race was becoming difficult to challenge. I thought about a book I'd seen in the University library called *The Races of Wales* with pictures of Welsh *peasants,* their features carefully categorised into types—probably all with black penises only it didn't say that.

RICE AND PEAS

Am I to be culturally marooned
and in white space cocooned
in my old girl days in Wales?
"So you put me in a home na?
Well who gun do me dreds
Get out me yellow cardie
to go wid me purple pants
maan, an' let me dance?

And the danglies and banglies
I wear
Who gun buy dem?
Where?

And wha' me go eat?
Not meat
wid peas and gravy!
Lord—save me!

Rice and peas
please . . . please?
Can me taalk loud?
Shout out me mout
'bout dis and dat?
Taalk back?

Damn place
got me heart but don't
recognise me face.
Just don't bury me white na?
Or sen' me back
I'm Welsh and I'm black.

Bacra-johnny

I am constantly pulled back to Guyana. There's a well-known Guyanese expression that goes "Eat labba, [41] drink creek water and you will always return." I can't remember ceremoniously partaking of the ritual but I had certainly eaten plenty of curried labba and there isn't a moment when I can't summon the earthy taste of creek water. There's a magnetism about the place that's for sure. *Hiraeth* we say in Wales, *hiraeth* calls you home.

When I went back the first time it wasn't quite with that type of longing. I hadn't seen Mal in months and I hadn't been in Guyana since that last eventful visit. I had a good deal of unfinished business rumbling around in my head.

I found him living alone in a small wooden cottage in Kingston, on the sea-wall side of Georgetown. It was the kind of cottage an ordinary black family in bygone days might have lived in. It was simple and tidy but a long way from the luxury of Delhi Street. It felt right. Mal looked well; the sun had worn kindly into his skin and he seemed at peace with himself. He was working for the Guyana Sugar Corporation at the head office in town but even

---

[41] A large rodent that lives in the bush; looks like a big guinea pig.

as a senior manager, his local salary still only covered the bare essentials. I was happy to see him settled in his new life.

The living room was sparsely but neatly furnished with locally made wooden furniture; a faded Welsh flag drooping from a hook on the wall the only concession to his expatriate status. The stifling heat and humidity had left the dragon looking tired. We sat in the front room looking out over the deserted midday road, too early yet for the gentle afternoon sea breeze to find its way through the shutters into the high roof space and provide a welcome relief from the scorching El Niño heat outside. He took a sip of beer from a bottle and went in search of a glass for mine. "The guys in work have nicknamed me Bacra-johnny," he chuckled. "I think it was the name originally given to lower-class, down-and-out whites! I think I like it; do you? Okay, so I never buy a round. Can't bloody afford it; my salary only buys the basics but it leaves a good taste in my mouth. I don't have to represent the British Empire any more, none of that adviser bollocks. I used to feel such a phony. Now I'm just trying to live a normal life, earn my bit like everyone else, and make whatever contribution I can. Don't get invited to cocktails with the High Commissioner any more though, now I've gone native!" He had a way of staying silent, enjoying my laughter while I laughed. He was happy that I had come to this Georgetown house, to see that this was a different return for both of us. I wanted to understand the sparse and simple life he'd chosen. I guessed he too had spent many hours thinking through how we had both got caught up in the crossfire on an old colonial battlefield. The wounds were deep for both of us.

With none of the privileges associated with his former expatriate status, finding a way to live an ordinary life wasn't proving so easy. Ordinary people lived a hard life in Georgetown and things were getting harder. "Hey Big Man!" a beggar, one of at least ten who arrived daily, called up to the window as we sat talking over our beer. He stood unsteadily in the road, red eyed, high on drugs, with a cutlass in his hand. "Big Man, gimmeh small piece nah? It meh birday." The next day the same beggar protested his mother was sick; the next day he shouted up "Meh mudder dead," and by the end of the week it was his birthday again. The wooden plank walls of Mal's house seemed thinner than ever. This down-town, downsized life would take some getting used to.

Water came intermittently to the house, rarely during the day but occasionally at night, when it meant having to get up to fill buckets and containers for the next day. Every drop of it for drinking purposes had to be boiled for ten minutes for fear of picking up some waterborne disease or worm. Mal had learned from experience to add a few drops of bleach to his bathing water because of the risk of skin irritations. As evening closed in he showed me how to bathe with just a half-bucket of water.

We lay listlessly in the heat of the bedroom talking about our *sea split*[42] marriage and carefully began to repair it. We had chosen to live on different sides of the Atlantic for a while. It helped. It's not too unusual to live like this in the Caribbean where lots of people have a wife or a husband living outside, sending money home to support the family. It's been happening this way for years and years; all those lives separated by water. The workers in Brit-ain's NHS and London Transport supported their families back

[42] Andrew Salkey, a friend of my father, first coined this phrase.

home till they could afford to send for them. Dad and Ma struggled to hold together a marriage across vast oceans for twenty years and more. Now it was our turn to experience the joys and punishments of separation, reunion and reconciliation.

"I'm not coming back to Wales," he announced that night. "Not yet anyway. I just don't feel like I belong there any more. I'd rather stay on here for the time being."

"Not sure that I do, but I feel I want to try," I answered him. "C'mon Mal, of course you belong, your family are all there. You were born there for God's sake. Look what we've invested. I want to see our girls grow up there." It sounded like Ma's Cwmdonkin Park speech all over again. I'd come to terms with the fact that the idea of Wales as home might always be inadequate, or at best double-edged. I still held too many uncertainties to say that I was reconciled with my motherland. The terms of the settlement contract I had struck with Wales might need renegotiating but there was no getting out of it. It was binding.

One Saturday afternoon we drove over to Wales village on the west bank of the Demerara River to visit a sister from Dad's second family. As we drove across the harbour bridge, the air was filled with smoke, the charred ash of sugar cane falling like black snow. Mal explained that the fields are burned in this way to remove all the unwanted green parts of the sugar plant—the "cabbage"—before the cane harvesters begin their early morning work. I had read a lot about the sugar history of Guyana, which made sense of the present.[43] Ordinary things about slave life that I never knew, built on the

---

[43] A beautifully written account is Emilia Viotti da Costa's *Crowns of Glory, Tears of Blood* (Oxford University Press, 1994).

patterns of African cultures. I realised that there were so many vestiges of Africa in the culture of the Caribbean: expressions, songs, attitudes, myths, magic, recipes that had been protected in resistance to the white man. It was the everyday things that presented no threat to the plantocracy that had survived, whilst those other things so vital to identity—language, name and place—were plundered. After slavery was abolished, East Indians became the exploited indentured labour of the sugar empires and deep racial divisions that continue to this day were provoked. Can there ever be reparation?

We recognised Morag's house by the flag of Zion fluttering from the gatepost, a symbol of her allegiance to Rastafari. But to the rest of the community Morag's home will always be referred to as "White Lady House", in acknowledgement of her mother Toni's presence in the village for more than fifteen years. Toni had been in Guyana over twenty-five years and raised all her children there, but still she was White Lady to them. She lived in a small house at the back of the compound whilst Morag and her family occupied the larger front house. Toni was digging the garden when we arrived. A strong and agile woman now in her late fifties, she was not the woman Ma held in her frozen memory. Aunt Lou, their housekeeper-cum-nanny, stood by my side in the kitchen looking down at Toni in the garden. "Look at she. She dig like she owe a buck for obeah," Aunt Lou said slowly and sucked in her teeth. Amerindian or "buck" obeah must be the strongest ju-ju of all because it seems Toni has been digging over the soil all her life in reparation for something.

Outside of Georgetown this small village life turned at a different pace. The family home had a sense of sanctuary about it like Beit-eel. I had imagined it as an isolated white mum/black children home like ours, but it was nothing of the kind. There was a whole community around to bolster the emotional security. And there was Aunt Lou, surrogate black mother, mother Africa, rich in the culture and traditions of the country, quietly guiding and shaping them all. The experience of Morag and her sisters and brothers must have been so different from ours.

Later in the day we all sat down in the yard between the two houses. Toni rested in the hammock with Morag's two small children Obena Kimani and Makeda lying across her. She was telling the children a story from her childhood and I was struck by how her Englishness was being passed on in such simple ways. Into Kimani's unconscious drift pieces of her grandmother. Obena Kimani, a little girl with an African name, her skin the colour of mahogany, growing up on the bosom of her English grandmother in a black village called Wales. How could anyone think a culture stands still? Or that we can hand it over intact like a book? It's more like the retelling of a story. It changes every time we put our own spin on it and pass it on. We add our own little bits, forget others and get some of the story completely mixed up.

The cane trucks rumbled by into the early evening. White Lady House shook on its pillars in response. Children from adjacent houses, their jobs for the day done, slowly wandered into the compound, curious about the visitors to the village. A tall, fine-boned young girl called Odine Welsh practised her newly learned Madonna song for them all; a strong sound from such an economical body. The other kids clapped and moved their hips in time to her tune. Her younger sister Tiffany stopped to examine me close by. She was concentrating on the moons of my nails, touching them over and over again and trying to rub them out with her small black fingers. She turned my hands over and looked at my palms. She had provided opportunity for Odine to move in, anxious to check out my hair at close quarters. The frizzy straggles must have been annoying them, their hair being so neat and styled. "She pretty but she need new hair style," she remarked determinedly to Aunt Lou. "Bring meh comb nah?" Tiffany and Kimani immediately presented themselves at her side, eager to help out. As Odine loosed out my full hair they all gasped at the revelation. "You's a mix?" Tiffany asked of me while directing her question to the whole audience, her wise seven-year-old eyes bulging with affected surprise. Up until that moment they had considered me white but now my hair contradicted their perceptions. Bursting with curiosity, she peeped below my blouse as if to confirm her suspicions. "She red outside but she white inside," she announced triumphantly. Everyone laughed, including me.

Odine worked with a skill passed down from generation to generation. Even the smallest of them can do the cornrows and the plaiting and the tatting of hair. "Even Kwesi know how," she told me, "an he a boy." This is one of those echoes of Africa, black women laying hands on black women; the gift of doing hair for one another, a tradition passed on like patchwork and quilting. I could have been back in Falolou Road. I felt the loss of that heritage keenly. I have none of those old skills. Yet I also felt in part retrieved with every sectioning and twisting action of the hair on my head. Odine's long black fingers worked my hair into a neat pattern and gently restored my soul. The rows emerged like the burned stripes on the sugar cane fields, black against the white of my scalp.

Odine wanted to know about Mal but she was too shy to talk to him directly. I told her how I was married when I was a teenager to a boy from my village in Wales and pointed across the room to Mal. "Yuh still marry tuh one an deh same man?" she asked with surprise.

"Yep, the same guy."

"He treat yuh good?"

"Yeh," I said rolling my eyes upwards and the children laughed and slapped their thighs in amusement.

"Meh nah marry til I is eighteen," announced Odine to the nodded approval of Aunt Lou. Aunt Lou was reading her Bible and not directly listening but she was clearly tuned in to everything going on around her. The children's chatter was mesmerising.

They argued over who should hold baby Makeda. Baby Makeda has eyes as black as jet. Kimani says that Tiffany can't hold the baby because she is not white like us. She points to herself and to me, the mulatto. Hierarchies of colour and the lines of difference are drawn over and over again in each generation.

Morag had made a batik dress for me. A purple dress with a bright golden sun bursting out of the front. The girls whooped with excitement at my hair and my new dress. They were claiming me and I was happy to go with it. Later still, under the house to the loud beat of reggae music, the children taught me to dance Guyanese style and my metamorphosis was complete. I felt a strong sense of belonging, however temporary. Things seemed familiar and that felt good. The house was filled with a generous inclusive spirit and there were memories that we shared, albeit from our different perspectives. I felt comfortable in a way I had not felt before in Georgetown.

When the night came I laid my head down on my bed with Malcolm snoring smoothly by my side. Sweet sleep. Only thin partitions separated the occupants of the house laid down to rest so that we are all one in our sleep, Toni with brown-skinned Kimani stretched out across her belly, Morag and Makeda, Aunt Lou, me and Bacra-johnny in White Lady House in black Wales.

I'd come a long way by then. I think I'd found a niche for myself in the order of things. I knew I had been chasing an idea of Guyanese-ness that would never be mine. I'd been too anxious to find a way in and at every turn I was refused entry. And the same went for Wales. Until I changed my perception of what it was to be Welsh or what it was to be Guyanese, or both, I would never feel the satisfaction of belonging. I would always feel a sham or somehow lacking against an unattainable ideal. I would have to accept my role as the spectre at the feast and stay in my limbo, in transit at Piarco Airport, somewhere and nowhere at all.

I felt more at ease with Wales. I felt I had exposed some of the connections and the contradictions that were meaningful to my position. I had begun to carve out the idea that there might just be a place for me there but I would have to make it. It might be an ongoing struggle but I wasn't giving up. And I reconciled myself to Mal. It was easy to be close to him again. He took a wrong turn in the road but I realised it was one I probably might have taken myself given enough time. It was more the fact that we had painfully disturbed some of the cracks in the foundations of our relationship that brought it tumbling down. Now it would be up to us to rebuild it on a surer footing. Could this ever be a relationship of equals?

Sunday morning and Wales village seemed a million miles away from Georgetown. I was glad for the time away from the city and its tensions. It was a very hot day; lingering smoke from last evening's burned cane making the air even thicker. Only the croaking of the frogs going off the night shift disturbed the rhythm of Jim Reeves floating across the cane fields. Driven out of bed before seven by the sheer sticky stillness of it all, I sat out on the back step drinking a mug of tea. A woman in the yard next door, still in her nightdress, hung out a second line of washing, her head a brightly coloured porcupine of curlers. Aunt Lou moved about the kitchen cooking ancestral food, the smell of salt-fish and bakes mixed with cane smoke touching something hidden deep within me. For the time it took to drink my tea and Jim to mend his broken heart, there was nowhere else on earth I'd rather be and I knew I would always return.

When we got back into Georgetown later that day, Mal's house had been broken into, the third time in the same number of months. But this time they'd really cleaned him out; everything that could possibly be carried had gone, even the fridge and some of the furniture. He had only the clothes he stood up in. He felt powerless against the tide of misfortunes. This is Georgetown now. Everyone tells the stories. A garage owner shot to death for just thirty thousand Guyana dollars—around one hundred and fifty pounds, a Canadian tourist hijacked on the East Coast Road and shot for a handful of nothing. Bacra-johnny's simple life was just not simple enough to deter the robbers. There was no one about at Brickdam police station when we went to report the break-in. A sign above the front desk read "No Limers, No Idlers". From somewhere in the back came the sound of the cricket commentary on the radio and the excited chatter of voices. Sunday or just Guyana? It was time to go home. To Wales.

ADVANCEMENT AND RETREAT

You've touched the breasts of freedom
Enchanted by her smile
You've shed the shackles of a life
That held you for a while

A spirit reborn in the smoothness of her skin
Moved by the sweetness in her voice
You felt the thrill within
That's left you little choice

Lain aside the mask of commitment
You toast a life renewed
In the sanctuary of her body
Your former self eschewed

So you've touched the breasts of freedom
Metamorphosis ensured
You cannot with your heart return
To the life you have obscured.

271

I goin' home

"I'm going to write about you when I get home, Paris. I think your trumpet story and the tomato farm and all that are brilliant. Just great. The Africans caught you off your guard eh? Like lots of us you were looking in the wrong direction, and then, boom, suddenly pulled right back into the tribe. Can I? Can I write your story?"

"You won't put what I said about Uncle Colin, will you?" he asks. "He was a great foster dad. He did his best, Auntie Eunice too."

"No, course not."

I think about the poem Curtis gave to me all that time ago by the river in Omai and how glad I am that I met Paris today because he's helped me make sense of such a lot of things. How do you hold on to the strangers you meet in these passing moments that leave such a marker in your life? There's no point promising to keep in touch. There's no point saying "If you're ever up in north Wales . . ." I don't need to meet up with Paris again, we've done the work, we both know it. We've tuned in to a kind of global consciousness that people like us must share.

"Why would you want to write about me anyway?"

272

"Well, because it's part of my story. You see, I think people like us have a lot in common and one of the things we have in common is our storytelling. It's a kind of place in itself isn't it—the story I mean—like home, a good place to be?"

"I get you."

"D'you know what I think?" I ask, gaining some momentum for my thesis, "I reckon we all find our own way of going back, going home, whatever you want to call it. It's not a myth like they say, but a very real part of what we are about. I've been going and coming so long now I can hardly see that this itself is my return, nothing to do with the places at all. I guess this is home for me, Paris."

"Here? What, y'mean Trinidad?"

"Here," I say tapping my forefinger on my temple. "Hey, d'you know about the man in Charles de Gaulle Airport?" I start up anxious to fill up some more of the time.

The call for my flight comes suddenly and unexpectedly. We've been waiting so long we have almost forgotten about travel. There's one collective celebratory cheer before people start moving fast towards the gate.

"That's me, Paris. Time's up! I'm outa here," I say gathering my stuff. "Hope you don't have to wait too long to get where you're going."

"I hope I don't as well," he smiles up at me.

"Really nice to meet you, Paris," I say, shaking his hand. "Take care man." As I walk off he calls after me, "Don't forget my grandma and the rice and peas, will you?"

The plane takes off, climbing steeply upward and below us Trinidad by night sparkles like a discarded carnival outfit on a navy blue carpet. There is a feeling of relief passing amongst the passengers on the plane now we are moving at last. Everyone is refreshed by the release from the holding space; some are thinking of beginnings and arrival, some of endings and leaving and many, like me, reconciled to a life of toing and froing, of coming and going. One big auntie has arranged her large frame two rows in front of me. I can see her contented profile; the triumph over the issue of the hand luggage giving way to battle plans for the impending encounter with the immigration officials. She dabs the sweat from her forehead with a large hanky, replaces her glasses, shuts her eyes and smiles. Wedged in to her left are two shorties; thin little guys aged about eight and ten with "unaccompanied minor" labels hanging around their necks. Not for long, I imagine. Auntie will shortly acknowledge her duty and take on a role that the flight attendants would never be able to emulate. She will talk them back home, or away, whichever, with stories about how her own children were "lef home wid meh own mudder" or "sen fo' when meh good an ready". I don't need to look around the plane to know that the whole spectrum of the Caribbean/Britain link will be represented: the tourist, the trader, the student, the expatriate kid going back to school, the consultant, the aid worker, the missionary, those going or coming because mommy is sick or to bury someone, the guy looking for his roots or reeling with the discovery of his rootlessness. The Bishop of Georgetown is on board, I glimpse his purple vestments. I recognise a government minister too, through the curtain dividing us from first class. She has her head down in a novel. Maybe Mighty Sparrow is on board. I feel at home.

I look out into the dark night sky. On one side of the Atlantic there is a room where my father is dying.

The room is cool and airy and the fan spins on like life, turning with deluded optimism. He lies on his bed, his eyes sealed off to the outside world but he lives for a while on our conversations. A trail of visitors slowly drains him. He visits and revisits episodes of his life with them, dropping in as an observer on scenes that are flashed before him. He corrects history in his accounting; things must fall out right now the end is near. No slur or criticism and no pain or bitterness will scar his journal now, Lobo is safe. His careful reminiscing finds tidy sequences and that comforts us all. We collude as we have so often done.

He has no pain despite his distended liver. Strangely, there is no taint of illness in the room, only the taint of disrepair, the consequence of all the years of neglect. It's as though he has been called and he must lie down and wait the final summoning. But first there is finishing work to do. I am touched and saddened over and over again by the precariousness of life in Guyana. I have found a small charity of hospice nurses in the town and they can offer some advice but no care. They are too stretched. Two nurses for a whole city. Evelyn has come and she and I will learn fast how to nurse him and give time for those conversations we never had. His new family has to go out to work to keep their jobs. Their lives must move on whilst we have the luxury of time. As the days pass we wash him, soothe him with skin freshener and oil and sit endlessly by his side. He tells Evelyn that she is his Mary Seacole. Her nursing is tireless. What she can't say in words she rubs deep into his skin and he receives it gratefully. She asks nothing of him, but these moments somehow salve the wounds in their shared past.

He lies in state like an African Oba. We bring our love to the room and he breathes it in. It is as if we seek out his last touches of approval and he gives generously. He is walking a peaceful path to a place of recalling. Days fold closed, and so do the pages of the great archive of his mind. I feel the loss. I feel a sense of desperation at what will not be said, at what I will never know. I cling to the phrases and pieces of him that he is still strong enough to give. I anticipate overwhelming losses. It is not just the passing away of a parent, although those losses are great enough. I begin that grief. A grief for the sound of him, for his presence and his overview of my life. I want to tell him about myself and to know that he knows me and those who mean something to me. I want him to be there and available. It's a grief for the time we lost, the potential of those twenty years we never had. There are things we might have done but now can't because it is too late.

It is a grief for what I lost through lack of his physical presence. I grieve my own isolation in that desperate white sand desert, the absence of black in my life, the absence of black experiences, the absence of black ways of thinking and being. I grieve for the loss of a great piece of myself. The loss of Lobo. I grieve the not knowing of his culture and the loss of access to it through him. Wasted years float across my mind. Great cavernous wastelands; huge spaces of emptiness and endless miles of barren landscapes.

The black in me begins to fade. I feel it draining away as the strength drains from him over the days. From an old sixties

record player rejected by the thieves on every visit, Paul Robeson
sings songs of redemption in an amber voice. "Swing low, sweet
chariot". Tears have formed at the corner of my father's eyes. I
hold his hand and mentally walk this small part of the path with
him towards his ancestral home. He is called back to his blood,
his soil and his people. His voyage seems clear and uncompli-
cated, a path that leads back through Joseph Williams his father,
to Moses Williams his grandfather and beyond, to the boats and
the sea crossings and to Africa. Will I lose this connection?

Eventually the trail of visitors thins as he becomes too weak to
receive them. The Bishop of Georgetown, an old schoolboy
friend, brings his booming voice and strong prayers into the room.
They don't need to remember their rift stemming back to Burnham days, when my father joined in government condemnation
of all the pomp and ceremony of the Church. "I don't want any
of that," Dad says. "Bury me in a simple way. I want to be buried
in St Sidwell's with my brother Everard and my school friend
Horace. Bury me amongst my people. And I don't want any kind
of noisy funeral parade from the Georgetown Cathedral with the
flag draped over my coffin; no bereted, red-coated soldiers leading
the parade to the trumpets of the police band playing Bach or
Handel. That's just colonial rubbish. Give me those people in the
clap-hand church; the ones who know their Africa." A sweet
smile of recognition comes to his lips. "My friend Horace said to
me, 'I know of all your achievements, Denis, but Sonny Williams,
that's who you are. You will always be Sonny Williams to me.' I
want to be buried Sonny Williams."

"Did you find Lobo?" I wanted to ask him. In some ways I'm

sure he had. He'd spent his life trying to shrug off the influences of the West; everything he did was a rejection of European domination. He had fled England for return to his Africa and in turn left Africa to return to a simple bush life in Guyana. He had contributed to his own country and finally married his own kind. Is that what Lobo meant for him? I thought about his kind of Lobo and his Lionel. They were, after all, one and the same person. They were the two sides of the predicament. The tension we would always have to straddle. I grieved for Lobo. I knew he was potentially my deepest and most profound loss.

How will I ever know Africa now? There is a flag of the Fante tribe of Africa that depicts a large fiery dragon like *Y Ddraig Goch* with a long twisting tail, a Union Jack and images of colonial struggle. In the book *Asafo! African Flags of the Fante*, the flag is accompanied by the caption, "*Will you fly or will you vanish?*" The Fante believe of this creature that "it can fly, it can dig in the ground, it can go anywhere". I hold on to the universality and indestructibility of that image, to its sense of integration and reconciliation of contradictory legacies of the past. There will always be an aching fear of disappearance amongst those of my generation. A fear of becoming invisible and watered down, a sense of the loss of heritage and an urgency about the need to preserve something. But what? What culture? How? So we return, we look back to the past. We look back so that we can recognise and retrieve a lost past, so that we can reaffirm all the elements of it. That way we manage to carry forward a sense of ourselves selecting and reinventing a culture and integrating it into the present. That's Lobo. Lobo is necessarily mixed.

In a room on the other side of the Atlantic a baby is born. She is a peach like Ma. Her eyes are Bethesda blue and her hair is corn-field yellow. My daughter names her Ruby and in moments I shift a whole generation. I shoulder the burden of memory as the generation of my father passes away and a new generation is born elsewhere. I can't write Ruby's history. Eventually she will pull together her own pieces and make sense of them in her present. I sit and wonder what exactly I must pass on to her. I try to piece together the parts of the collective memory, the essence of my generation that may be meaningful to hers. Is it our quest to dig, to pull down the heritage in some way, but not to fix it? Is it to carry the idea of return like a faulty gene; is it the sea stories and the stories of movement; is it the story of unbelonging? The story of global connections and yet local attachment, of boundary disputes, of challenging the very idea of race? What is it that binds us? How will we reinvent this heritage together?

I was born into a long journey. I've crossed huge physical and psychological spaces to bind the great triangle of Africa and the Caribbean and Britain and I know my journey isn't over. It is a journey of constantly grappling with the landscapes we encounter, changing them and redefining them, of corrupting the pure. It has taken me a long time to puzzle out the half–half alternative that was offered; to understand that to be mixed race is not to be half of anything; mixed but not mixed up. We may look to Africa or the Caribbean for our inspirational cues, we may inherit fragments of a traditional culture from our parents, but these we reformulate and reinvent and locate in our home places.

I dream Ruby's Wales, a future Wales where the search for one voice gives way to a chorus of voices that make up what it is to be Welsh. I know why it is that I like Wales. I like it because it is fragmented, because there is a loud bawling row raging, because its inner pain is coming to terms with its differences and its divisions, because it realises it can't hold on to the myth of sameness, past or present. I ponder what is to come. I hope for a place where we won't be just a curiosity to be tolerated like the Congo boys, or somewhere where we are paraded as a quirky interest like the black person who speaks Welsh, or a team of black mountain climbers or a black ballerina. Just a normal space will do. And I hope that it won't be a place where we will have to listen to an endless round of "first-tos" and "been-tos" boasting amongst ourselves. The first black Welsh man to have done this or the first black Welsh woman to have been there.

I am reminded of a parable by Chinweizu called "The Been-tos and the First-tos". It's a tale about a gathering of African namedroppers who get into a round of boasting about which of them has been the first to do certain things or the only one to have been to certain places. One boasted that he was the first African "ever to read Sanskrit diagonally whilst standing on his head". Another that he was the first African "ever to be buggered by a turbaned Arab in the market at Baghdad right after the noonday prayer, on a perfumed rug embroidered in Samarkand gold". Finally an albino spoke out—his claim more outrageous than any that had gone before. He claimed to be the first African ever to be reborn in the image of God. He related how he had jumped into a boiling cauldron and emerged with burns so severe they took a year to heal. Yet all this suffering was worthwhile, he maintained, because now he looked white and clean like an angel, and anytime he wanted to he could pass as a European, even in daylight.

It's a priceless tale and a sobering one. Maybe I did lose Lobo but I reckon I'm not scalded.

The flight attendant brings round the drinks and I am lost in a round of new concerns about where I am going. I think about Bacra-johnny, about Wales, about Wales village in Guyana. I want to experience the smell of fermenting cane again. I want to sit and chat with Gwen Llewelyn and Barry Cadwalladar and get to the bottom of my puzzle about their names. I want to keep making the links that make home. I want to swim brown skin in the brown waters of the rivers and tributaries that cross Guyana in a great network and meet and join in curious connections as they eddy and flow into the mighty Essequibo and out into the Atlantic. And I want to tell Ruby all about it.

Acknowledgements

In the telling of my story I acknowledge my enormous gratitude to those close to me, above all my husband Malcolm, without whom I might never have put pen to paper. His commitment, generosity and patience are immense. I have known him since I was sixteen and he is my life-long love and sponsor.

This collection of thoughts, memories and ideas was bound together under a number of influences, most notably the writings and paintings of my father, Denis Williams. He is an established figure in the Caribbean for his numerous artistic contributions, his writings and significantly his archaeological work. But it is the influences of his early work in his Africa phase that so shaped me. I would like to acknowledge two paintings in particular, *Human World* and *The Moolit*, and two books, *Other Leopards* (Heinemann, 1963), and *Icon and Image—A Study of Sacred and Secular Forms of African Classical Art* (Allen Lane, 1974) as providing some deep foundations to my existence.

My thanks go to Mr Ivor Wynne Jones, a dear friend and something of an adopted Welsh father figure, for introducing me to the graves of the Congo boys and William Hughes' account of their story *Dark Africa and the Way Out*. Other books that engaged me are A. Hardy's 1913 account of a trip to British Guiana called *Life and Adventure in the Land of Mud*, Chinweizu's *Voices from Twentieth-Century Africa*, in particular his *Parables on the African Condition*, Peter Fryer's *Staying Power* and Wilfred Cartey's essays *Whispers from the Caribbean, I Goin' Away, I Goin' Home*, which I read for the first time in the skies somewhere over the Atlantic.

I would like to thank John Barnie for initiating and encouraging this project. My thanks also go to Glenda Carr, who provided the wonderful translation of the Talhaiarn poem *Brenin y Canibalyddion* and pointed me towards a number of Welsh hymns.

I dedicate my humble account to those strong women in my life: to my daughters Naiomi and Phoebe, my sisters Janice, Evelyn, Isabel and Beatrice, and my granddaughter Ruby. And of course, especially to Ma, who sadly died before this book was finished.

BLACK BRITAIN: WRITING BACK

Selected by Booker Prize-winning author
Bernardine Evaristo, this series rediscovers
and celebrates pioneering books from black
Britain and the diaspora, which remap the
nation and reframe our history.

Read on for titles in the *Black Britain: Writing
Back* series, each containing an introduction
from Evaristo.

MINTY ALLEY C. L. R. JAMES

It is the 1920s in the Trinidadian capital, and Haynes's world has
been upended. His mother has passed away, and his future of
gleaming opportunity has disappeared with her.

Unable to afford his former life, he finds himself moving into the
bustling barrack yard of Minty Alley. With outrageous love affairs
and passionate arguments a daily fixture, Haynes begins to slip
from curious observer to the heart of the action.

A gloriously observed portrayal of class and community, *Minty
Alley* is a modern classic from one of the twentieth century's
greatest Caribbean thinkers.

'A rich literary rendering of working-class life in colonial
Trinidad . . . its rediscovery and republication is an important
event' *Arts Desk*

INCOMPARABLE WORLD S. I. MARTIN

In the years after the American Revolution, London was the unlikely refuge for thousands of black Americans who fought for liberty on the side of the British.

Buckram, Georgie and William have earned their freedom and escaped their American oppressors, but on the streets of London, poverty awaits with equal cruelty. Forced into a life of crime, their only hope for a better future is to concoct a scheme so daring it will be a miracle if it pays off.

Pulsating with energy and vivid detail, *Incomparable World* boldly uncovers a long-buried narrative of black Britain.

'A brilliant singular work' Irenosen Okojie

BERNARD AND THE CLOTH MONKEY

JUDITH BRYAN

When Anita finally returns to London, everything has changed. Her father is dead, her mother has disappeared, and she is alone with her sister Beth for the first time in years.

Tentatively, they reach out to each other for connection, but the house echoes with words unspoken. Can they confront the pain of the past together?

Dazzling and heartbreaking, *Bernard and the Cloth Monkey* is a shattering portrait of family, a rebellion against silence and a testament to the human capacity for survival.

'An important contribution to the literary landscape' *Bad Form*

THE FAT LADY SINGS JACQUELINE ROY

It is the 1990s, and Gloria is living in a London psychiatric ward. She is unapologetically loud, audacious and eternally on the brink of bursting into song. After several months of uninterrupted routine, she is joined by another young black woman – Merle – who is full of silences and fear.

Unable to confide in their doctors, they agree to journal their pasts. Whispered into tape recorders and scrawled ferociously at night, the remarkable stories of their lives are revealed.

Tender, life-affirming and fearlessly hopeful, Roy tells an unforgettable story of two women navigating a system that fails to protect them and finding strength in their shared vulnerability.

'A strong and humane work of fiction' Jackie Kay

THE DANCING FACE MIKE PHILLIPS

University lecturer Gus knows that stealing the priceless Benin mask, The Dancing Face, from a museum at the heart of the British establishment will gain an avalanche of attention. But such risky theft will also inevitably capture the attention of characters with more money, more power and fewer morals.

Naively entangling his loved ones in his increasingly dangerous pursuit of righteous reparation, is Gus prepared for what it will cost him?

'Brutal, deep, cunning and unbearably beautiful' *Independent*

WITHOUT PREJUDICE NICOLA WILLIAMS

Lee Mitchell is a thirty-year-old barrister from a working-class Caribbean background: in the cut-throat environment of the courtroom, everything is stacked against her.

After she takes on the high-profile case of notorious millionaire playboy Clive Omartian – arrested along with his father and step-brother for eye-wateringly exorbitant fraud – the line between her personal and professional life becomes dangerously blurred.

Spiralling further into Clive's trail of debauchery and corruption, she finds herself in alarmingly deep waters. Can she survive her case, let alone win it?

'Impressive and unique' Bernardine Evaristo

A BLACK BOY AT ETON DILLIBE ONYEAMA

Dillibe Onyeama was the first black boy to graduate from Eton College, and only the second to join when he started in 1965. Written at just twenty-one, this is a deeply personal, revelatory account of the racism he endured during his time as a student at the world-famous institution.

A Black Boy at Eton is a searing, groundbreaking book that provides a unique insight into the reverberating impact of colonialism on traditional British institutions, and paints an intimate picture of a boy growing into a man in an extraordinary environment.

'A frank and reflective memoir . . . An important story to tell' *Guardian*

BRITONS THROUGH NEGRO SPECTACLES

A. B. C. MERRIMAN-LABOR

In *Britons Through Negro Spectacles* Merriman-Labor takes us on a joyous, intoxicating tour of London at the turn of the twentieth century. Slyly subverting the colonial gaze usually placed on Africa, he introduces us to the citizens, culture and customs of Britain with a mischievous glint in his eye.

This incredible work of social commentary provides unique insights into the intersection between empire, race and community at this important moment in history.

'Merriman-Labor was clearly way ahead of his time with this razor-sharp satire' *Buzz Magazine*

GROWING OUT BARBARA BLAKE HANNAH

Travelling over from Jamaica in the 1960s, Barbara finds her footing in TV and blossoms, travelling around the world and covering incredible celebrity stories. But with the responsibility of being the first black woman reporting on TV comes an enormous amount of pressure, and a flood of hateful complaints that eventually cost her the job.

In the aftermath of this fallout, she goes through a period of self-discovery that allows her to celebrate her black identity, rather than feeling suffocated in her attempts to conform to the culture around her.

Growing Out provides a dazzling, revelatory depiction of race and womanhood in the swinging 60s from an entirely unique perspective.

'A fascinating book' *Telegraph*

SEQUINS FOR A RAGGED HEM

AMRYL JOHNSON

Amryl Johnson came to England from Trinidad when she was eleven. As an adult in 1983, she embarks on a journey through the Caribbean searching for home, searching for herself.

Landing in Trinidad as carnival begins, she instantly surrenders to the collective pulsating rhythm of the crowd, euphoric in her total freedom. This elation is shattered when she finds the house where she was born has been destroyed: she cannot escape from the inheritance of colonialism.

In intoxicating, lyrical prose, *Sequins for a Ragged Hem* is an astonishingly unique memoir, interrogating the way our past and present selves live alongside each other.

'A powerful and unusual book' *Guardian*

MY FATHERS' DAUGHTER

HANNAH-AZIEB POOL

In her twenties, Hannah-Azieb Pool is given a letter that unravels everything she knows about her life. Adopted from an orphanage in Eritrea and brought to the UK, she believed she did not have any surviving relatives. In truth, her birth father is alive, and her Eritrean family are desperate to meet her. She is faced with a critical choice. Should she go?

With radiant warmth, courage and wisdom, Pool takes us on an extraordinary journey of self-discovery, as she travels to Eritrea and disentangles the concepts of identity, family and home.

'What a story. So vivid, honest and moving' Andrea Levy

He just wanted a decent book to read ...

Not too much to ask, is it? It was in 1935 when Allen Lane, Managing Director of Bodley Head Publishers, stood on a platform at Exeter railway station looking for something good to read on his journey back to London. His choice was limited to popular magazines and poor-quality paperbacks – the same choice faced every day by the vast majority of readers, few of whom could afford hardbacks. Lane's disappointment and subsequent anger at the range of books generally available led him to found a company – and change the world.

'We believed in the existence in this country of a vast reading public for intelligent books at a low price, and staked everything on it'
Sir Allen Lane, 1902–1970, founder of Penguin Books

The quality paperback had arrived – and not just in bookshops. Lane was adamant that his Penguins should appear in chain stores and tobacconists, and should cost no more than a packet of cigarettes.

Reading habits (and cigarette prices) have changed since 1935, but Penguin still believes in publishing the best books for everybody to enjoy. We still believe that good design costs no more than bad design, and we still believe that quality books published passionately and responsibly make the world a better place.

So wherever you see the little bird – whether it's on a piece of prize-winning literary fiction or a celebrity autobiography, political tour de force or historical masterpiece, a serial-killer thriller, reference book, world classic or a piece of pure escapism – you can bet that it represents the very best that the genre has to offer.

Whatever you like to read – trust Penguin.